Visual C#® Express For Kids

A Computer Programming Tutorial

12th Edition
Illustrated

By Philip Conrod & Lou Tylee

Kidware Software LLC
PO Box 701
Maple Valley, WA 98038

KIDWARE SOFTWARE

http://www.computerscienceforkids.com
http://www.kidwaresoftware.com

Kidware Software LLC
PO Box 701
Maple Valley, Washington 98038
1.425.413.1185
www.kidwaresoftware.com
www.computerscienceforkids.com
www.biblebytebooks.com

Printed in the United States of America

ISBN-13: 978-1-937161-91-0 (Adobe Glassbook Edition)
978-1-937161-59-0 (Printed Edition)

Previous edition published as "Visual C# Express For Kids – 11th Edition"

Library of Congress Control Number: 2014906959

Copy Editor: Jessica Conrod
Book Cover: Stephanie Conrod
Compositor: Michael Rogers
Illustrations: Kevin Brockschmidt

This guide was developed for the course, "Visual C# Express For Kids," produced by Kidware Software, Maple Valley, Washington. It is not intended to be a complete reference to the Visual C# language. Please consult the Microsoft website for detailed reference information.

About The Authors

Philip Conrod has authored, co-authored and edited numerous computer programming books for kids, teens and adults. Philip holds a BS in Computer Information Systems and a Master's certificate in the Essentials of Business Development from Regis University. He also holds a Certificate in Programming for Business from WarrenTech. Philip has been programming computers since 1977. He has also held various Information Technology leadership roles in companies like Sundstrand Aerospace, Safeco Insurance Companies, FamilyLife, Kenworth Truck Company, PACCAR and Darigold Inc. In his spare time, Philip serves as the President & Publisher of Kidware Software, LLC. He and his beautiful family live in Maple Valley, Washington.

Lou Tylee holds BS and MS degrees in Mechanical Engineering and a PhD in Electrical Engineering. Lou has been programming computers since 1969 when he took his first Fortran course in college. He has written software to control suspensions for high speed ground vehicles, monitor nuclear power plants, lower noise levels in commercial jetliners, compute takeoff speeds for jetliners, locate and identify air and ground traffic and to let kids count bunnies, learn how to spell and do math problems. He has written several on-line texts teaching Visual Basic, Visual C# and Java to thousands of people. He taught a beginning Visual Basic course for over 15 years at a major university. Currently, Lou works as an engineer at a major Seattle aerospace firm. He is the proud father of five children and proud husband of his special wife. Lou and his family live in Seattle, Washington.

Acknowledgements

I want to thank my three wonderful daughters - Stephanie, Jessica and Chloe, who helped with various aspects of the book publishing process including software testing, book editing, creative design and many other more tedious tasks like finding errors and typos. I could not have accomplished this without all your hard work, love and support. I want to also thank my best friend Jesus, who has always been there by my side giving me wisdom and guidance. Without you, this book would have never been printed and published.

I also want to thank my multi-talented co-author, Lou Tylee, for doing all the real hard work necessary to develop, test, debug, and keep current all the 'beginner-friendly' applications, games and base tutorial text found in this book. Lou has tirelessly poured his heart and soul into so many previous versions of this tutorial and there are so many beginners who have benefited from his work over the years. Lou is by far one of the best application developers and tutorial writers I have ever worked with. Thank you Lou for collaborating with me on this book project.

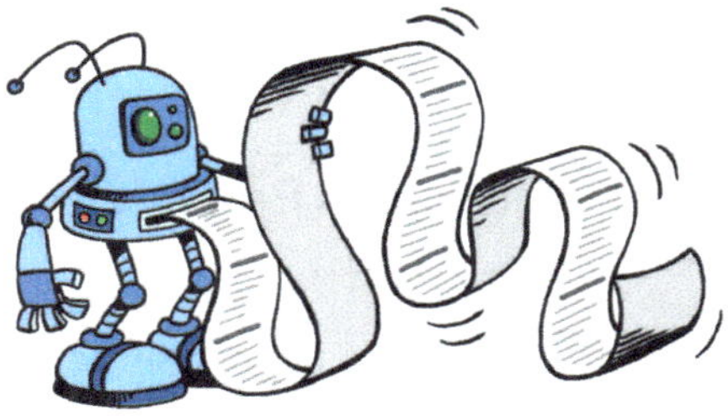

3. Your First Visual C# Express Project

4. Project Design, Forms, Buttons

5. Labels, Text Boxes, Variables

6. UpDown Control, Decisions, Random Numbers

7. Icons, Group Boxes, Check Boxes, Radio Buttons

9. Picture Boxes, Arrays

10. Timers, Animation, Keyboard Events

Bonus Projects

Course Description:

Visual C# Express for Kids is an interactive, self-paced tutorial providing a complete introduction to the Visual C# Express programming language and environment. The tutorial consists of 10 lessons explaining (in simple, easy-to-follow terms) how to build a Visual C# Express application. Numerous examples are used to demonstrate every step in the building process. The tutorial also includes detailed computer projects for kids to build and try. **Visual C# Express for Kids** is presented using a combination of course notes (written in Microsoft Word format) and many Visual C# Express examples and projects.

Course Prerequisites:

To use **Visual C# Express for Kids**, you should be comfortable working within the Windows environment, knowing how to find files, move windows, resize windows, etc. No programming experience is needed. The course material should be understandable to kids aged 10 and up. You will also need the ability to view and print documents saved in Adobe Acrobat format.

Software Requirements

To use Visual C# Express, you (and your potential users) must be using Windows 7 or Windows 8. And, of course, you need to have the Visual C# Express 2012 product installed on your computer. It is available for free download from Microsoft. Follow this link for complete instructions for downloading and installing Visual C# Express on your computer:

http://www.kidwaresoftware.com/viscse.htm

A Brief Word on the Course:

Though this course is entitled "Visual C# Express for Kids," it is not necessarily written in a kid's vocabulary. Computer programming has a detailed vocabulary of its own and, since adults developed it, the terminology tends to be very adult-like. In developing this course, we discussed how to address this problem and decided we would treat our kid readers like adults, since they are learning what is essentially an adult topic. We did not want to 'dumb-down' the course. You see this in some books. We, quite frankly, are offended by books that refer to readers as dummies and idiots simply because they are new to a particular topic. We didn't want to do that here. Throughout the course, we treat the kid reader as a mature person learning a new skill. The vocabulary is not that difficult, but there may be times the kid reader needs a little help. Hopefully, the nearest adult can provide that help.

Installing and Using the Downloadable Solution Files:

If you purchased this directly from our website you received an email with a special and individualized internet download link where you could download the compressed Program Solution Files. If you purchased this book through a 3rd Party Book Store like Amazon.com, the solutions files for this tutorial are included in a compressed ZIP file that is available for download directly from our website at:

http://www.kidwaresoftware.com/vcsekids-registration.html

Complete the online web form at the webpage above with your name, shipping address, email address, the exact title of this book, date of purchase, online or physical store name, and your order confirmation number from that store. After we receive all this information we will email you a download link for the Source Code Solution Files associated with this book.

Warning: If you purchased this book "used" or "second hand" you are not licensed or entitled to download the Program Solution Files. However, you can purchase the Digital Download Version of this book at a discounted price which allows you access to the digital source code solutions files required for completing this tutorial.

Using Visual C# Express for Kids:

The course notes and code for **Visual C# Express for Kids** are included in one or more ZIP files. Use your favorite 'unzipping' application to write all files to your computer. The course is included in the folder entitled **VCSEKids**. This folder contains two other folders: **VCSEK Notes** and **VCSEK Projects**. The **VCSEK Projects** folder includes all the Visual C# Express projects developed during the course.

How To Take the Course:

Visual C# Express for Kids is a self-paced course. The suggested approach is to do one class a week for ten weeks. Each week's class should require about 3 to 6 hours of your time to grasp the concepts completely. Prior to doing a particular week's work, open the class notes file for that week and print it out. Then, work through the notes at your own pace. Try to do each example as they are encountered in the notes. Work through the projects in Classes 3 through 10 (and the Bonus class). If you need any help, all completed projects are included in the **VCSEK Projects** folder.

Forward By Alan Payne, A Computer Science Teacher

What is Visual C# For Kids ... and how it works.

These lessons in Visual C# For Kids are a highly organized and well-indexed set of tutorials in the Visual C# programming environment *meant for children aged 10 and above*. Visual C# is a programming environment which allows the user to drag and drop buttons, text boxes, scroll bars, timers and dozens of other visual "controls" to make programs which look like "Windows" programs The controls are combined to provide the user with a GUI – a graphical user interface.

The tutorials provide the benefit of completed age-appropriate applications for children - fully documented projects from the teacher's or parents' point of view. That is, while full solutions are provided for the adults' (and child learner's) benefit, the projects are presented in an easy-to-follow set of lessons explaining the rational for the form layout, coding design and conventions, and specific code related to the problem. The child-learner may follow the tutorials at their own pace. Every bit of the lesson is remembered as it contributes to the final solution to a kid-friendly application. The finished product is the reward, but the student is fully engaged and enriched by the process. This kind of learning is often the focus of teacher training. Every computer science teacher knows what a great deal of work is required for projects to work in this manner, and with these tutorials, the work is done by an author who understands the classroom *and parenting* experience. That is extremely rare!

Graduated Lessons for Every Project ... Lessons, examples, problems and projects. Graduated learning. Increasing and appropriate difficulty... Great results.

With these projects, there are lessons providing a comprehensive, kid-friendly background on the programming topics to be covered. Once understood, concepts are easily applicable to a variety of applications. Then, specific examples are drawn out so that a young learner can practice with the Visual C# form designer. Then specific coding for the example is provided so that the user can see all the parts of the project come together for the finished product.

By presenting lessons in this graduated manner, students are fully engaged and appropriately challenged to become independent thinkers who can come up with their own project ideas and design their own forms and do their own coding. Once the process is learned, then student engagement is unlimited! I have seen literacy improve dramatically when students cannot get enough of what is being presented.

Indeed, lessons encourage *accelerated* learning - in the sense that they provide an enriched environment to learn computer science, but they also encourage *accelerating* learning because students cannot put the lessons away once they start! Computer science provides this unique opportunity to challenge students, and it is a great testament to the authors that they are successful in achieving such levels of engagement with consistency.

My History with Kidware Software products.

I have used Kidware's Programming Tutorials for over a decade to keep up my own learning. By using these lessons, I am able to spend time on things which will pay off in the classroom. I do not waste valuable time ensconced in language reference libraries for programming environments – help screens which can never be fully remembered! These projects are examples of how student projects should be as final products - thus, the pathway to learning is clear and immediate in every project.

If I want to use or expand upon some of the projects for student use, then I take advantage of site-license options. I have found it very straight forward to emphasize the fundamental computer science topics that form the basis of these projects when using them in the classroom. I can list some computer science topics which everyone will recognize, regardless of where they teach – topics which are covered expertly by these tutorials:

- Data Types and Ranges
- Scope of Variables
- Naming Conventions
- Decision Making
- Looping
- Language Functions – String, Date, Numerical
- Arrays, Control Arrays

Writing Your own Methods (subroutines) and more… it's all integrated into the tutorials.

In many States or Provinces, the above-listed topics would not be formally introduced in Middle School computer studies, but *would* form the basis of most projects undertaken by students. With these tutorials, you as the teacher or parent may choose where to put the emphasis, to be sure to cover the curricular expectations of your curriculum documents.

Any further Middle school computer programming topics derive directly from those listed above. Nothing is forgotten. All can be integrated with the lessons provided.

Quick learning curve for teachers!

How teachers can use the product:

Having projects completed ahead of time can allow the teacher to present the design aspect of the project FIRST, and then have students do all of their learning in the context of what is required in the finished product. This is a much faster learning curve than if students designed all of their own projects from scratch. Lessons concentrating on a unified outcome for all makes for much more streamlined engagement for students (and that is what they need, in Middle school, and in grades 9 and 10), as they complete more projects within a short period of time and there is a context for everything that is learned.

After the process of form-design, naming controls and coding has been mastered for a given set of Visual C# controls, then it is much more likely that students can create their own problems and solutions from scratch. Students are ready to create their own summative projects for your computer science course – or just for fun, and they may think of projects for their other courses as well! And what could be wrong with asking the students' other teachers what they would like to see as project extensions?

Meet Different State and Provincial Curriculum Expectations and More

Different states and provinces have their own curriculum requirements for computer science. With the Kidware Software products, you have at your disposal a series of projects which will allow you to pick and choose from among those which best suit your curriculum needs. Students focus upon design stages and sound problem-solving techniques from a computer-science, problem-solving perspective. In doing so, they become independent problem-solvers, and will exceed the curricular requirements of Middle schools everywhere.

Useable projects - Out of the box!

The specific projects covered in the Visual C# for Kids tutorials are suitable for students aged 10 and above. Specific kid-friendly tutorials and projects are found in the Contents document, and include

Bonus Projects

As you can see, there is a high degree of care taken so that projects are age-appropriate.

You as a parent or teacher can begin teaching the projects on the first day. It's easy for the adult to have done their own learning by starting with the solution files. Then, they will see how all of the parts of the lesson fall into place. Even a novice could make use of the accompanying lessons.

How to teach students to use the materials.

In a Middle school situation, parents or teachers might be tempted to spend considerable amounts of time at the projector or computer screen going over the tutorial – but the best strategy is to present the finished product first! That way, provided that the adult has covered the basic concepts listed in the table of contents, then students will quickly grasp how to use the written lessons on their own. Lessons will be fun, and the pay-off for younger students is that there is always a finished product which is fun to use!

Highly organized reference materials for student self-study!

Materials already condense what is available from MSDN *(which tends to be written for adults)* and in a context and age-appropriate manner, so that younger students remember what they learn.

The time savings for parents, teachers and students is enormous as they need not sift through pages and pages of on-line help to find what they need.

How to mark the projects.

In a classroom environment, it is possible for teachers to mark student progress by asking questions during the various design and coding stages. In the early grades (grades 5 to 8) teachers can make their own oral, pictorial review or written pop quizzes easily from the reference material provided as a review strategy from day to day. I have found the requirement of completing projects (mastery) sufficient for gathering information about student progress - especially in the later grades (grades 10 to 12).

Lessons encourage your own programming extensions.

Once concepts are learned, it is difficult to NOT know what to do for your own projects. This is true even at the Middle school level – where applications can be made in as short as 10 minutes (a high-low guessing game, or a temperature conversion program, for example), or 1 period in length – if one wished to expand upon any of the projects using the "Other Things to Try" suggestions.

Having used Kidware's tutorials for the past decade, I have to say that I could not have achieved the level of success which is now applied in the variety of many programming environments which are currently of considerable interest to kids! I thank Kidware Software and its authors for continuing to stand for what is right in the teaching methodologies which work with kids - even today's kids where competition for their attention is now so much an issue.

Regards,

Alan Payne
Computer Science Teacher
T.A. Blakelock High School
Oakville, Ontario
http://chatt.hdsb.ca/~paynea

1

Introducing Visual C# Express

A Story About Bill and Paul

Back in the early 1970's, Bill and Paul were friends at Lakeside School in Seattle, Washington. Bill and Paul enjoyed working with computers and wrote many games they could play - games like Tic-Tac-Toe and moon landing games. These computer games were written in a computer language called **BASIC** (which stands for **B**eginner's **A**ll-Purpose **S**ymbolic **I**nstruction **C**ode). When the first small computer was developed in the mid 1970's, Bill and Paul had just started college. They had improved their computer skills by then and were able to tell that new computer how to use the BASIC language. They actually sold their version of the BASIC language to other people (it cost $350 and was stored on a cassette tape). They started making money selling BASIC and decided to start a company. You may have heard of their company - Microsoft! Bill is Bill Gates, who still runs Microsoft and is worth many billions of dollars, and Paul is Paul Allen, who no longer works for Microsoft, but has his own business ventures including computers and software, professional sports teams, and real estate development.

One of the first products sold by Microsoft was the BASIC computer programming language. Since then they have developed many other products and many other programming languages. The product you will learn in this set of notes is called **Visual C# Express**. The word **Visual** means you will build Windows-based applications that a user can see and interact with. The term **C#** (pronounced "cee sharp") refers to the particular language used within the Visual C# Express environment. This language was developed using pieces of other languages called C, C++ and Java. And, the term **Express** is used to indicate this is a special version of another Microsoft product called Visual C# .NET. The Express version has been developed for beginners like yourself (providing you with a "speedy" way to learn programming). Visual C# Express is one of the easiest programming languages to learn. Yet, even though it is easy to learn and to use, Visual C# Express can also be used to develop very powerful computer programs. Visual C# Express provides a sophisticated environment for building and testing Windows-based applications. You've used Windows-based applications before. Microsoft's programs like Word, Excel, Internet Explorer and the windows that appear within these applications (to open and save files, to print files) are all Windows-based applications. These applications are not written in Visual C# Express (they are written in a language called C++), but they do demonstrate the functionality you can put in your Visual C# Express applications.

So, why learn Visual C# Express? There are several reasons for doing this. First, if you know how to program, you will have a better understanding of just how computers work. Second, writing programs is good exercise for your thinking skills – you must be a very logical thinker to write computer programs. You must also be something of a perfectionist – computers are not that smart and require exact, perfect instructions to do their jobs. Third, computer programmers are in demand and make a lot of money. And, last, writing computer programs is fun. It's rewarding to see your ideas for a certain computer program come to life on the computer screen. In these notes, you will learn how to use Microsoft's Visual C# Express to write your own Windows-based applications. You may not become a billionaire like Bill and Paul, but hopefully you'll have some fun learning a very valuable skill.

Let's Get Started

Learning how to use Visual C# Express to write a computer program (like learning anything new) involves many steps, many new terms, and many new skills. We will take it slow, describing each step, term, and skill in detail. Before starting, we assume you know how to do a few things:

- You should know how to start your computer and use the mouse.
- You should have a little knowledge on working with your operating system.
- You should know how to resize and move windows around on the screen.
- You should know how to run an application on your computer by using the **Start Menu**.
- You should know how to fill in information in Windows that may pop up on the screen.
- You should know about folders and files and how to find them on your computer.
- You should know what file extensions are and how to identify them. For example, in a file named **Example.ext**, the three letters **ext** are called the extension.
- You should know how to click on links to read documents and move from page to page in such documents. You do this all the time when you use the Internet.

You have probably used all of these skills if you've ever used a word processor, spreadsheet, or any other software on your computer. If you think you lack any of these skills, ask someone for help. They should be able to show you how to do them in just a few minutes. Actually, any time you feel stuck while trying to learn this material, never be afraid to ask someone for help. We were all beginners at one time and people really like helping you learn.

Let's get going. And, as we said, we're going to take it slow. In this first class, we will learn how to get Visual C# Express started on a computer, how to load a program (or project) into Visual C# Express, how to run the program, how to stop the program, and how to exit from Visual C# Express. It will be a good introduction to the many new things we will learn in the classes to come.

Starting Visual C# Express

We assume you have Visual C# Express installed and operational on your computer. If you don't, you need to do this first. Again, this might be a good place to ask for someone's help if you need it. Visual C# Express is available for free download from Microsoft.

Visual C# Express is included as a part of **Microsoft Visual Studio Express for Windows Desktop** (the current version is **VS Express for Desktop 2013**). Visual Studio Express includes not only Visual C# Express, but also Visual C++ Express and Visual Basic Express. All three languages use the same development environment. Follow this link for complete instructions for downloading and installing Visual C# Express on your computer:

http://www.kidwaresoftware.com/viscse.htm

Once installed, to start Visual C# Express:

- Click on the **Start** button on the Windows task bar.
- Select **Programs**, then **Microsoft Visual Studio 2013 Express**
- Then **Microsoft Visual C# 2013 Express**

The Visual C# Express program should start. Several windows will appear on the screen, with the layout depending on settings within your product.

Upon starting, my screen shows:

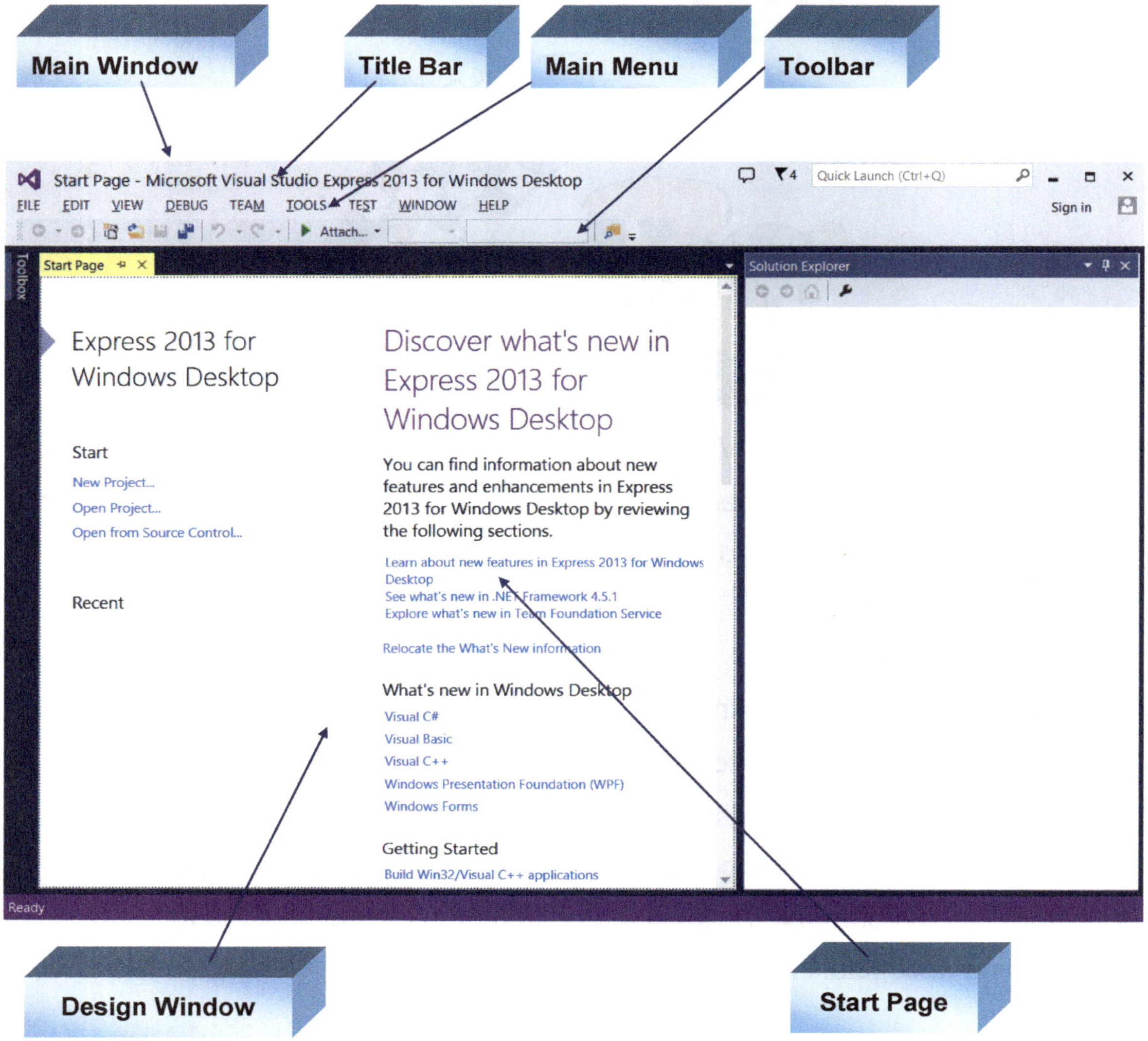

This screen displays the Visual C# Express **Integrated Development Environment (IDE)**. This is where we build, run and work with our applications. Let's point out just a few items on the screen. There are many windows on the screen. At the top of the screen is the Visual C# Express **Main Window**. At the top of the main window is the **Title Bar**. The title bar gives us information about what program we're using and what Visual C# Express program we are working with. Below the title bar is the **Main Menu** from where we can control the Visual C# Express program. You should be familiar with how menus work from using other programs like word processors and games. Under the main menu is a

Toolbar. Here, little buttons with pictures also allow us to control Visual C# Express, much like the main menu. If you put the mouse cursor over one of these buttons for a second or so, a little 'tooltip' will pop up and tell you what that particular button does - try it! Almost all Windows applications (spreadsheets, word processors, games) have toolbars that help us do different tasks. This is the purpose of the Visual C# Express toolbar. It will help us do most of our tasks. In the middle of the screen is the **Start Page**, contained in the **Design Window**. This page has many helpful topics you might be interested in pursuing as you learn more about Visual C# Express. – especially note the topics under **Getting Started**.

At any time, your particular screen may look different than ours. The Visual C# Express environment can be customized to an infinite number of possibilities. This means you can make things look anyway you want them to. You can 'dock' windows or 'float' windows. You can move windows wherever you want or you can completely delete windows. And, different windows will appear at different times. As you become more experienced with Visual C# Express, you will learn ways you want things to be. We encourage you to try different things. Try moving windows. Try docking and floating. We won't talk a lot about how to customize the development environment. (We will, however, always show you how to find the particular window you need.)

Opening a Visual C# Express Project

What we want to do right now is **open a project**. Windows applications written using Visual C# Express are referred to as **solutions**. A solution is made up of one or more **projects**. Projects include all the information we need for our computer program. In this course, our applications (solutions) will be made up of a single project. Because of this, we will use the terms application, solution and project interchangeably. Included with these notes are many Visual C# Express projects you can open and use. Let's open one now.

We will open a project using the main menu. Follow these steps:

- Select **File** from the main menu, then click **Open**, then select **Open Project**. An **Open Project** window will appear:

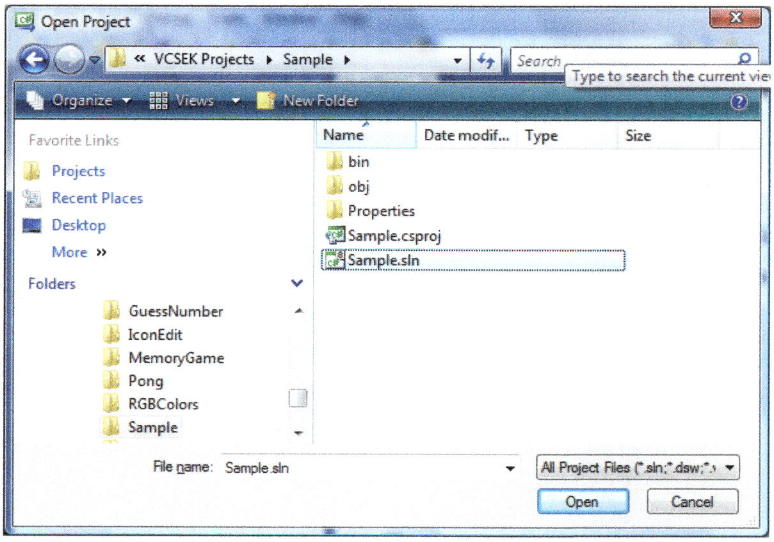

- Find the folder named **VCSEKids** (stands for **Visual C# (Sharp) Express** for **Kids**). This is the folder that holds the notes and projects for this course. Open that folder.
- Find and open the folder named **VCSEK Projects.** This folder holds all the projects for the course

Remember how you got to this folder. Throughout the course, you will go to this folder to open projects you will need. Open the project folder named **Sample**.

In this project folder, among other things is a **Visual Studio Solution** file named **Sample** (with **sln** extension) and a **Visual C# Express Project** file named **Sample** (with **csproj** extension). Open the **Sample** solution file (as shown in the example Open Project window). Since there is only one project in this solution, you could also open the project file and get the same results, but it is better to always open the solution file.

Once the project is opened, many windows are now on the screen:

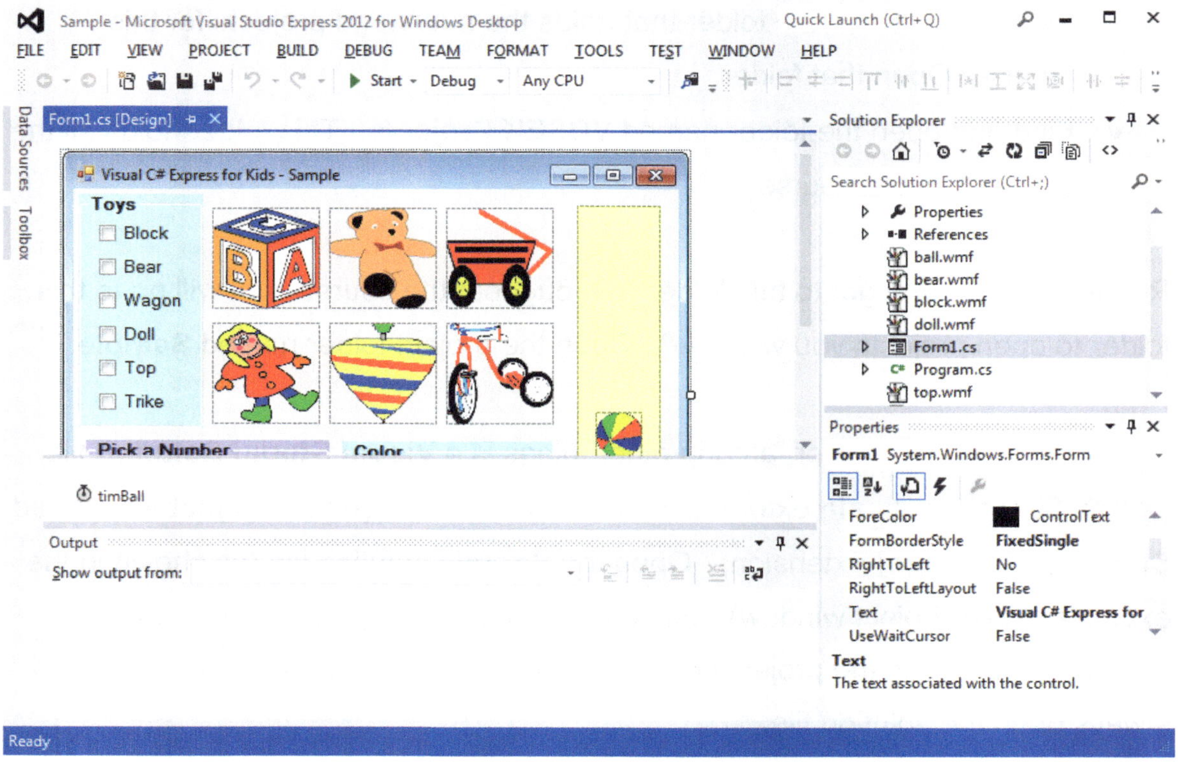

Look for the **Solution Explorer** window (if it is not there, choose **View** in the menu and select **Solution Explorer**). This lists the files in our solution. Right-click the file **Form1.cs** and choose **Open**.

In the **Design** window will appear a window that looks something like this:

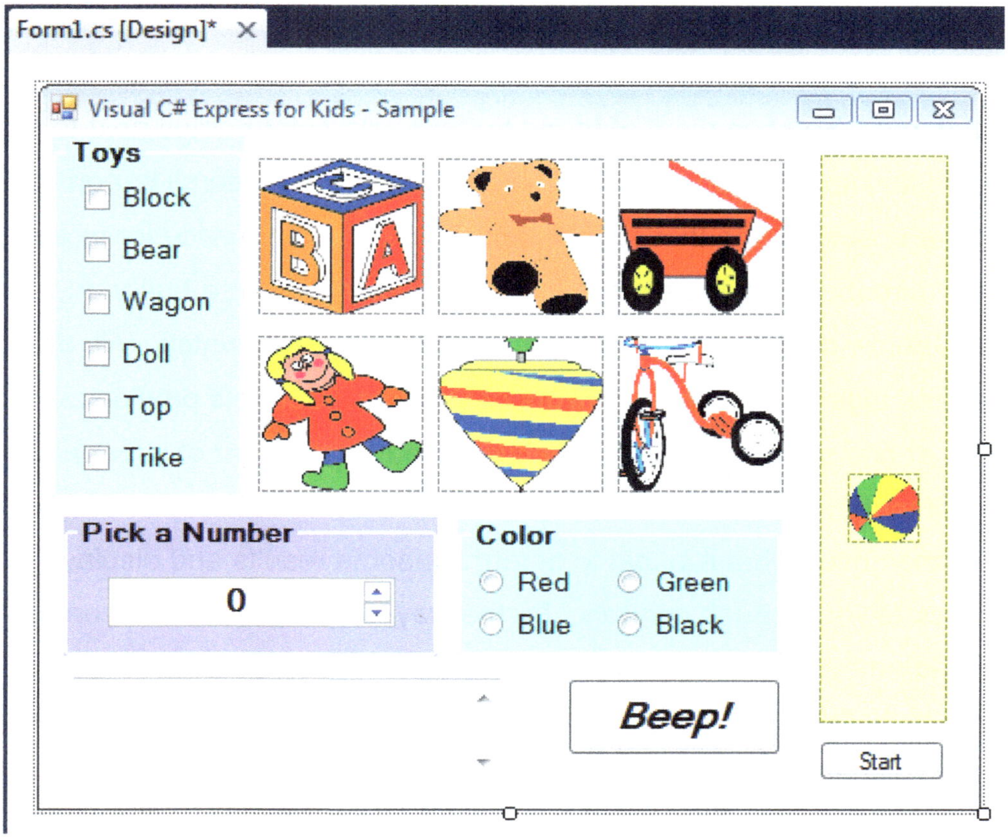

This is our project named **Sample**. We're going to spend a bit of time explaining everything that is displayed here. This will introduce you to some of the words, or vocabulary, we use in Visual C# Express. There are lots of terms used in Visual C# Express. Don't try to memorize everything - you'll see these new words many times through the course.

We call the displayed project window a **Form**. All Visual C# Express projects or programs are built using forms. In fact, you have probably noticed that all Windows applications are built using forms of some type. At the top of the form is the **Title Bar**. It has an **icon** (little picture) related to the form, a description of what the form does (**Visual C# Express for Kids - Sample**), and three smaller buttons that control form appearance (we won't worry about these buttons right now). There are lots of other things on the form. These other things are the 'heart' of a Visual C# Express computer program.

You see a set of square buttons with toy names next to them. You see pictures of toys. You see a set of round buttons with color names next to them. There is a little box you can type in with something called a scroll bar on the right side. There's a big button that says **Beep!** There's a little device for picking the value of a number. And, there's a ball in a big rectangle with a button that says **Start** and, below the form, a little thing that looks like a stopwatch. We call all of these other things on the form **Controls** or **Objects**. Controls provide an **interface**, or line of communication, between you (or the user of your program) and the computer. You use the controls to tell the computer certain things. The computer then uses what it is told to determine some results and displays those results back to you through controls. By the way, the form itself is a control. If you've used any Windows applications, you've seen controls before - you probably just didn't know they were called controls. As examples, buttons on toolbars are controls, scroll bars to move through word processor documents are controls, menu items are controls, and the buttons you click on when opening and saving files are controls.

I think you get the idea that controls are a very important part of Visual C# Express, and you're right. They are the most important part of Visual C# Express - they are what allow you to build your applications. We will spend much of this course just learning about controls. Right now, though, let's run this program and get some insight into how a Visual C# Express project (and its controls) works.

Running a Visual C# Express Project

After developing a Visual C# Express project, you want to start or run the program. This gets the program going and lets the user interact with the **controls** on the form and have the computer do its assigned tasks. We can run a project using the toolbar under the Visual C# Express menu. Look for a button that looks like the **Play** button on a VCR, CD player, or cassette tape player:

Start Project
Toolbar Button

- Click this button to run **Sample** (the project we opened previously).

You can also run a project by: (1) selecting the **Debug** menu heading, then clicking **Start**, or (2) pressing the **<F5>** function key.

The project form will appear and look something like this. Your form may appear slightly different depending on the particular Windows operating system you are using. We use both Windows Vista (seen here) and Windows XP in these notes:

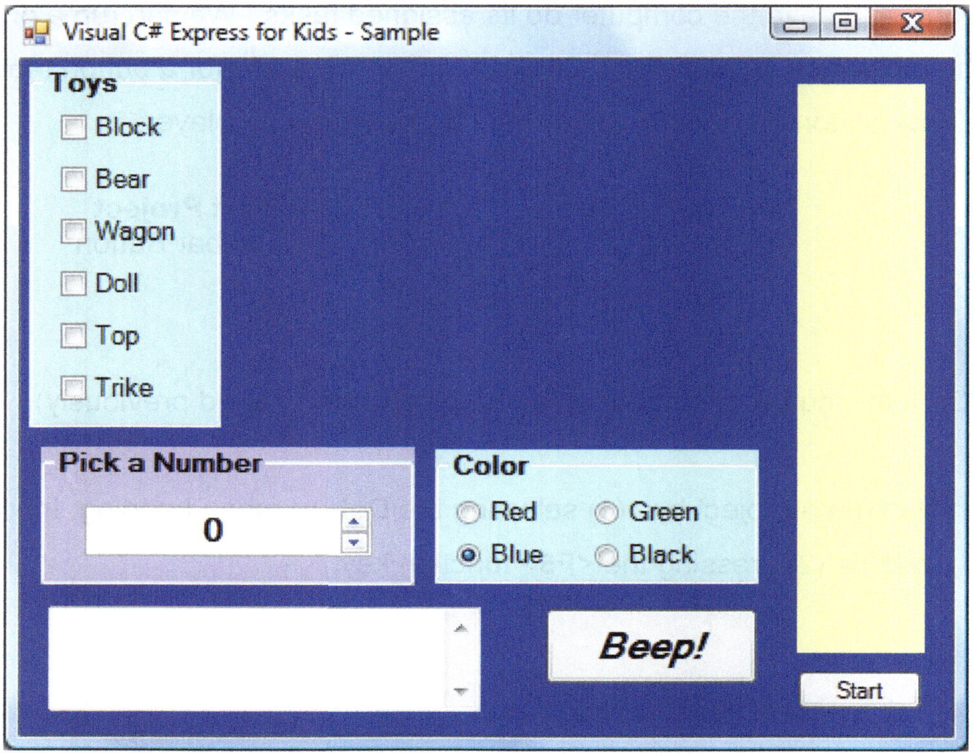

Notice a few things have changed. All the toys have disappeared. The background color of the form is blue. The circle button next to **Blue** has a black dot in it. The little stopwatch control is not visible. The little ball has moved near the top of the big rectangle. What happened? We'll find out how and why all this happened as we learn more about Visual C# Express. Also, notice in the Visual C# Express title bar (in the main window) that the word **Running** appears in parentheses next to the project name. It is important to always know if you are running (in run mode) or designing a program (in design mode) – this indication in the title bar will tell you.

The project is now running, but what is it doing? Nothing is happening, or is it? At this point, Visual C# Express is waiting for you, the user, to do something. We say your Visual C# Express project is waiting for an **event** to occur. Nothing can happen in a Visual C# Express program until an event occurs. We call Visual C# Express an **event-driven** programming language. So, let's cause an event.

An event occurs when you do something on the form - click on something with the mouse, type something in places where words can go, or maybe drag an object across the form. In the upper left corner of the form is a group of six boxes within a rectangular region with the heading **Toys**. Each little box has a toy name printed next to it. Click on one of these boxes. Notice what happens. A check appears in the selected box, indicating box selection, and the toy named by that box appears on the screen. When we click on a box, we cause an event, called a **CheckedChanged** event (this means the 'checked' status of the box has changed). The computer recognizes the event and does what you have told it to do (through your computer program) if that particular event occurs. In this case, the event tells the computer to display the selected toy. Click on the box again. The check mark and the toy disappear. You have caused another event and told the computer to make the toy disappear. This particular control is called a **check box**. Notice you can check as many boxes as you want, picking which toys (if any) you want displayed on your screen. Check boxes are used when you want to select items from a list. Two other controls are used in this example. The rectangular region the check boxes are contained is called a **group box**. The region each toy picture is displayed in is called a **picture box** control. Now, let's look at causing events with the other controls on the form.

Near the middle of the screen is a group of four round buttons in a group box with the heading **Color**. Each button has a color name printed next to it. The **Blue** button has a black dot in it, indicating it is the currently selected color (notice the form is blue). Click on another of these buttons. Notice what happens. The form color changes to the selected color. This **CheckedChanged** (meaning the 'checked' or actually 'dotted' status of the button has changed) event tells the computer to change the form background color. Notice that when you select a new color, the black dot appears in the selected button and disappears in the previously selected button. Unlike the check boxes we saw earlier, you can only select one of these buttons. This makes sense - the form can only be one color! These round buttons are called **radio buttons**. Radio buttons are used when you need to choose exactly one option from a list of many. They are called radio buttons because, on a radio, you can only choose one option (station) at a time.

Under the **Toys** group box is another group box with the heading **Pick a Number**. There we see a control called a **numeric up-down** control. There is a **label** area displaying a number and next to the number is another control with one arrow pointing up and one pointing down (a **scroll bar**). You've probably seen scroll bars in other applications you have used. The scroll bar is used to change the displayed number. Click on the arrow on the top of the scroll bar. The displayed value will increase by 1. Continued clicking on that arrow will continue to increase the value. Clicking the lower arrow will decrease the value. In this example, the computer is responding to the numeric up-down control's **ValueChanged** event, which occurs each time an arrow is clicked, changing the displayed value.

Under the **Pick a Number** group box is a region with a scroll bar on the right side. This control is called a **text box**. You can click in it, then type in any text you want. Try it. The text box is like a little word processor in itself. Each time you type something in the text box, several events occur. There is a **KeyPress** event when you press a key and a **Change** event that is called each time the text in the box changes.

Next to the text box is a button that says **Beep!** Click the button and you should hear a beep on your

computer's speaker. This control is called a **button** and is one of the most widely used controls in Visual C# Express. The **Click** event told the computer to make the speaker beep.

The last thing on our form is a tall, yellow, rectangular control called a **panel** that contains a **picture box** control displaying a beach ball. Under the panel is a button that says **Start**. Click on that button, that is, cause a **Click** event. The ball starts moving down. It continues moving down until it hits the bottom of the panel, then starts moving back up. It will continue to do this until you click the button that now says **Stop**. Remember the little stopwatch that was below our form in design mode, but disappeared when we ran the project. It is being used by the bouncing ball example - it is called a **timer** control. The Click event on the button, in addition to changing what the button says to **Stop**, also started this timer control. The timer control generates **Tick** events all by itself at preset time intervals. In this example, a **Tick** event is generated every 1/10th of a second and, in that event, the ball position is changed to give the appearance of movement. Notice that even while the ball is bouncing, you can change the form color, make toys appear and disappear, type text, and make the computer beep. So, Visual C# Express even has the capability of handling multiple events.

Obviously, this project doesn't do much more than demonstrate what can be done with Visual C# Express, but that is a important concept. It points out what you will be doing in building your own Visual C# Express projects. A project is made up of the controls that let the user provide information to the computer. By causing events with these controls, the computer will generate any required results. We haven't worried about how to use the events to determine these results, but we will in all the later classes. By the time you have finished this course, you will be able to build projects that do everything (and more) that the **Sample** project does. Let's look now at how to stop the project.

Stopping a Visual C# Express Project

There are many ways to stop a Visual C# Express project. We will use the toolbar. Look for a button that looks like the **Stop** button on a VCR, CD player, or cassette tape player (you may have to move the project form down a bit on the screen to see the toolbar):

- Click on this button (you may have to click it twice). The project will stop and Visual C# Express will return to design mode.

Alternate ways to stop a project are:

- Selecting the **Debug** menu heading, then clicking **Stop Debugging**
- Click the **Close** button found on the form. It is the little button that looks like an **X** in the upper right corner of the form.

Stopping Visual C# Express

When you are done working with a Visual C# Express project, you want to leave the Visual C# Express program and the design environment. It is the same procedure used by nearly all Windows applications:

- Select **File** in the main menu.
- Select **Exit** (at the end of the File menu).

Stop Visual C# Express now. Visual C# Express will close all open windows and you will be returned to the Windows desktop. In stopping Visual C# Express with **Sample** active, you may be asked if you want to save certain files. Answer **No**. Like with stopping a project, an alternate way to stop Visual C# Express is to click on the close button in the upper right hand corner of the main window. It's the button that looks like an **X**.

Whew! Are you tired? We covered a lot of new material here, so if you are, that's OK. As we said earlier, you learned a lot of new words and concepts. Don't worry if you don't remember everything we talked about here. You will see the material many times again. It's important that you just have some concept of what goes into a Visual C# Express project and how it works. And you know how to start and stop Visual C# Express itself.

In summary, we saw that a Visual C# Express project is built upon a **form**. **Controls** (also called **objects**) are placed on the form that allow the user and computer to interact. The user generates **events** with the controls that allow the computer to do its job. In the next class, you will begin to acquire the skills that will allow you to begin building your own Visual C# Express projects. You will see how the parts of a project fit together. Using project **Sample** as an example, you will learn how to locate important parts of a project. Then, in Class 3, you will actually build your first project!

2

The Visual C# Express Design Environment

Review and Preview

In Class 1, we learned the important parts of a Visual C# Express **project**. We saw that a project is built on a **form** using **controls** (also called **objects**).

By interacting with the controls using **events**, we get the computer to do assigned tasks via instructions we provide. In this second class, we will learn the beginning steps of building our own Visual C# Express projects by looking at the different parts of the project and where they fit in the Visual C# Express design environment. Like Class 1, there are also a lot of new terms and skills to learn.

Parts of a Visual C# Express Project

In Class 1, we saw that there are four major components in a Visual C# Express application: the solution, the project, the form, and the controls. A **solution** can contain multiple projects. In this course, solutions will only contain a single project, so the words solution and project are used interchangeably. **Project** is the word used to encompass everything in a Visual C# Express project. Other words used to describe a project are **application** or **program**. The **form** is the window where you create the interface between the user and the computer. **Controls** are graphical features or tools that are placed on forms to allow user interaction (text boxes, labels, scroll bars, command buttons). Recall the form itself is a control. Controls are also referred to as **objects**. Pictorially, a project is:

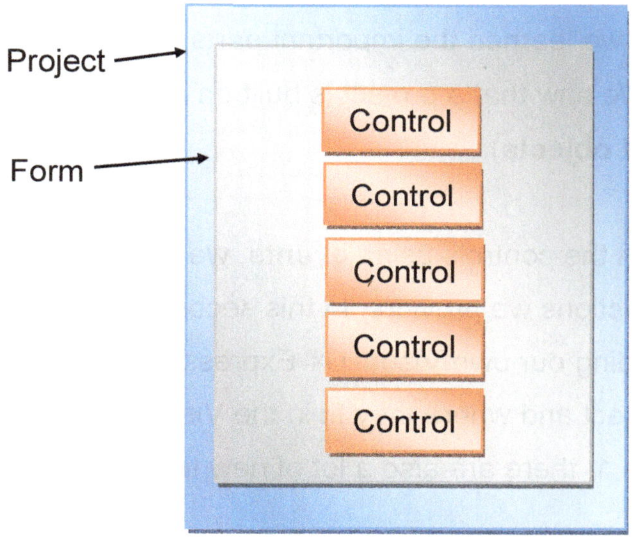

So, in simplest terms, a project consists of a form containing several (and some projects contain hundreds) controls.

Every characteristic of a control (including the form itself) is specified by a **property**. Example control properties include names, any text on the control, width, height, colors, position on the form, and contents. Properties are used to give your project the desired appearance. For each control studied in this class, we will spend a lot of time talking about properties.

In Class 1, we saw that by interacting with the controls in the **Sample** project (clicking buttons, choosing different options, typing text), we could make things happen in our project by generating control **events**. We say that Visual C# Express is an **event-driven** language and it is governed by an **event processor**. That means that nothing happens in a Visual C# Express project until some event occurs. Once an event is detected, the project finds a series of instructions related to that event, called an **event method**. That method is executed, then program control is returned to the event processor:

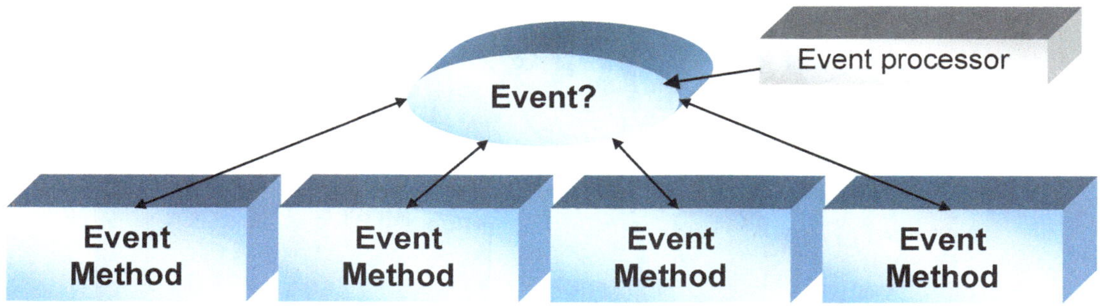

Event methods associated with various controls are where we do the actual computer programming. These methods are where we write C# language statements. You will learn a lot of programming and C# language in this class.

In summary, the major parts of a Visual C# Express project are:

- **form**
- **controls**
- control **properties**
- control **event methods**

Now, let's take a look at the Visual C# Express programming environment and identify where we can access each of these project components.

Parts of the Visual C# Express Environment

Visual C# Express is more than just a computer language. It is a project building environment. Within this one environment, we can begin and build our project, run and test our project, eliminate errors (if any) in our project, and save our project for future use. With other computer languages, many times you need a separate text editor to write your program, something called a compiler to create the program, and then a different area to test your program. Visual C# Express integrates each step of the project building process into one environment. Let's look at the parts of the Visual C# Express environment. To help in this look, we first need to get a new project started. We won't do anything with this project. We just use it to identify parts of the Visual C# Express environment.

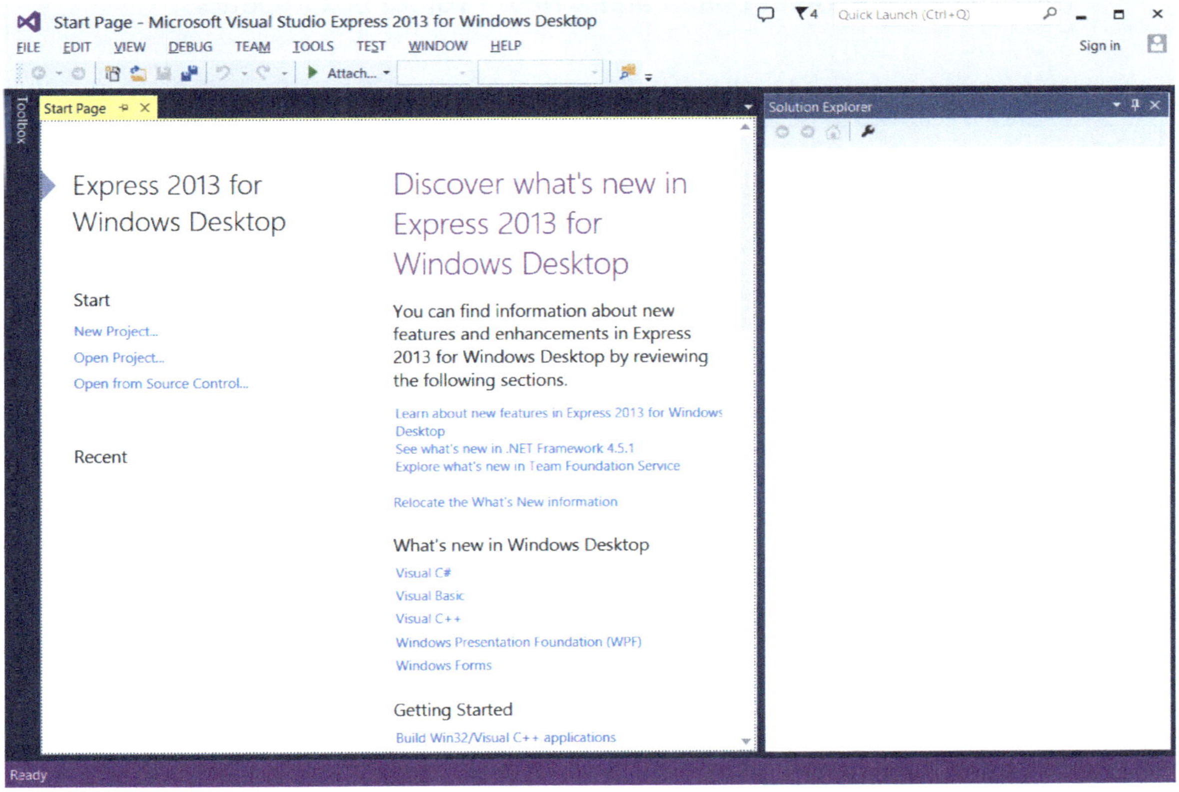

Starting a New Visual C# Express Project

Every time you want to build a project using Visual C# Express, a first step is to create a new project. Start Visual C# Express using the procedure learned in Class 1. We will start a new project using the toolbar under the Visual C# Express menu. Look for this button (the first button on the left):

You can also start a new project by selecting **File** from the menu, then clicking **New Project**.

Click the **New Project** button and a **New Project** box appears:

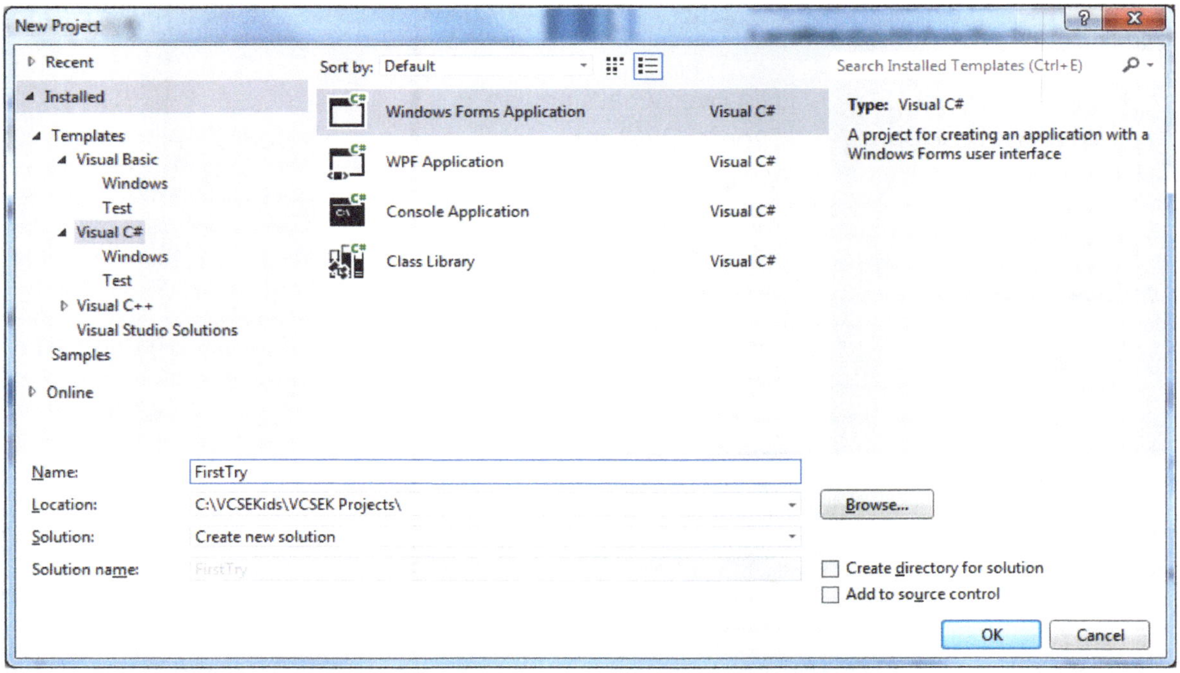

Under **Installed Templates**, make sure **Visual C#** is selected. We will always be building windows applications, so select **Windows Forms Application**.

This window also asks where you want to save your project. In the **Name** box, enter the name (I used **FirstTry**) of the folder to save your project in. **Location** should show the directory your project folder will be in. You can **Browse** to an existing location or create a new directory by checking the indicated box. For these notes, we suggest saving each of your project folders in the same directory. For the course notes, all project folders are saved in the **\BeginVCSE\BVCSE Projects** folder. Once done, click **OK**. Your new project will appear in the Visual C# Express environment, displaying several windows.

Main Window

The **Main Window** is used to control most aspects of the Visual C# Express project building and running process:

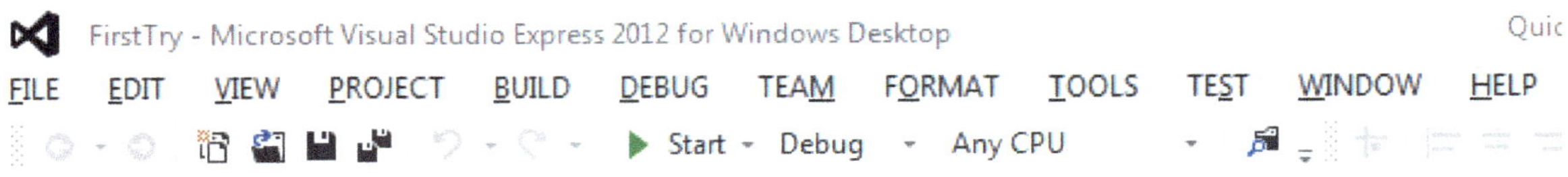

The main window consists of the title bar, menu bar, and toolbars. The title bar indicates the project name (here, **FirstTry**). The menu bar has drop-down menus from which you control the operation of the Visual C# Express environment. The toolbars have buttons that provide shortcuts to some of the menu options. You should be able to identify the **New Project** button. Also, look for the button we used in Class 1 to start a project.

Solution Explorer Window

The **Solution Explorer Window** shows which files make up your project:

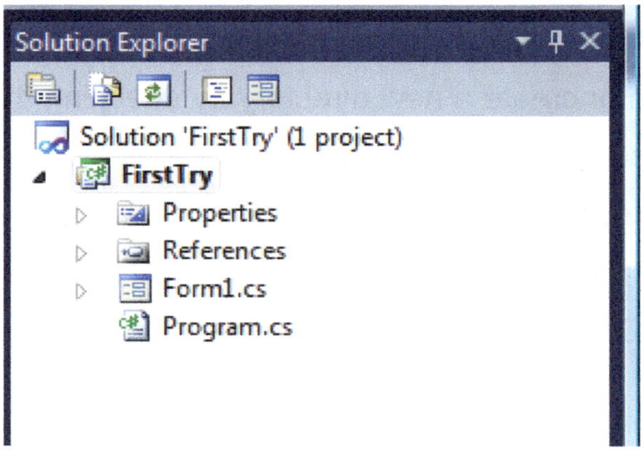

If the Solution Explorer window is not present on the screen, click **View** on the main menu, then **Solution Explorer**. As an alternate, if the window does not show up, press the **R** key while holding down **<Ctrl>**. If you select the form file (**Form1.cs**), you can obtain a view of the project form by clicking the **View Designer** button at the top of the window. Or, you see the actual C# coding within a form by clicking the **View Code** button. We will look at this code window soon.

Design Window

The **Design Window** is central to developing Visual C# Express applications. It is where you build your form and write actual code. You should see a blank form in this window:

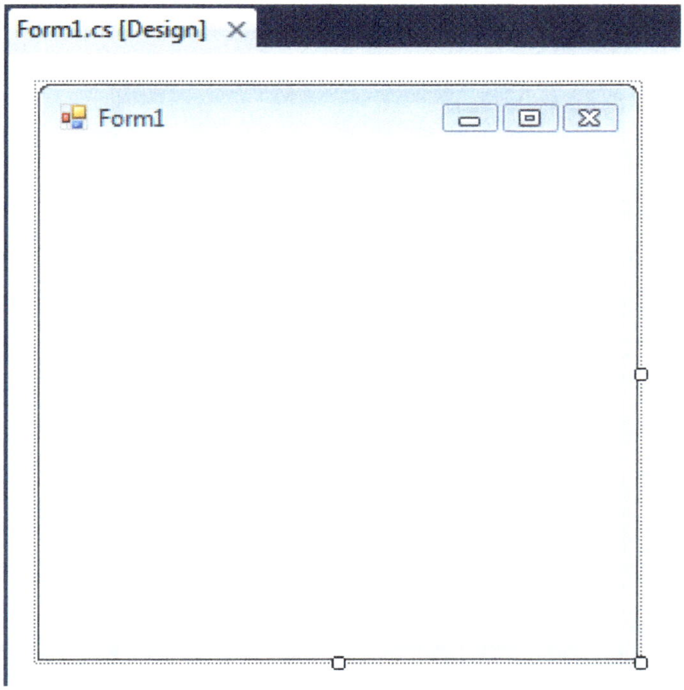

If the form is not present on the screen, select **Form1.cs** in the **Solution Explorer** window. Then, click **View** on the main menu, then **Designer**. Or, press the **<F7>** function key while holding down **<Shift>.**

Toolbox Window

The **Toolbox Window** is the selection menu for controls used in your application. Many times, controls are also referred to as **objects** or **tools**. So, three words are used to describe controls: objects, tools, and, most commonly, controls.

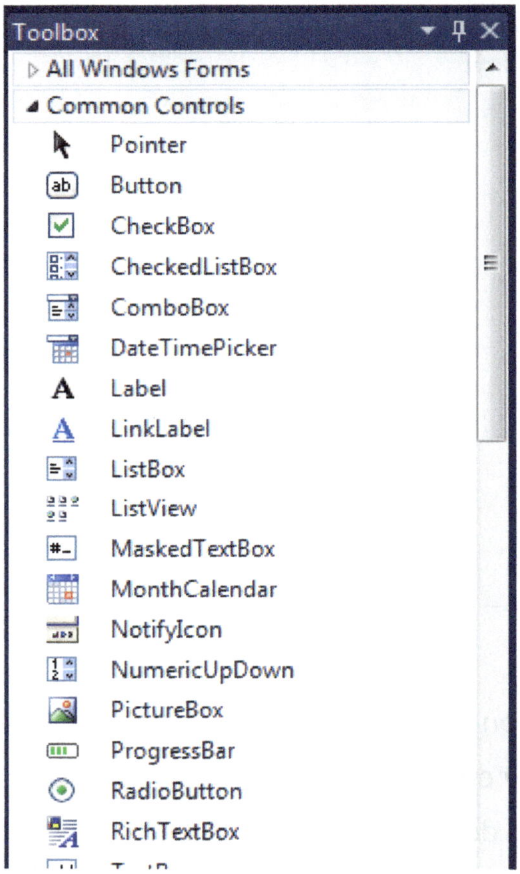

If the toolbox window is not present on the screen, click **View** on the main menu, then **Toolbox**. Make sure you are viewing the **Common Controls**. See if you can identify some of the controls we used in Class 1 with our **Sample** project.

Properties Window

The **Properties Window** is used to establish initial property values for controls. It is also used to establish control **events** (we will see how in Class 3) – for now, we just look at the properties – to do this make sure the **Properties** toolbar button (in the properties window) is selected and not the **Events** button (see the picture below):

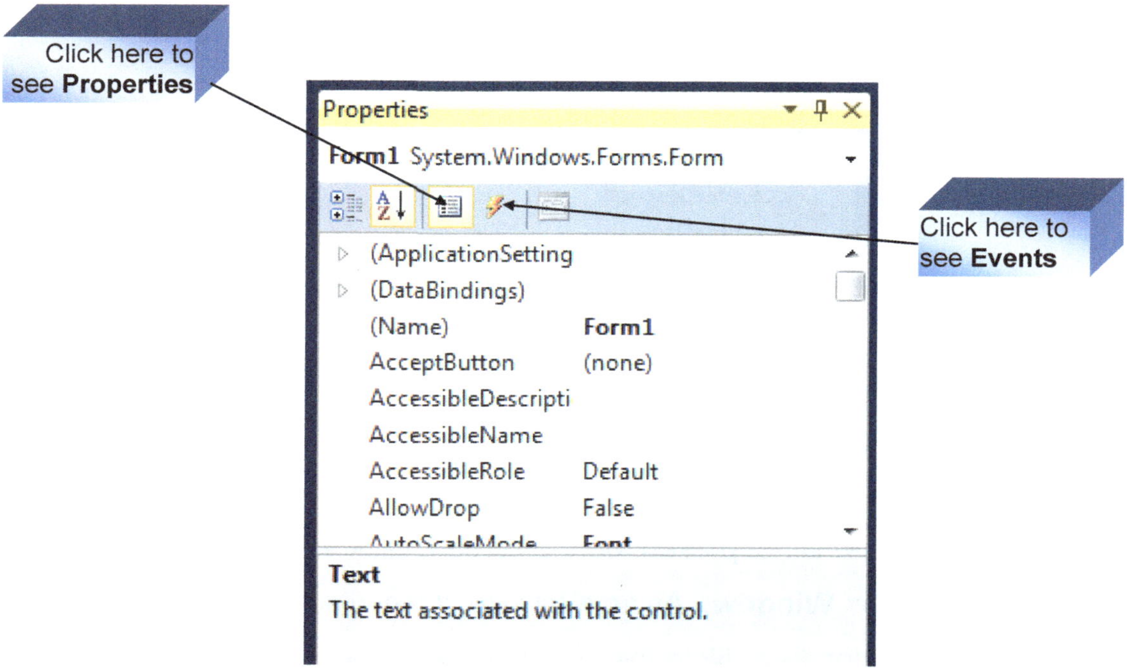

The drop-down box at the top of the window lists all controls on the current form. Under this box are the available properties for the currently selected object (the **Form** in this case). Different views of the properties are selected using the toolbar near the top of the window. Two views are available: **Alphabetic** and **Categorized**. We will always used the Alphabetic view.

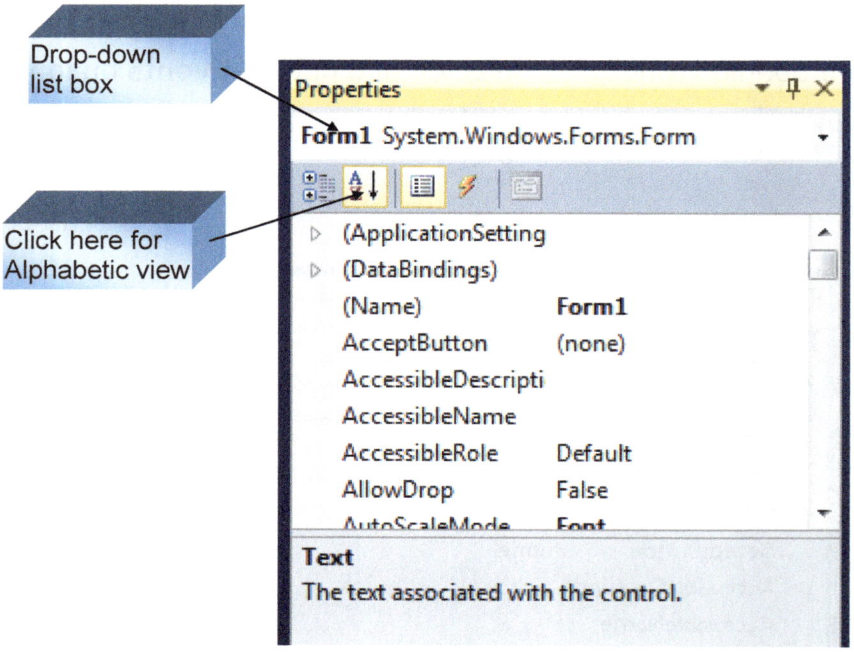

If the properties window is not present on the screen, click **View** on the main menu, then **Properties Window**. As an alternate, if the window does not show up, press the **F4** function key. Note the properties window will only display when the form and any controls are displayed in the Design window.

You should be familiar with each of the Visual C# Express environment windows and know where they are and how to locate them, if they are not displayed. Next, we'll revisit the project we used in Class 1 to illustrate some of the points we've covered here.

Moving Around in Visual C# Express

Solution Explorer Window

Open the project named **Sample** that we used in Class 1 (use the **File** menu option, then select **Open** and **Project/Solution** reviewing the steps in Class 1 if needed). Once **Sample** is opened (recall it is in the **Sample** folder in the **\VCSEKids\VCSEK Projects** folder), find and examine the **Solution Explorer** window:

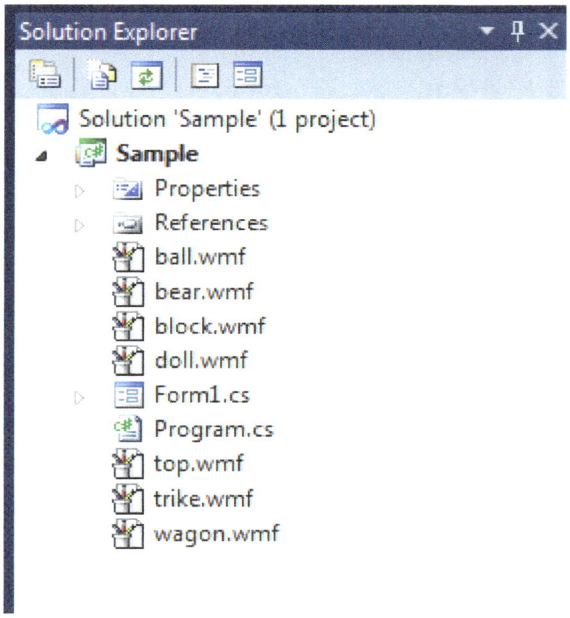

The Solution Explorer window indicates we have a solution with a project file named **Sample.** The project contains a single form saved as **Form1.cs**. The project also includes folders named **Properties** and **References** and a file named **Program.cs**. There are also several graphics files (the ones with **wmf** extensions). The only file we're really worried about for now is the form.

Properties Window

Find the **Properties** window. Remember it can only be shown when the form is displayed. So, you may have to make sure the form is displayed first. Review the steps that get the desired windows on your screen. Make sure the properties and not the events are displayed.

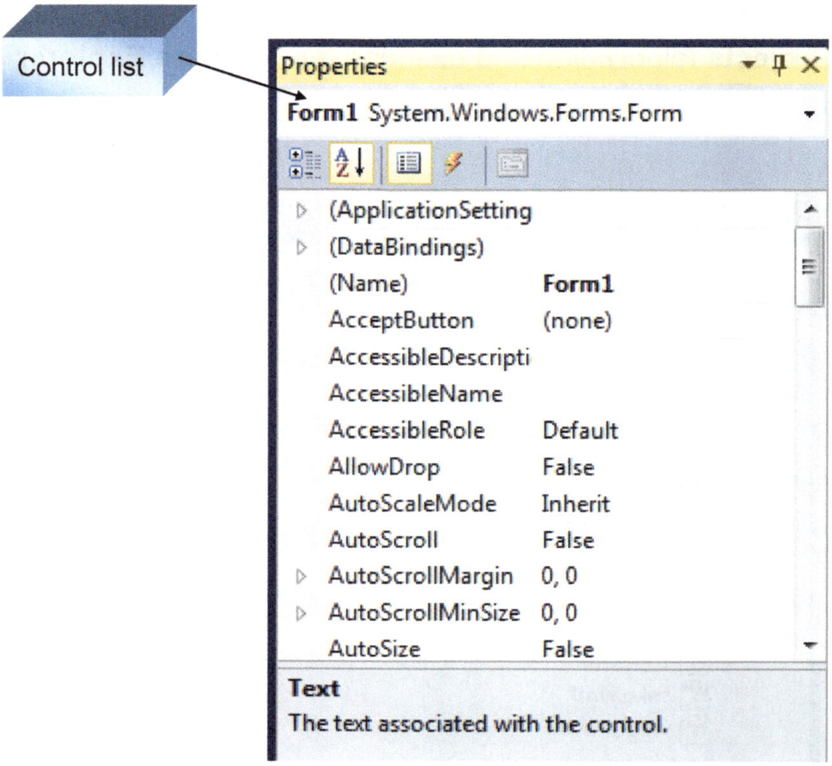

The drop-down box at the top of the properties window is called the **control list**. It displays the name (the **Name** property) of each control used in the project, as well as the type of control it is. Notice, as displayed, the current control is the **Form** and it is named **Form1**. The properties list is directly below this box. In this list, you can scroll (using the scroll bar) through the properties for the selected control. The property name is on the left side of the list and the current property value is on the right side. Scroll through the properties for the form. Do you see how many properties there are? You'll learn about many of these as you continue through the course. Don't worry about them for now, though.

Click on the down arrow in the control list (remember that's the drop-down box at the top of the properties window):

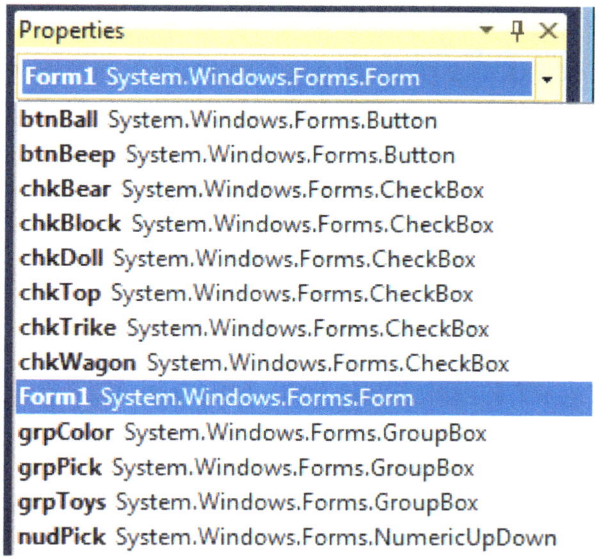

Scroll through the displayed list of all the controls on the form. There are a lot of them. Notice the assigned names and control types. Notice it's pretty easy to identify which control the name refers too. For example, **picBear** is obviously the **picture box** control holding a picture of a bear. We always want to use proper control naming - making it easy to identify a control just by it's name. We'll spend time talking about control naming in the later classes.

Select a control and scroll through the properties for that control. Look at the properties for several controls. Notice every control has many properties. Most properties are assigned by default, that is the values are given to it by Visual C# Express. We will change some properties from their default values to customize them for our use. We will look at how to change properties in Class 3.

Code Window

Let's look at a new window. Recall Visual C# Express is event-driven - when an event is detected, the project goes to the correct **event method**. Event methods are used to tell the computer what to do in response to an event. They are where the actual computer programming (using the C# language) occurs. We view the event methods in the **Code Window**. There are many ways to display the code window. One way is to use the **View Code** button found in the Solution Explorer window. Another is to click **View** on the main menu, then **Code**. Or, as an alternate, press the **F7** function key. Find the code window for the **Sample** project. It will appear in the design window under the **Form1.cs** tab:

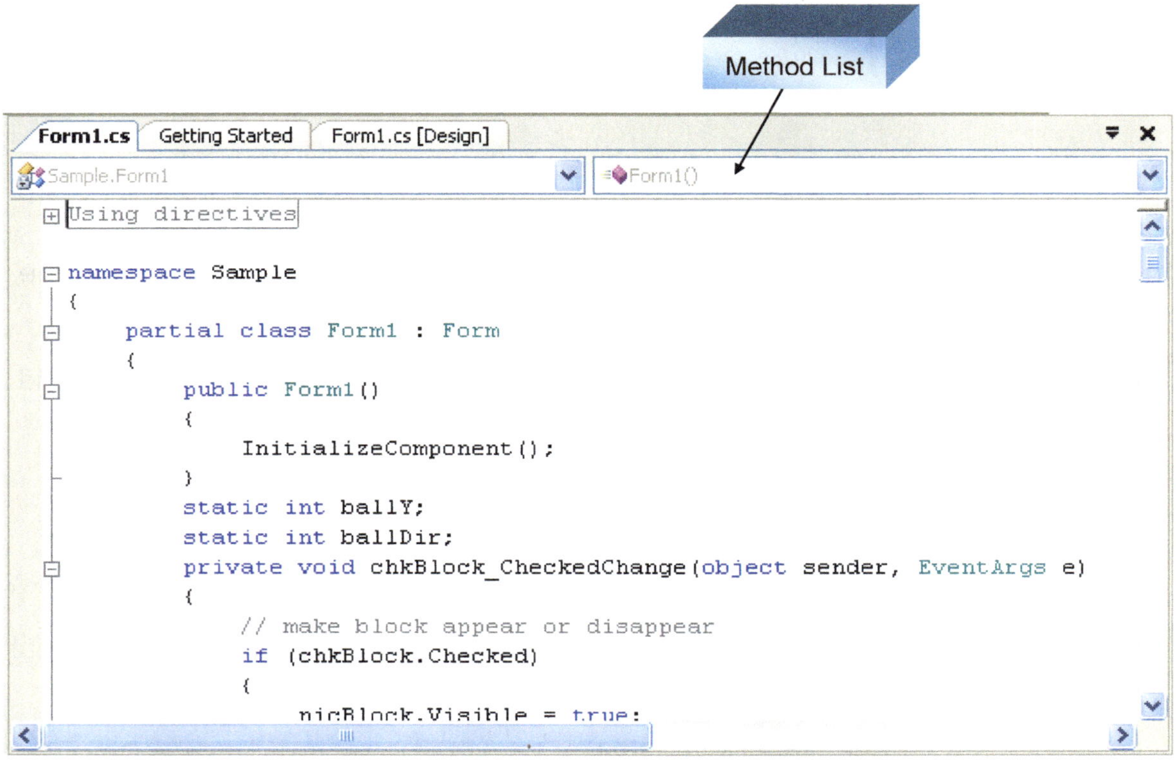

At the top of the code window are two drop-down boxes. The one on the right side is the **method lists**. It lists all the methods (including event methods) used in the code. Click on the drop-down arrow in the methods list. Select **rdoBlue_CheckedChanged** as the method. You should see this:

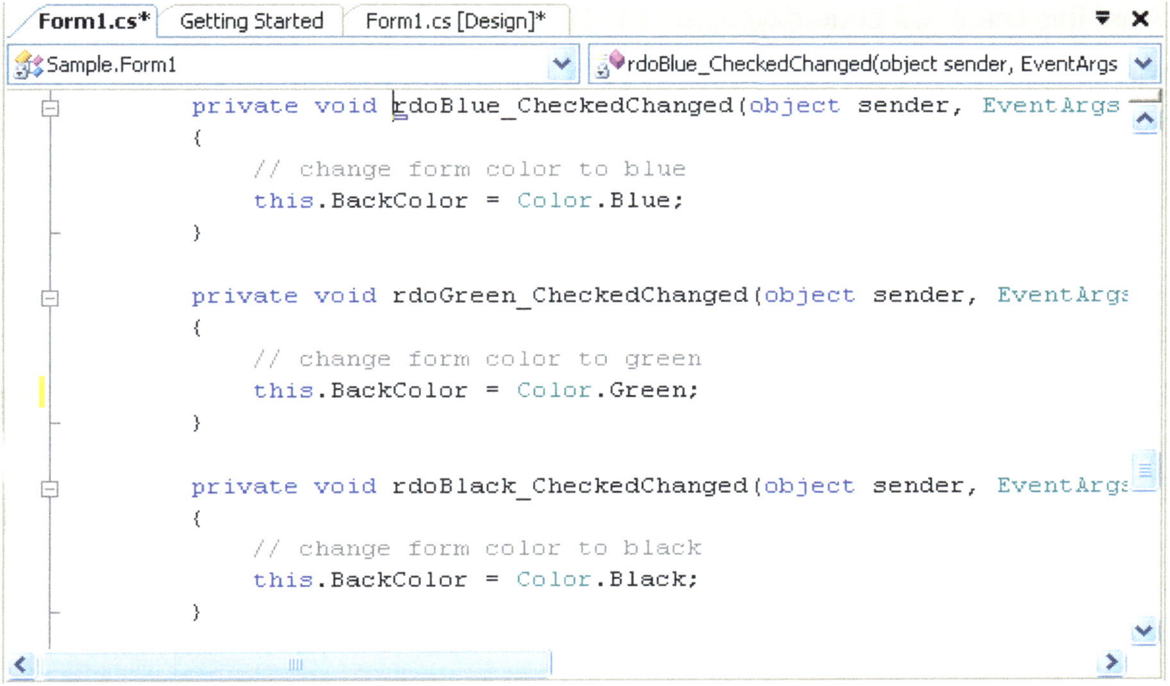

Near the top of the code window is the **CheckedChanged** event method for the control name **rdoBlue**. And even though you may not know any C# right now, you should be able for figure out what is going on here. Since we will be careful in how we name controls, you should recognize this control to be the radio button (one with a little circle) with the word **Blue** next to it (the word next to a radio button is its **Text** property). The status of a radio button (whether it is selected or not) is called its **Checked** property. So, this event method is called whenever we click on the Blue radio button and change its Checked property.

Notice the procedure has a single line of instruction (ignore the other lines for now):

```
this.BackColor = Color.Blue;
```

What this line of C# code says is set the **BackColor** property of the control named **this** (a word used by Visual C# Express to refer to the form) to Blue (represented by the words **Color.Blue**). Pretty easy, huh?

Scroll through the other code in the code window. Much of this code might look like a foreign language right now and don't worry - it should! You'll be surprised though that you probably can figure out what's going on even if you don't know any C#. In subsequent classes, you will start to learn C# and such code will become easy to read. You'll see that most C# code is pretty easy to understand. Writing C# code is primarily paying attention to lots of details. For the most part, it's very logical and obvious. And, you're about to start writing your own code!

In this second class, we've learned the parts of the Visual C# Express environment and how to move around in that environment. We've also learned some important new terms like **properties** and **event methods**. You're now ready to build your first Visual C# Express project. In the next class, you'll learn how to place controls on a form, move them around, and make them appear just like you want. And, you will learn the all-important step of how to put C# code in the event methods.

3

Your First Visual C# Express Project

Review and Preview

In the first two classes, you learned about **forms**, **controls**, **properties**, and **event methods**. In this class, you're going to put that knowledge to work in building your first simple Visual C# Express project. You'll learn the steps in building a project, how to put controls on a form, how to set properties for those controls, and how to write your own event methods using a little C#.

Steps in Building a Visual C# Express Project

There are three primary steps in building a Visual C# Express Project:

1. Place (or draw) **controls** on the form.
2. Assign **properties** to the controls.
3. Write **event methods** for the controls.

Each of these steps is done with Visual C# Express in **design** mode.

Start Visual C# Express and start a new project (review the steps covered in Class 2, if necessary, naming it whatever you choose). Open the created form in the **Design** window. You should see something like this:

You can resize the form if you want. This is one of the 'Windows' techniques you should be familiar with. Notice the form has a 'sizing handle' in the lower right corner. If you move the cursor over this handles, a little 'double-arrow' will appear. At that point, you can click and drag the corner to its desired position. This allows you to increase the width and height of the form at the same time. If you hold the cursor over the right or lower edge (until the arrow appears), you can resize the width and height, respectively. Practice sizing the form.

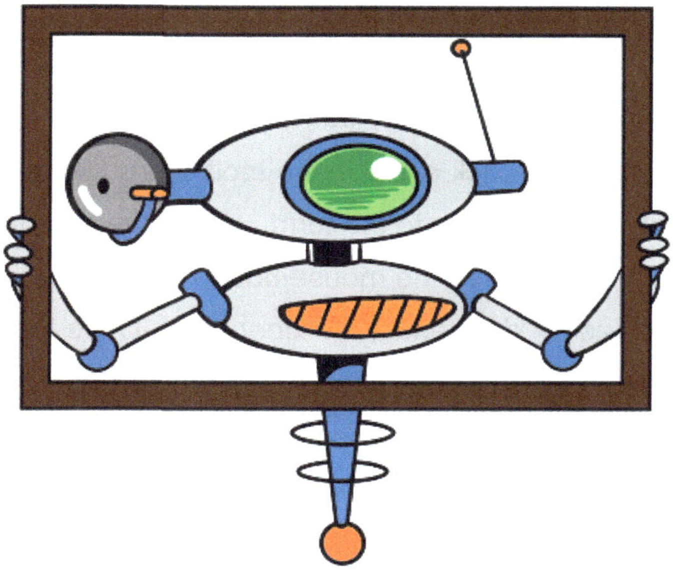

Placing Controls on the Form

The first step in building a Visual C# Express project is to place controls on the form in their desired positions. So, at this point, you must have decided what controls you will need to build your project. Many times, this is a time-consuming task in itself. And, I guarantee, you will change your mind many times. Right now, we'll just practice putting controls on the form.

Controls are selected from the Visual C# Express **Toolbox** window (**Windows Form** controls). Click a tool in the toolbox and hold the mouse button down. Drag the selected tool over to the form. When the cursor pointer is at the desired upper left corner, release the mouse button and the default size control will appear. This is the classic "drag and drop" operation. Once the control is on the form, you can still move or resize the control. To **move** a control, left-click the control to select it (crossed-arrows will appear). Drag it to the new location, then release the mouse button. To **resize** a control, left-click the control so that it is selected. If you move the cursor over one its four sizing handles, a little 'double-arrow' will appear. At that point, you can click and drag the corresponding edge or corner to its desired position.

There are other ways to place a control on the form – you will learn them as you progress in your programming skills. One way is to simply double-click the control in the toolbox and it will appear in the upper left corner of the form. We prefer the drag and drop method since the control is placed where you want it.

Example

Make sure Visual C# Express is still running and there is a form on the screen as well as the **Toolbox** (click **View** on the main menu, then **Toolbox** if it is not there). Go to the toolbox and find the **button** control. It looks like this:

Drag and drop the button onto the form. Your form should look something like this:

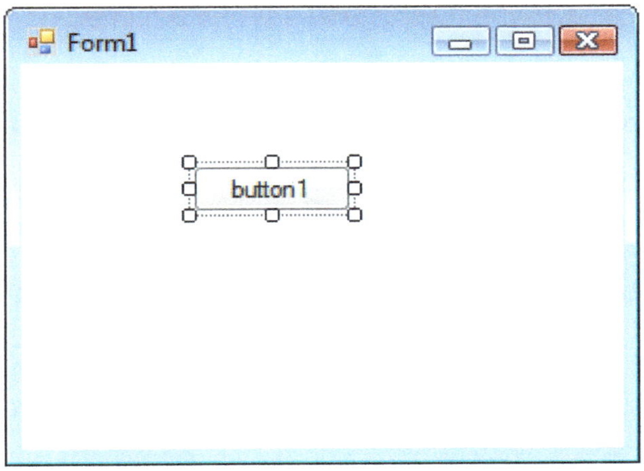

Notice the sizing handles around the button. This indicates this is the **active** control. Click on the form and those handles disappear, indicating the form is now the active control. Click on the button again to make it active.

As mentioned, controls can always be moved and resized. To **move** a control you have drawn, click the object on the form (a cross with arrows will appear). Now, drag the control to the new location. Release the mouse button. To **resize** a control, click the control so that it is selected (active) and sizing handles appear. Use these handles to resize the object.

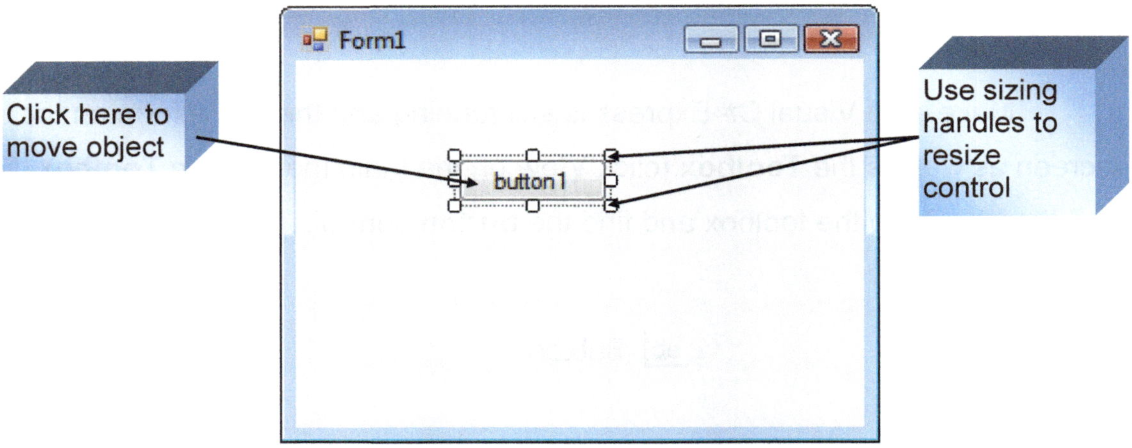

Move the button around and try resizing it. Make a real big button, a real short button, a real wide button, a real tall button. Try moving the button around on the form.

Drag and drop another button control on the form. Move and resize it. Click from button to button noticing the last clicked control has the sizing handles, making it the active control. Spend some time placing controls on the form. Use other controls like labels, text boxes, radio buttons, and check boxes. Move them around, resize them. Try to organize your controls in nicely lined-up groups. These are skills that will be needed in building Visual C# Express projects.

You also need to know how to remove controls from a form. It is an easy process. Click on the control you want to remove. It will become the active control. Press the **Del** (delete) key on your keyboard. The control will be removed. Before you delete a control, make sure you really want to delete it. Delete any controls you may have placed on the form.

Setting Control Properties (Design Mode)

Once you have the desired controls on the form, you will want to assign properties to the controls. Recall properties specify how a control appears on the form. They establish such things as control size, color, what a control 'says', and position on the form. When you place a control on the form, it is given a set of default properties by Visual C# Express. In particular, its geometric properties (governing size and location) are set when you place and size the control on the form. But, many times, the default properties are not acceptable and you will want to change them. This is done using the **Properties Window**.

If Visual C# Express is not running on your computer, start it now. Start another new project. There should be a blank form in the design window. If it's not there, select the **View** menu and choose **Designer**. Find the **Properties Window** (press <**F4**> if it's not there):

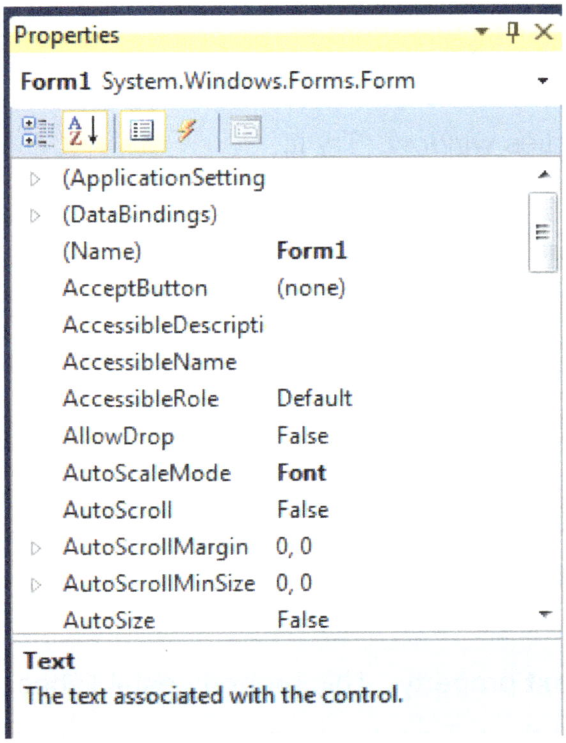

Click the **Alphabetic** view (the button with A-Z on it) if **Categorized** properties are displayed. Also make sure the **Properties** button, next to the Alphabetic view button is depressed (always make sure this button is pressed when working with properties). Recall the box at the top of the properties window is the **control list**, telling us which controls are present on the form. Right now, the list only has one control, that being the form itself. Let's look at some of the form's properties.

First, how big is the form? All controls are rectangular in shape and two properties define the size of that rectangle. Scroll down the list of properties and find the **Size** property. You will see two numbers listed separated by commas. The first number is the **Width** of the form in pixels (a pixel is a single dot on the form). The second number is the **Height** of the form in pixels. Click on the little plus sign (+) in the box next to the Size property. The Width and Height properties will be displayed individually. Resize the form and notice the Height and Width properties change accordingly. You can also change the width and height of the form by typing in values for the desired property in the Properties window. Try it.

Scroll to the **BackColor** property. You probably guessed that this sets the background color of the form. The value listed for that property is probably **Control** (a light gray). To change the BackColor property, click on BackColor, then on the drop-down arrow that appears in the property side of the list. Choose one of the three 'tabs' that appear: **Custom**, **Web**, or **System**, then choose a color. My favorite is Custom. With this choice, a palette of colors will appear, you can choose a new color and notice the results.

Scroll to the **Text** property. This property establishes what is displayed in the form's title bar. Click on Text, then type in something on the right side of the property window and press **<Enter>**. Notice the new Text appears in the form title bar.

That's all there is to setting control properties. First, select the control of interest from the control list. Then, scroll down through properties and find the property you want to change. Click on that property. Properties may be changed by typing in a new value (like the Width and Height values and the Text property) or choosing from a list of predefined options (available as a drop-down list, like color values).

Let's look at some of the **button** properties. Add a button control to your form. Select the button in the control list of the properties window. Like the form, the button is also rectangular. Scroll down to the **Size** property and click on the little plus (+) sign to expand this property. The **Width** property gives its width in pixels and **Height** gives its height in pixels. Two other properties specify the location of the button on the form. Scroll down to the **Location** property and expand it. Values for **X** (the **Left** property) and **Y** (the **Top** property) are displayed. **Left** gives the horizontal position (in pixels) of the left side of the button relative to the left side of the form. Similarly, **Top** is the vertical position (in pixels) of the top side of the button relative to the top of the form (the top of the form being defined as the lower part of the title bar). For a single button, these properties are:

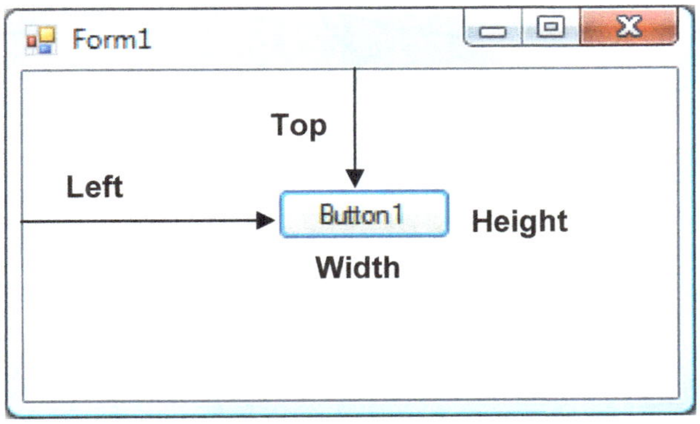

Another important property for a button is the **Text** property. The text appearing on the button is the Text. It should indicate what happens if you click that button. Change the **Text** property of your button. Put a couple more buttons on the form. Move and size them. Change their Text and BackColor properties, if you want.

We have seen that to change from one control to another in the properties window, we can click on the down arrow in the controls list and pick the desired control. A shortcut method for switching the listed properties to a desired control is to simply click on the control on the form, making it the **active** control. Click on one of the buttons. Notice the selected control in the properties window changes to that control. Click on another button - note the change. Click on the form. The selected control becomes the form. You will find this shortcut method of switching from one control to another very useful as you build your own Visual C# Express projects.

Naming Controls

The most important property for any control is its **Name**. Because of its importance, we address it separately. When we name a control, we want to specify two pieces of information: the **type** of control and the **purpose** of the control. Such naming will make our programming tasks much easier.

In the Visual C# programming community, a rule has been developed for naming controls. The first three letters of the control name (called a **prefix**) specify the type of control. Some of these prefixes are (we will see more throughout the class):

Control	Prefix
Button	**btn**
Label	**lbl**
Text Box	**txt**
Check Box	**chk**
Radio Button	**rdo**

After the control name prefix, we choose a name (it usually starts with an upper case letter to show the prefix has ended) that indicates what the control does. The complete control name can have up to 40 characters. The name must start with a letter (this is taken care of by using prefixes) and can only contain letters (lower or upper case), numbers, and the underscore (_) character. Even though you can have 40 character control names, keep the names as short as possible without letting them lose their meaning. This will save you lots of typing.

Let's look at some example control names to give you an idea of how to choose names. These are names used in the **Sample** project looked at in Class 1 and Class 2. Examples:

btnBeep - Button that causes a beep
txtType- Text box where information could be typed
rdoBlue - Radio button that changes background color to Blue
chkTop - Check box that displays or hides the toy top
picTop – Picture box that has the picture of a toy top

This should give you an idea of how to pick control names. We can't emphasize enough the importance of choosing proper names. It will make your work as a programmer much easier.

It is important to note that the Visual C# language is case sensitive. This means the names **picTop** and **PICTOP** are not treated the same. Make sure you assign unique names to each control. We suggest mixing upper and lower case letters in your control names for improved readability. Just be sure when you type in control names that you use the proper case.

Setting Properties in Run Mode

To illustrate the importance of proper control names, let's look at a common task in Visual C# Express. We have seen one of the steps in developing a Visual C# Express project is to establish control properties in design mode. You can also establish or change properties while your project is in run mode. For example, in the **Sample** project, when you clicked on a radio button, the **BackColor** property of the form was changed. When you clicked on a toy name, that toy either appeared or disappeared. To change a property in run mode, we need to use a line of C# code (you're about to learn your first line of C#!). The format for this code is:

```
controlName.PropertyName = PropertyValue;
```

That is, we type the control's name, a dot (same as a period or decimal point), the name of the property we are changing (found in the properties window), an equal sign (called an assignment operator), and the new value. Such a format is referred to as **dot notation**. Make sure the line ends with a semi-colon (;) – almost every line of code in Visual C# will end with a semi-colon.

In **Sample**, the code used to display the toy top on the form is:

```
picTop.Visible = true;
```

The **Visible** property of a control can be **true** (control is displayed) or **false** (control is not displayed). Notice proper control naming makes this line of code very understandable, even if you don't know any C#. It says that the picture box displaying the top has been made visible.

One exception to the rule we just used is when we set **Form** properties. To set a form property at run-time, you use the Visual C# Express keyword **this** to refer to the form. For example, in Sample, to set the background color of the form to blue, we use:

```
this.BackColor = Color.Blue;
```

How Control Names are Used in Event Methods

Another place the importance of proper control naming becomes apparent is when we write event methods (discussed next). We have seen that event methods are viewed in the code window. The structure for event methods is:

```
private void controlName_EventName(object sender, EventArgs
e)
{
            [C# code goes here]
}
```

Header line

There's a lot to look at. The first, long line that takes up two lines here (due to margin constraints), is the **header** line. Then the method begins with a left curly brace (**{**) and ends with a right curly brace (**}**). You will see lots of braces in C#. The actual C# code goes between these two braces.

Let's look at the header, ignoring the information in parentheses for now. Notice the control name is used as is the event name. Can you see that, with proper naming, we can easily identify each control's event method?

As an example, using **Sample** again, the **CheckedChanged** event method for the **rdoBlue** control is:

```
private void rdoBlue_CheckedChanged(object sender, EventArgs
e)
{
    // change form color to blue
    this.BackColor = Color.Blue;
}
```

We recognize this is the code that is executed when the user changes the **Checked** property (clicks on) of the **rdoBlue** radio button. Proper naming makes identifying and reading event methods very easy. Again, this will make your job as a programmer much easier. Now, let's write our first event method.

Writing Event Methods

The third step in building a Visual C# Express application is to write event methods for the controls on the form. To write an event method, we use the code window. Review ways to display the code window in your project. This step is where we need to actually write C# code or do computer programming. You won't learn a lot of C# right now, but just learn the process of finding event methods and typing code.

Each control has many possible events associated with it. You don't write C# code for each event method - only the ones you want the computer to respond to. Once you decide an event is to be 'coded,' you decide what you want to happen in that event method and translate those desires into actual lines of C# code. As seen earlier, the format for each event method is:

```
private void controlName_EventName(object sender, EventArgs
e)
{

            [C# code goes here]

}
```

In the header line (remember it's one long line), the word '**private'** indicates this method is private to the form (only usable by the form - don't worry about what this means right now). The word **void** indicates nothing is being computed by the method. The words enclosed in parentheses tell us what information is provided to the event method. These values are known as the method **arguments** and we won't concern ourselves with them right now. The code goes between the curly braces following this header line.

Writing the C# code is the creative portion of developing a Visual C# Express application. And, it is also where you need to be very exact. Misspellings, missing punctuation, and missing operators will make your programs inoperable. You will find that writing a computer program requires exactness. So, the process to write event methods is then:

- Decide which events you want to have some response to
- Decide what you want that response to be
- Translate that response into C# code
- Establish the event method in the code window
- Type in the C# code

And, it is a process best illustrated by example. This example project is saved as **FirstCode** in the course projects folder (**\VCSEKids\VCSEK Projects**).

Example

If Visual C# Express is not running on your computer, start it and begin a new project. Name it **FirstCode**.

- Put a single button on the form.
- Set the **Text** property of the form to **My First Code**.
- Set the **Name** property of the button to **btnBeep**.
- Set the **Text** property of the button to **Beep!!**

At this point in the design process, your form should look something like this:

We want to write a single event method - the method that responds to the **Click** event of the button. When we click on that button, we want to computer to make a beep sound. Let's look at how to establish the event method.

Display the code window (pressing <**F7**> is one way; choose **View**, then **Code** in the menu is another):

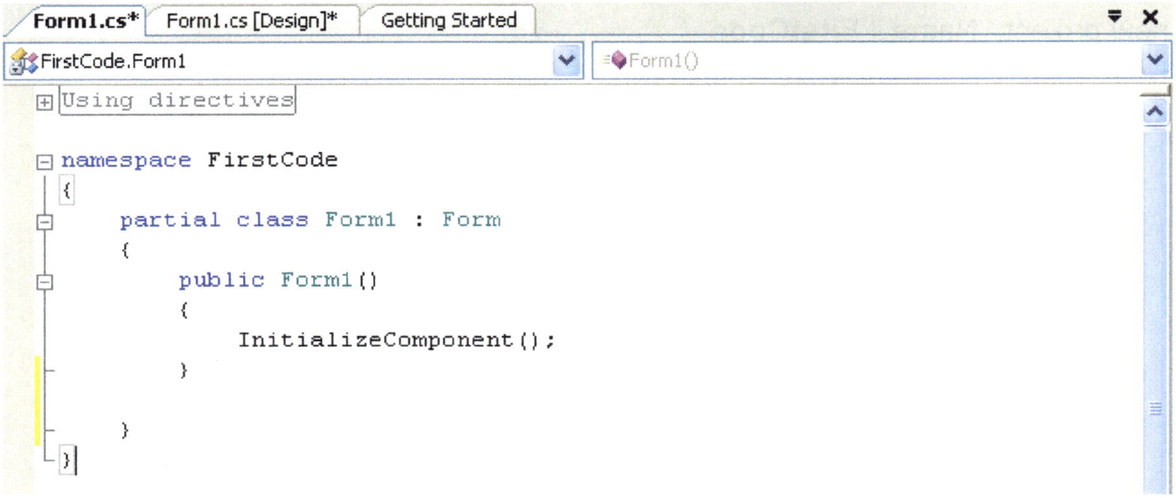

The header line (**namespace FirstCode**) starts the code. In Visual C# Express, everything that makes up your project is called a **namespace**. Your form is called a **class**. The line **public Form1()** begins the form **constructor**. The constructor consists of a single line saying **InitializeComponent();**. This code accesses a routine written by the Visual C# Express environment to set up the form that you designed. Notice again the use of curly braces to start and end code segments. You don't have to worry much about any of this code – just don't change any of it. The only code we will change is associated with event methods we establish and write. Let's do that now for the button control.

Recall when we looked at the properties window, we mentioned that, in addition to establishing control properties, that window is also used to establish event methods. Be aware that since the properties window has these two purposes, you should always be aware whether the **Properties** or **Events** button is selected in the window's toolbar. The steps to establish a blank event method for a particular control are:

- View the application form in design mode.
- Make desired control active, so its name appears at top of properties window.
- Go to properties window – select **Events** button (looks like a lightning bolt).
- Find event of interest.
- Double-click the event name.

At this point, the code window will open displaying the newly formed event method. Let's follow these steps for our button control.

We want to write code for the button control **Click** event. Display the form design window. Select the button control (**btnBeep**) in the properties window drop-down box (or click the button control on the form) to make it active. Scroll down the events list and highlight the Click event:

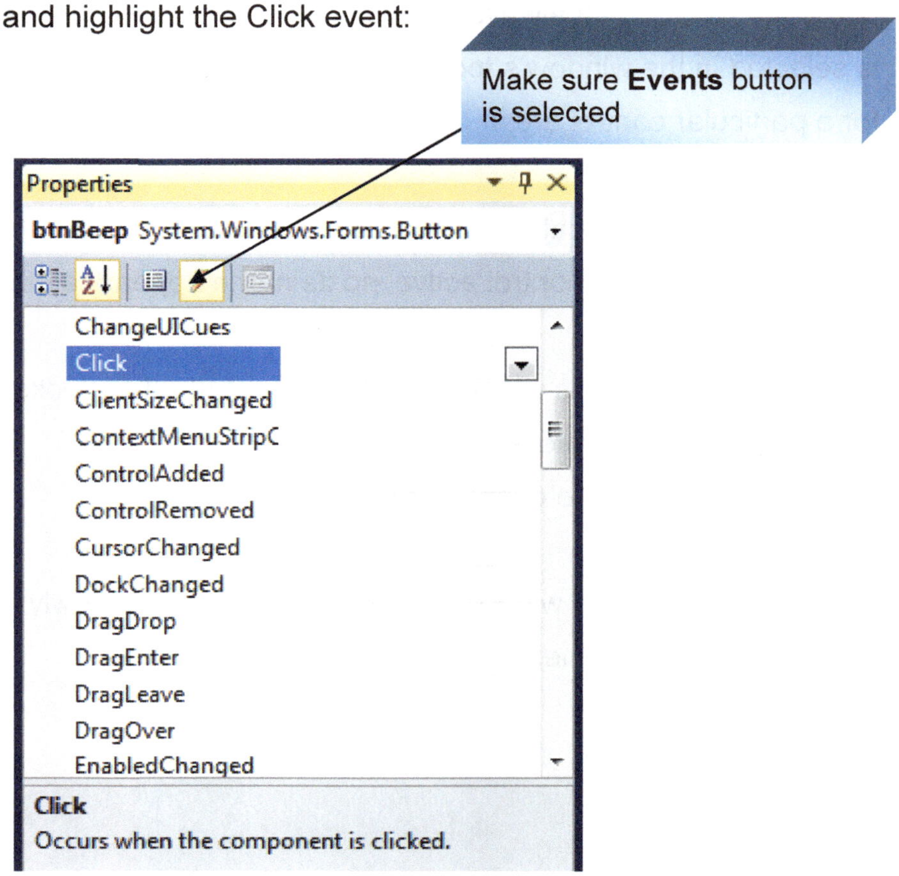

Any name already assigned to the **Click** event method would be listed on the right side of the properties window. There should be no name in that area – a name will be automatically assigned. Double-click the word **Click** in the properties window.

The code window should open and appear as:

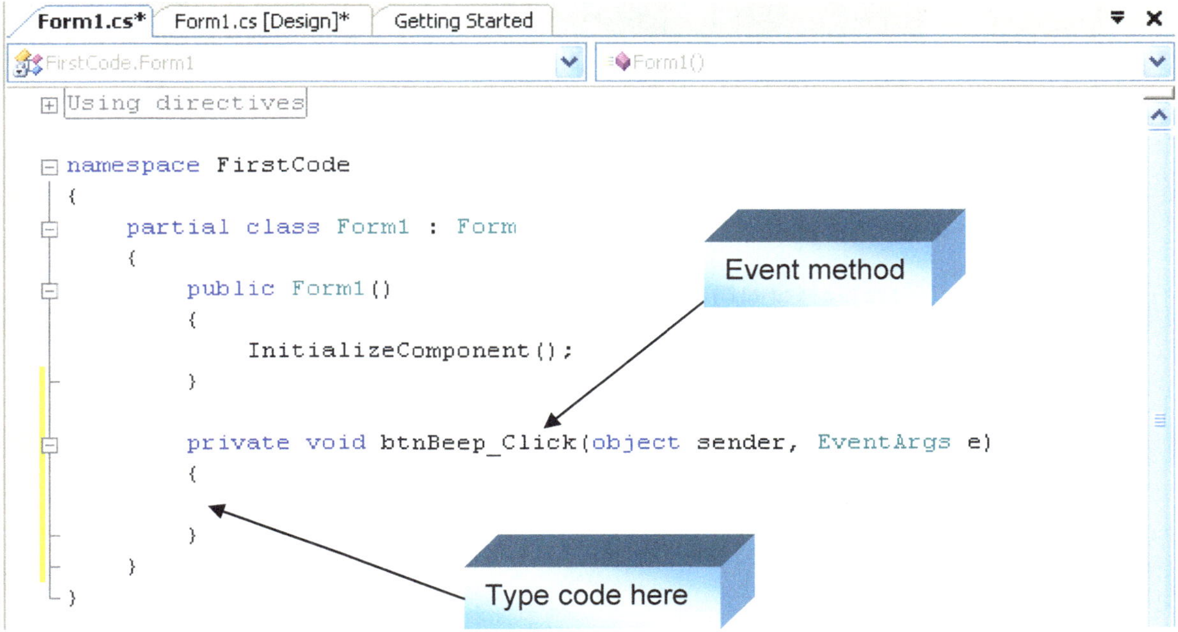

Notice the **Click** method for the **btnBeep** button is now displayed under the form constructor code. This is where all event methods will appear. If your return to the properties window, the method name **btnBeep_Click** will appear next to the Click event. We type the code to make the computer beep between the two curly braces following the method header line.

The code window acts like a word processor. You can type text in the window and use many of the normal editing features like cut, paste, copy, find, and replace. As you become a more proficient programmer, you will become comfortable with using the code window. Click on the region between the two braces. Type the single line exactly as shown:

```
System.Media.SystemSounds.Beep.Play();
```

The code window should now look like this:

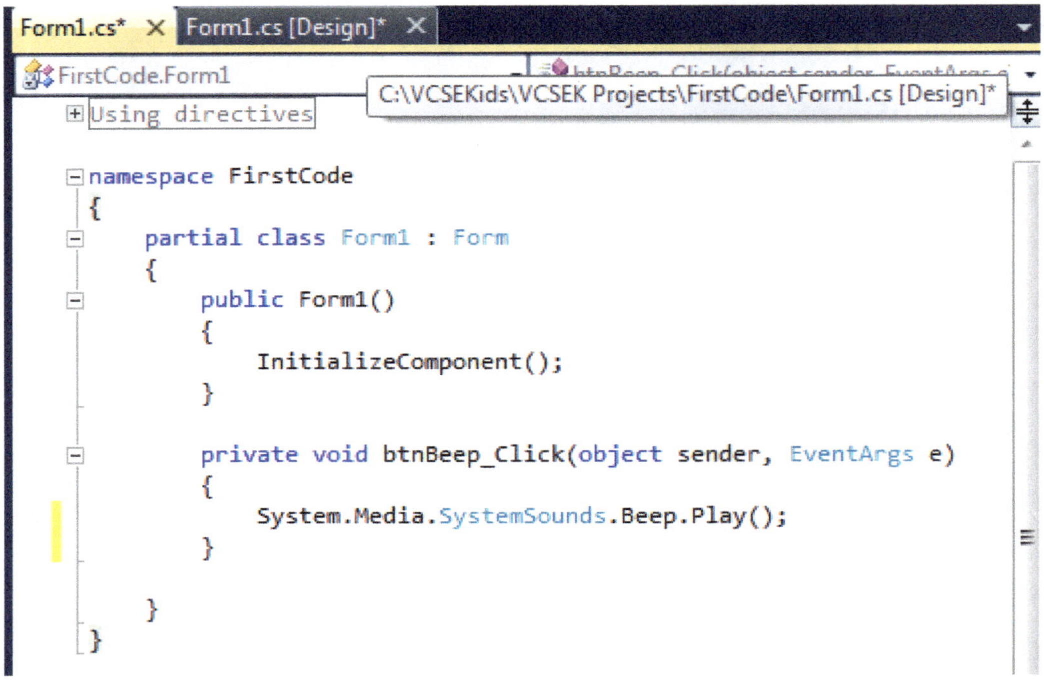

Notice after you typed the line, it was indented and parentheses were added at the end (indicating this is a built-in function). The Visual C# Express environment does this additional 'formatting.' The long line of code:

```
System.Media.SystemSounds.Beep.Play();
```

is a C# instruction that simply tells the computer to beep. You have now written your first line of C# code.

Your project is now ready to run. **Run** the project (click the **Start** button on the toolbar or press <**F5**>). The form will appear:

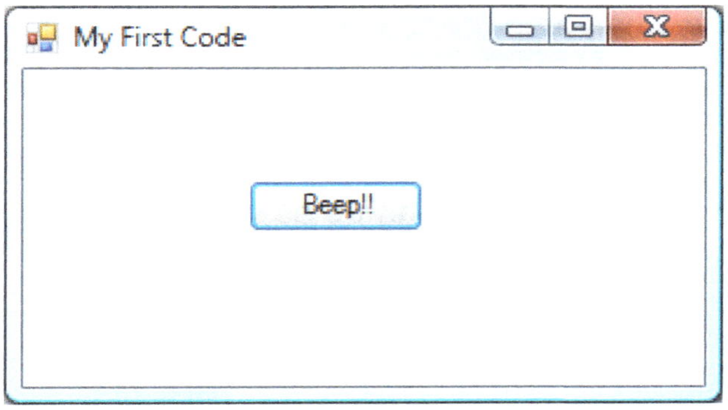

(If it doesn't, go back and make sure you've done all steps properly). Click the button. The computer should beep or some sound like a beep should be heard. You caused a **Click** event on the **btnBeep** control. The computer recognized this and went to the **btnBeep_Click** event method. There it interpreted the line of code [Console.Beep();] and made the computer beep. Stop your project. Go back to the code window and find the btnBeep_Click event. After the 'beep' line, add this line:

```
btnBeep.BackColor = Color.Blue;
```

Make sure you type it in exactly as shown, paying particular attention to letter case – code in computer programs must be exact. Run the project again. Click on the button. Explain what happens in relation to the control, the event method, and the C# code. Stop your project.

You may have noticed when you added this second line of code that as soon as you typed **btnBeep**, then a dot, a little window popped up with lots of choices for completing the line (**BackColor** was one of them). Similarly, once you typed **Color**, then a dot, a choice of colors (including **Blue**) popped up. This is the Visual C# Express **Intellisense** feature (you probably also noticed it when typing the code to make the computer beep). It helps a lot when it comes to typing code. Intellisense is a very useful part of Visual C# Express. You should become acquainted with its use and how to select suggested values. You usually just scroll down the list (you can type the first few letters of a choice for faster scrolling), pick the desired item and continue typing. The choice will be inserted in the proper location. We tell you about the Intellisense feature now so you won't be surprised when little boxes start popping up as you type code.

You have now finished your first complete Visual C# Express project. You followed the three steps of building an application:

1. Place controls on the form
2. Assign control properties
3. Write control event methods

You follow these same steps, whether building a very simple project like the one here or a very complicated project.

Now, knowing these steps, you're ready to start working your way through the Visual C# Express toolbox, learning what each control does. You can now begin learning elements of the C# language to help you write programs. And, you can begin learning new features of the Visual C# Express environment to aid you in project development. In each subsequent class, you will do just that: learn some new controls, learn some C#, and learn more about Visual C# Express.

4

Project Design, Forms, Buttons

Review and Preview

You have now learned the parts of a Visual C# Express project and the three steps involved in building a project:

1. Place controls on the form.
2. Set control properties.
3. Write desired event methods.

Do you have some ideas of projects you would like to build using Visual C# Express? If so, great. Beginning with this class, you will start to develop your own programming skills. In each class to come, you will learn some new features of the Visual C# Express environment, some new controls, and elements of the C# language. In this class, you will learn about project design, the form and button controls, and build a complete project.

Project Design

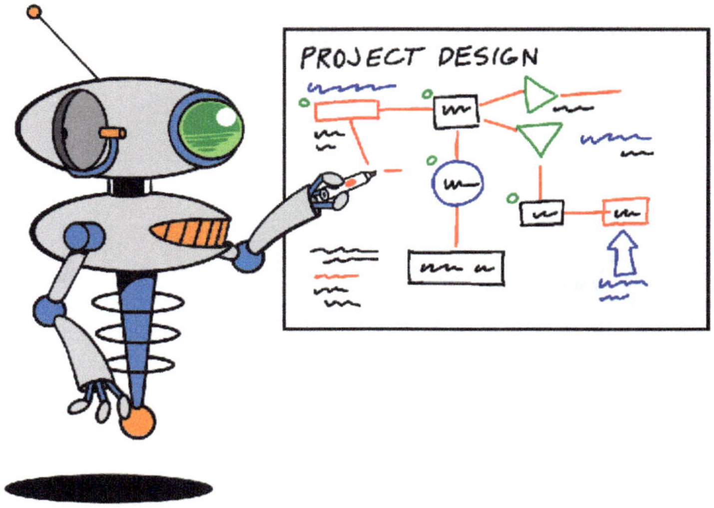

You are about to start developing projects using Visual C# Express. We will give you projects to build and maybe you will have ideas for your own projects. Either way, it's fun and exciting to see ideas end up as computer programs. But before starting a project, it's a good idea to spend a little time thinking about what you are trying to do. This idea of proper **project design** will save you lots of time and result in a far better project.

Proper project design is not really difficult. The main idea is to create a project that is easy to use, easy to understand, and free of errors. That makes sense, doesn't it? Spend some time thinking about everything you want your project to do. What information does the program need? What information does the computer determine? Decide what controls you need to use to provide these sets of information. Design a nice user interface (interface concerns placement of controls on the form). Consider appearance and ease of use. Make the interface consistent with other Windows applications, if possible. Familiarity is good in Windows based projects, like those developed using Visual C# Express.

Make the C# code in your event methods readable and easy to understand. This will make the job of making later changes (and you will make changes) much easier. Follow accepted programming rules - you will learn these rules as you learn more about C#.

Make sure there are no errors in your project. This may seem like an obvious statement, but many programs are not error-free. The Windows operating system has many errors floating around!

The importance of these few statements about project design might not make a lot of sense right now, but they will. The simple idea is to make a useful, clearly written, error-free project that is easy to use and easy to change. Planning carefully and planning ahead helps you achieve this goal. For each project built in this course, we will attempt to give you some insight into the project design process. We will always try to explain why we do what we do in building a project. And, we will always try to list all the considerations we make.

Saving a Visual C# Express Project

When a project is created in Visual C# Express, it is automatically saved in the location you specify. If you are making lots of changes, you might occasionally like to save your work prior to running the project. Do this by clicking the **Save All** button in the Visual C# Express toolbar. Look for a button that looks like several floppy disks. (With writeable CD's so cheap, how much longer do you think people will know what a floppy disk looks like? – many new machines don't even have a floppy disk drive!)

Save All
Toolbar Button

Always make sure to save your project before running it or before leaving Visual C# Express.

On-Line Help

Many times, while working in the Visual C# Express environment, you will have a question about something. You may wonder what a particular control does, what a particular property is for, what events a control has, or what a particular term in C# means. A great way to get help when you're stuck is to ask someone who knows the answer. People are usually happy to help you - they like the idea of helping you learn. You could also try to find the answer in a book and there are lots of Visual C# Express books out there! Or, another great way to get help is to use the Visual C# Express **On-Line Help** system.

Most Windows applications, including Visual C# Express, have help files available for your use. To access the Visual C# Express help system, click the **Help** item in the main menu, then **Contents**. At that point, you can search for the topic you need help on or scroll through all the topics. The Visual C# Express help system is just like all other Windows help systems. If you've ever used any on-line help system, using the system in Visual C# Express should be easy. If you've never used an on-line help system, ask someone for help. They're pretty easy to use. Or, click on **Start** on your Windows task bar, then choose **Help**. You can use that on-line help system to learn about how to use an on-line help system!

A great feature about the Visual C# Express on-line help system is that it is 'context sensitive.' What does this mean? Well, let's try it. Start Visual C# Express and start a new project. Go to the properties window. Scroll down the window displaying the form properties and click on the word **BackColor**. The word is highlighted. Press the **<F1>** key. A screen of information about the **Form.BackColor** property appears:

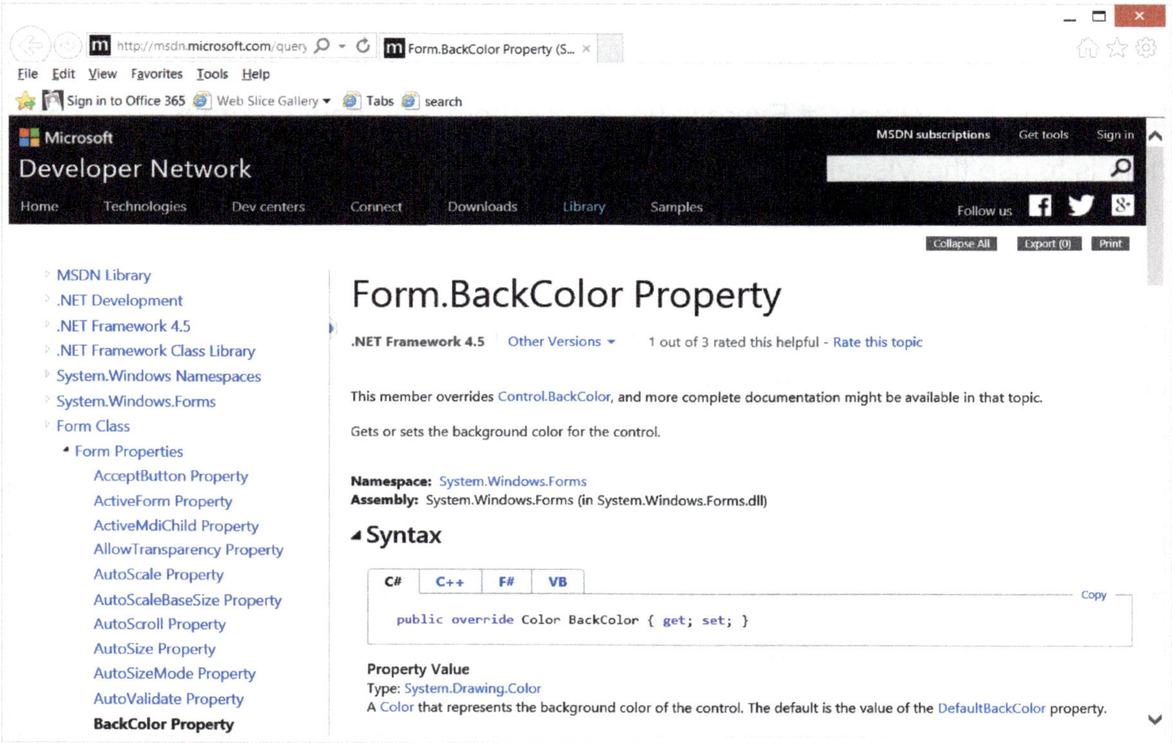

The help system has intelligence. It knows that since you highlighted the word BackColor, then pressed **<F1>** (**<F1>** has always been the key to press when you need help), you are asking for help about BackColor. Anytime you press **<F1>** while working in Visual C# Express, the program will look at where you are working and try to determine, based on context, what you are asking for help about. It looks at things like highlighted words in the properties window or position of the cursor in the code window. As you work with Visual C# Express, you will find you will use 'context-sensitive' help a lot. Many times, you can get quick answers to questions you might have. Get used to relying on the Visual C# Express on-line help system for assistance.

That's enough new material about the Visual C# Express environment. Now, let's look, in detail, at two important controls: the form itself and the button. Then we'll start our study of the C# language and build a complete project.

The Form Control

We have seen that the **form** is the central control in the development of a Visual C# Express project. Without a form, there can be no project! Let's look at some important properties and events for the form control. The form appears when you begin a new project.

Properties

Like all controls, the form has many (over 40) properties. Fortunately, we only have to know about some of them. The properties we will be concerned with are:

Property	Description
Name	Name used to identify form. In this course, we will always use the default **Form1** for the name.
Text	Text that appears in the title bar of form.
BackColor	Background color of form.
Icon	Reference to icon that appears in title bar of form (we'll look at creating icons in Class 7).

Width	Width of the form in pixels.
Height	Height of form in pixels.
FormBorderStyle	Form can either be sizable (can resize using the mouse) or fixed size.
StartPosition	Determines location of form on computer screen when application begins (we usually use a value of **CenterScreen**).

The form is primarily a 'container' for other controls. Being a container means many controls (the button control, studied next, is an exception) placed on the form will share the **BackColor** property. To change this behavior, select the desired control (after it is placed on the form) and change the color.

Example

To gain familiarity with these properties, start Visual C# Express and start a new project with just a form. Set the Height and Width property values (listed under **Size** in the properties window) and see their effect on form size. Resize the form and notice how those values are changed in the properties window. Set the Text property. Pick a new background color using the selection techniques discussed in Class 3. Try centering the form by changing the StartPosition property. To see the effect of the BorderStyle property, set a value (either **Fixed Single** or **Sizable;** these are the only values we'll use in this course) and run the project. Yes, you can run a project with just a form as a control! Try resizing the form in each case. Note the difference. Stop this example project.

Events

The form does support events. That is, it can respond to some user interactions. We will only be concerned with three form events in this course:

Event	Description
Click	Event executed when user clicks on the form with the mouse.
Load	Event executed when the form first loads into the computer's memory. This is a good place to set initial values for various properties and other project values.
FormClosing	Event called when the project is ending. This is a good place to 'clean up' your project.

Recall, to create any corresponding event method, make the form the active control, choose Events in the properties window, then double-click the name of the event. The event method will appear in the code window. To view an 'already-created' method in the code window, use the Methods List drop-down box at the top of the code window.

Typical Use of Form Control

For each control in this, and following chapters, we will provide information for how that control is typically used. The usual design steps for a **Form** control are:

- Set the **Text** property to a meaningful title.
- Set the **StartPosition** property (in this course, this property will almost always be set to **CenterScreen**)
- Set the **FormBorderStyle** to some value. In this course, we will mostly use **FixedSingle** forms.
- Write any needed initialization code in the form's **Load** event.
- Write any needed finalization code in the form's **FormClosing** event.

Button Control

The **button** is one of the more widely used Visual C# Express controls. Buttons are used to start, pause, or end particular processes. The button is selected from the toolbox. It appears as:

In Toolbox:

On Form (default properties):

Properties

A few useful properties for the button are:

Property	Description
Name	Name used to identify button. Three letter prefix for button names is **btn**.
Text	Text (caption) that appears on the button.
TextAlign	How the caption text is aligned on the button.
Font	Sets style, size, and type of caption text.

BackColor	Background color of button.
ForeColor	Color of text on button.
Left	Distance from left side of form to left side of button (referred to by X in properties window).
Top	Distance from top side of form to top side of button (referred to by Y in properties window).
Width	Width of the button in pixels.
Height	Height of button in pixels.
Enabled	Determines whether button can respond to user events (in run mode).
Visible	Determines whether the button appears on the form (in run mode).

Example

Start Visual C# Express and start a new project. Put a button on the form. Move the button around and notice the changes in X and Y properties (listed under **Location** in the properties window). Resize the button and notice how Width and Height change. Set the Text property. Change BackColor and ForeColor properties.

Many controls, in addition to the button, have a Font property, so let's take a little time to look at how to change it. Font establishes what the Text looks like. When you click on Font in the properties window, a button with something called an **ellipsis** will appear on the right side of the window:

Click this button and a **Font Window** will appear:

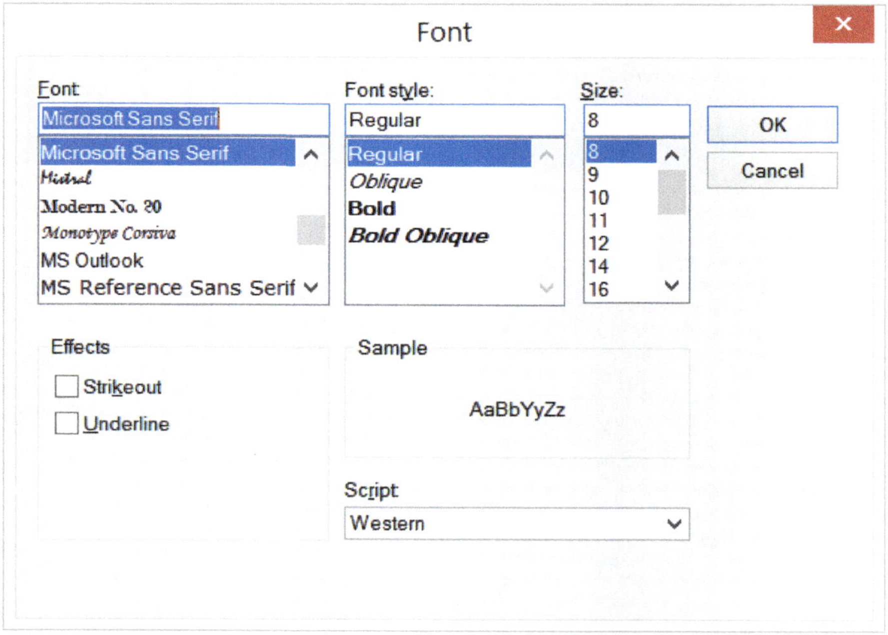

With this window, you can choose three primary pieces of information: **Font**, **Font Style**, and **Size**. You can also have an underlined font. This window lists information about all fonts stored on your computer. To set the Font property, make your choices in this window and click **OK**. Try different fonts, font styles, and font size for the button Text property.

Two other properties listed for the button are Enabled and Visible. Each of these properties can either be **True** (On) or **False** (Off). Most other controls also have these properties. Why do you need these?

If a control's Enabled property is False, the user is unable to access that control. Say you had a stopwatch project with a Start and Stop button:

You want the user to click Start, then Stop, to find the elapsed time. You wouldn't want the user to be able to click the Stop button before clicking the Start button. So, initially, you would have the Start button's Enabled property set to True and the Stop button's Enabled property set to False. This way, the user can only click Start. Once the user clicked Start, you would swap property values. That is, make the Start button's Enabled property False and the Stop button's Enabled property True. That way, the user could now only click Stop.

The effects of a False Enabled property are only evident when Visual C# Express is in run mode. When a button is not Enabled (Enabled is False), it will appear 'hazy' and the user won't be able to click it. When Stop is not Enabled on the stopwatch, it looks like this:

So, use the Enabled property when you want a control on the form to be temporarily disabled. This is a decision made in the project design process we discussed earlier.

The Visible property is a bit more drastic. When a control's Visible property is set to False (its default value is True), the control won't even be on the form! Now, why would we want a control we just placed on the form, set properties for, and wrote event methods for, to be invisible? The answer is similar to that for the Enabled property. Many times in a project, you will find you want a control to temporarily go away. Remember the **Sample** project in Class 1 where check boxes controlled whether toys were displayed or not. The display of the toys was controlled via the picture box control's Visible property. Or, in the little stopwatch example, instead of setting a button's Enabled property to False to make it 'unclickable,' we could just set the Visible property to False so it doesn't appear on the form at all. Either way, you would obtain the desired result. This is another project design decision. One more thing - like the Enabled property, the effects of Visible being False are only evident in run mode. This makes sense. It would be hard to design a project with invisible controls!

Now, play with the Enabled and Visible properties of the button in the example you have been working with. Once you set either property, run the project to see the results. Note with Enabled set to False, you can't click the button. Note with Visible set to False, the button isn't there. When done, stop the example project.

Events

There is only one button event of interest, but it is a very important one:

Event	Description
Click	Event executed when user clicks on the button with the mouse.

Every button will have an event method corresponding to the Click event.

Typical Use of Button Control

The usual design steps for a button control are:

- Set the **Name** and **Text** property.
- Write code in the button's **Click** event.
- You may also want to change the **Font**, **Backcolor** and **Forecolor** properties.

C# - The First Lesson

At long last, we are ready to get into the heart of a Visual C# Express project - the C# language. You have seen that, in a Visual C# Express project, event methods are used to connect control events to actual actions taken by the computer. These event methods are written using C#. So, you need to know C# to know Visual C# Express. In each subsequent class in this course, you will learn something new about the C# language.

Event Method Structure

You know, by now, that event methods are created using the properties window and viewed in the Visual C# Express code window. Each event method has the same general structure. First, there is a **header** line of the form:

```
private void controlName_EventName(object sender, EventArgs
e)
```

This tells us we are working with a **private** (only accessible from our form) method, returning no information (word **void**), that is executed when the event **EventName** occurs for the control **controlName**. Makes sense, doesn't it? Again, for now we will ignore the information contained in the parentheses.

The event method code is enclosed in a matched set of curly braces that follow the header line. The event method code is simply a set of line-by-line instructions to the computer, telling it what to do. The computer will process the first line, then the second, then all subsequent lines.

Some C# Programming Rules

The event method code is written in the C# language. C# is a set of keywords and symbols that are used to make the computer do things. There is a lot of content in C# and we'll try to look at much of it in this course. Just one warning at this point. We've said it before, but it's worth saying again. Computer programming requires exactness - it does not allow errors! The Visual C# Express environment can point out some errors to you, but not all. You must especially be exact when typing in event methods. Good typing skills are a necessity in the computer age. As you learn Visual C# Express programming, you might like also to improve your typing skills using some of the software that's available for that purpose. The better your typing skills, the fewer mistakes you will make in building your Visual C# Express applications.

Here are some rules to follow as you type in your C# code:

- C# code requires perfection. All keywords must be spelled correctly. If you type **BckColor** instead of **BackColor**, a human may know what you mean, but a computer won't.
- C# is case-sensitive, meaning upper and lower case letters are considered to be different characters. When typing code, make sure you use upper

and lower case letters properly. In C#, the words **Blue** and **blue** are completely different.

- Curly **braces** are used for grouping. They mark the beginning and end of programming sections. Make sure your C# code has an equal number of left and right braces. We call the section of code between matching braces a **block**.
- It is good coding practice to **indent** code within a block. This makes code easier to follow. Notice in examples we've seen, each block is indented 4 spaces. The Visual C# Express editor automatically indents code in blocks for you.
- Every C# statement will end with a semicolon. A **statement** is a program expression that generates some action (for example, the statement used to make the computer beep in the previous class). Note that not all C# expressions are statements (for example, the line defining an event method has no semicolon).

We'll learn a lot more C# programming rules as we progress.

Assignment Statement

The simplest, and most used, statement in C# is the **assignment** statement. It has this form:

```
leftSide = rightSide;
```

The symbol **=** is called the **assignment operator**. You may recognize this symbol as the equal sign you use in arithmetic, but it's not called an equal sign in computer programming. Why is that?

In an assignment statement, we say whatever is on the left side of the assignment statement is replaced by whatever is on the right side. The left side of the assignment statement can only be a single term, like a control property. The right side can be just about any legal C# expression. It might have some math that needs to be done or something else that needs to be evaluated. If there are such evaluations, they are completed <u>before</u> the assignment. We are talking in very general terms right now and we have to. The idea of an assignment statement will become very obvious as you learn just a little more C#.

Property Types

Recall a property describes something about a control: size, color, appearance. Each **property** has a specific **type** depending on the kind of information it represents. When we use the properties window to set a value in design mode, Visual C# Express automatically supplies the proper type. If we want to change a property in an event method using the C# assignment statement, we must know the property type so we can assign a properly typed value to it. Remember we use something called 'dot notation' to change properties in run mode:

```
controlName.PropertyName = PropertyValue;
```

controlName is the Name property assigned to the control, PropertyName is the property name, and PropertyValue is the new value we are assigning to PropertyName. We will be concerned with four property types.

The first property type is the **int** (stands for integer) type. These are properties that are represented by whole, non-decimal, numbers. Properties like the **Top**, **Left**, **Height**, and **Width** properties are integer type. So, if we assign a value to an integer type property, we will use integer numbers. As an example, to change the width property of a form to 1,100 pixels, we would write in C#:

```
this.Width = 1100;
```

Recall the keyword **this** is used to refer to the form. This says we replace the current Width of the form with the new value of 1100. Notice you write 1,100 as 1100 in C# - we can't use commas in large numbers.

A second property type involves **colors**. We need this to set properties like BackColor. Fortunately, Visual C# Express has a set of built-in colors to choose from. To set a control color (described by **ColorPropertyName**), we type:

```
controlName.ColorPropertyName = Color.ColorName;
```

As soon as we type the word **Color** and a dot on the right side of the assignment statement, a entire list of color names to choose from magically appears. To change the form background color to blue, use:

```
this.BackColor = Color.Blue;
```

Another property type is the **bool** (stands for Boolean) type. It takes its name from a famous mathematician (Boole). It can have two values: **true** or **false**. We saw that the Enabled and Visible properties for the button have Boolean values. So, when working with Boolean type properties, we must insure we only assign a value of true or a value of false. To make a form disappear (not a very good thing to do!), we would use the assignment statement:

```
this.Visible = false;
```

This says the current Visible property of the form is replaced by the Boolean value false. We could make it come back with:

```
this.Visible = true;
```

There is one possible point of confusion when working with Boolean values. When setting a Boolean value using the properties window, the two choices are **True** or **False**. When setting Boolean values using C# code, the two choices are

true or **false**. That is, in one case, upper case words are used and in the other, lower case words are used. Be aware of this when writing code. A common error is to use upper case values, rather than the proper lower case values.

The last property type we need to look at here is the **string** type. Properties of this type are simply what the definition says - strings of characters. A string can be a name, a string of numbers, a sentence, a paragraph, any characters at all. And, many times, a string will contain no characters at all (an empty string). The Text property is a string type property. We will do lots of work with strings in Visual C# Express, so it's something you should become familiar with. When assigning string type properties, the only trick is to make sure the string is enclosed in quotes ("). You may tend to forget this since string type property values are not enclosed in quotes in the properties window. To give our a form a caption in the title bar, we would use:

```
this.Text = "This is a caption in quotes";
```

This assignment statement says the Text property of the form is replaced by (or changed to) the string value on the right side of the statement. You should now have some idea of how assignment statements work.

Comments

When we talked about project design, it was mentioned that you should follow proper programming rules when writing your C# code. One such rule is to properly comment your code. You can place non-executable statements (ignored by the computer) in your code that explain what you are doing. These **comments** can be an aid in understanding your code. They also make future changes to your code much easier.

To place a comment in your code, use the comment symbol, two slashes (//). Anything written after the comment symbol will be ignored by the computer. You can have a comment take up a complete line of C# code, like this:

```
// Change form to blue
this.BackColor = Color.Blue;
```

Or, you can place the comment on the same line as the assignment statement:

```
this.BackColor = Color.Blue; // Makes form blue
```

You, as the programmer, should decide how much you want to comment your code. We will try in the projects provided in this course to provide adequate comments. Now, on to the first such project.

Project - Form Fun

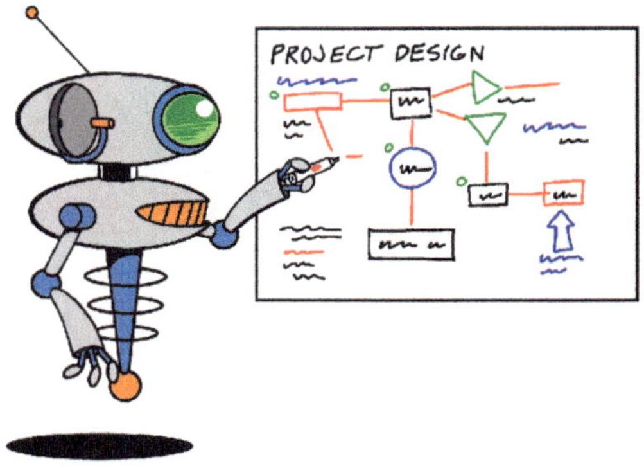

Project Design

In this project, we will have a little fun with form properties using buttons. We will have a button that makes the form grow, one that makes the form shrink, and two buttons that change the form color. We'll even have a couple of buttons that make the other buttons disappear and reappear. This project is saved as **FormFun** in the course projects folder (**\VCSEKids\VCSEK Projects**).

Place Controls on Form

Start a new project in Visual C# Express. Size the form so six buttons will fit on the form. Place six buttons on the form. Resize and move the buttons around until the form looks something like this:

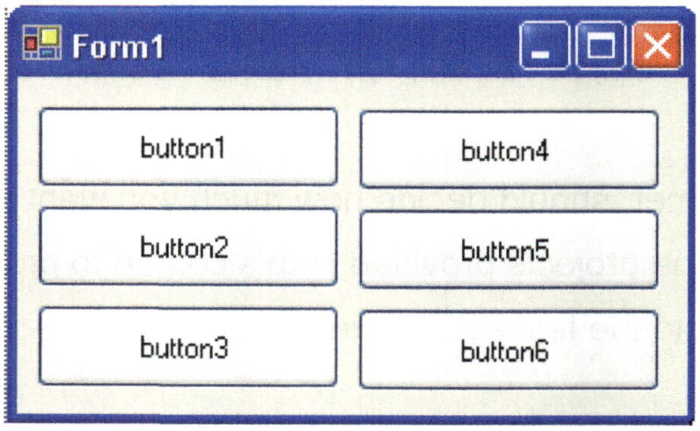

If you've used Windows applications for a while, you have probably used the edit feature known as **Copy** and **Paste**. That is, you can copy something you want to duplicate, move to the place you want your copy and then paste it. This is something done all the time in word processing. You may have discovered, in playing around with Visual C# Express, that you can copy and paste controls. Try it here with the button controls and in other projects if you like. It works pretty nicely.

Set Control Properties

Set the control properties using the properties window. Remember that to change the selected control in the properties window, you can either use the controls list at the top of the window or just click on the desired control. For project control properties, we will always list controls by their default names (those assigned by Visual C# Express when the control is placed on the form).

Form1 Form:

Property Name	**Property Value**
StartPosition	CenterScreen
Text	Form Fun

button1 Button:

Property Name	**Property Value**
Name	btnShrink
Text	Shrink Form

button2 Button:

Property Name	**Property Value**
Name	btnGrow
Text	Grow Form

button3 Button:

Property Name	**Property Value**
Name	btnHide
Text	Hide Buttons

button4 Button:

Property Name	**Property Value**
Name	btnRed
Text	Red Form

button5 Button:

Property Name	**Property Value**
Name	btnBlue
Text	Blue Form

button6 Button:

Property Name	**Property Value**
Name	btnShow
Text	Show Buttons
Visible	False

You can change other properties if you want - maybe change the Font property of the buttons. When you're done setting properties, your form should resemble this:

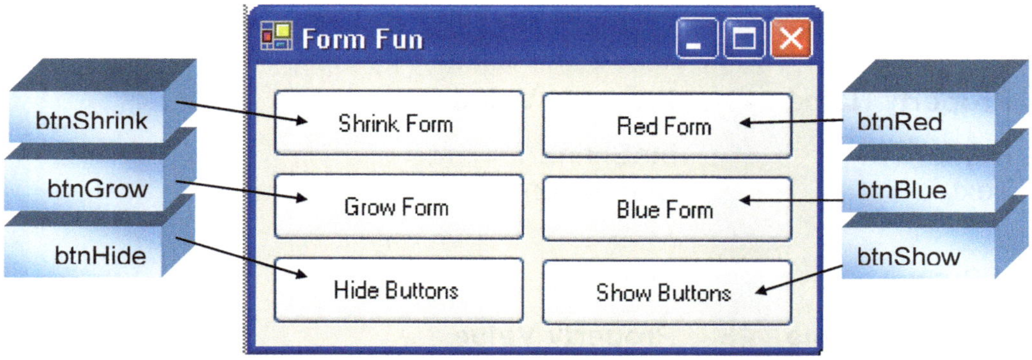

What we have are six buttons, two to change the size of the form, two to change form color, one to make buttons go away, and one to make buttons reappear. Notice the **Show Buttons** button has a Visible property of False. We don't want it on the form at first, since the buttons will already be there. When we make the buttons go away (by changing their Visible property) by clicking the **Hide Buttons** control, we will make the **Show Buttons** button appear. Makes sense, doesn't it? But, why is the **Show Buttons** button there if its Visible property is False? Remember a False Visible property will only be seen in run mode.

Write Event Methods

We have six buttons on our form. We need to write code for the **Click** event method for each of these buttons. We'll also want to write a **Click** event method for the form - we'll explain why. We have a button on the form that makes the form shrink. What if we shrink it so much, we can't click on the button to make it grow again? We can avoid that by allowing a click on the form to also grow the form. This 'thinking ahead' is one of the project design concepts we talked about.

Each event method is created using the properties window. To create the method, select the desired control on the form and go to the properties window. Click the **Events** button in the toolbar, scroll down to the desired event (**Click** in each case here) and double-click the event name. The code window will open with the method displayed. Then click in the region between the curly braces following the header line and start typing code. It's that easy. But, again, make sure you type in everything just as written in these notes. You must be exact!

First, let's type the **btnShrink_Click** event method. In this event method, we decrease the form height by 10 pixels and decrease the form width by 10 pixels:

```
private void btnShrink_Click(object sender, EventArgs e)
{
    // Shrink the form
    // Decrease the form height by 10 pixels
    this.Height = this.Height - 10;
    // Decrease the form width by 10 pixels
    this.Width = this.Width - 10;
}
```

Before looking at the other event methods, let's look a bit closer at this one since it uses a few ideas we haven't clearly discussed. This is the event method executed when you click on the button marked **Shrink Form**. You should easily recognize the comment statements. The non-comment statements change the form height and width. Look at the statement to change the height:

```
this.Height = this.Height - 10;
```

Recall how the assignment operator (=) works. The right side is evaluated first. So, 10 is subtracted (using the - sign) from the current form height. That value is assigned to the left side of the expression, this.Height. The result is the form Height property is replaced by the Height property minus 10 pixels. After this line of code, the Height property has decreased by 10 and the form will appear smaller on the screen.

This expression also shows why we call the assignment operator (=) just that and not an equal sign. Anyone can see the left side of this expression cannot possibly be equal to the right side of this expression. No matter what this.Height is, the right side will always be 10 smaller than the left side. But, even though this is not an equality, you will often hear programmers read this statement as "this.Height equals this.Height minus 10," knowing it's not true! Remember how assignment statements work as you begin writing your own programs.

Now, let's look at the other event methods. The **btnGrow_Click** event method increases form height by 10 pixels and increases form width by 10 pixels:

```
private void btnGrow_Click(object sender, EventArgs e)
{
    // Grow the form
    // Increase the form height by 10 pixels
    this.Height = this.Height + 10;
    // Increase the form width by 10 pixels
    this.Width = this.Width + 10;
}
```

The **btnRed_Click** event method changes the form background color to red:

```
private void btnRed_Click(object sender, EventArgs e)
{
    // Make form red
    this.BackColor = Color.Red;
}
```

while the **btnBlue_Click** event method changes the form background color to blue:

```
private void btnBlue_Click(object sender, EventArgs e)
{
    // Make form blue
    this.BackColor = Color.Blue;
}
```

The **btnHide_Click** event method is used to hide (set the **Visible** property to **false**) all buttons except **btnShow**, which is made **Visible** (note the use of lower case **true** and **false** when writing code):

```
private void btnHide_Click(object sender, EventArgs e)
{
    // Hide all buttons but btnShow
    btnGrow.Visible = false;
    btnShrink.Visible = false;
    btnHide.Visible = false;
    btnRed.Visible = false;
    btnBlue.Visible = false;
    // Show btnShow button
    btnShow.Visible = true;
}
```

and the **btnShow_Click** event method reverses these effects:

```
private void btnShow_Click(object sender, EventArgs e)
{
    // Show all buttons but btnShow
    btnGrow.Visible = true;
    btnShrink.Visible = true;
    btnHide.Visible = true;
    btnRed.Visible = true;
    btnBlue.Visible = true;
    // Hide btnShow button
    btnShow.Visible = false;
}
```

Lastly, the **Form1_Click** event method is also used to 'grow' the form, so it has the same code as **btnGrow_Click**:

```
private void Form1_Click(object sender, EventArgs e)
{
    // Grow the form
    // Increase the form height by 10 pixels
    this.Height = this.Height + 10;
    // Increase the form width by 10 pixels
    this.Width = this.Width + 10;
}
```

Save your project by clicking the **Save All** button (the multiple floppy disks button) in the toolbar.

You should easily be able to see what's going on in each of these methods. Pay special attention to how the Visible property was used in the **btnHide** and **btnShow** button click events. Notice too that many event methods are very similar in their coding. For example, the **Form1_Click** event is identical to the **btnGrow_Click** event. This is often the case in Visual C# Express projects. We encourage the use of editor features like Copy and Paste when writing code. To copy something, highlight the desired text using the mouse - the same way you do in a word processor. Then, select **Edit** in the Visual C# Express main menu, then **Copy**. Move the cursor to where you want to paste. You can even move to other event methods. Select **Edit**, then **Paste**. Voila! The copy appears. The pasted text might need a little editing, but you will find that copy and paste will save you lots of time when writing code. And, this is something you'll want to do since you probably have noticed there's quite a bit of typing in programming, even for simple project such as this. Also useful are **Find** and **Replace** editor features. Use them when you can.

The **Intellisense** feature of Visual C# Express is another way to reduce your typing load and the number of mistakes you might make. While you are writing C# in the code window, at certain points little boxes will pop up that display information that would logically complete the statement you are working on. This way, you can select the desired completion, rather than type it.

Run the Project

Go ahead! Run your project - click the **Start** button on the Visual C# Express toolbar. If it doesn't run properly, the only suggestion at this point is to stop the project, recheck your typing, and try again. We'll learn 'debugging' techniques in the next class. Here's a run I made where I grew the form and made it red:

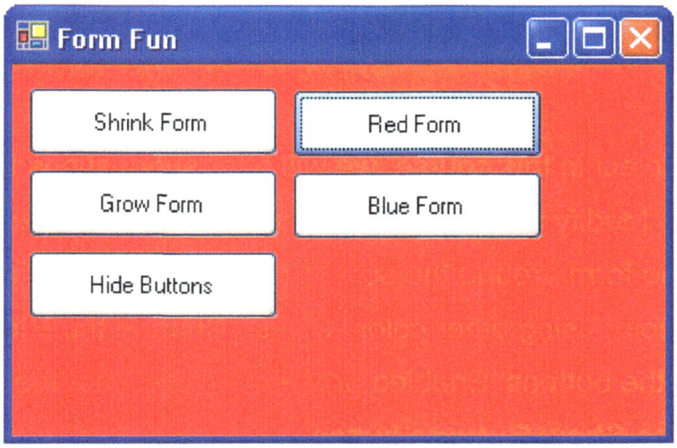

Try all the buttons. Grow the form, shrink the form, change form color, hide the buttons, make the buttons reappear. Make sure you try every button and make sure each works the way you want. Make sure clicking the form yields the desired result. This might seem like an obvious thing to do but, for large projects, sometimes certain events you have coded are never executed and you have no way of knowing if that particular event method works properly. This is another step in proper project design - thoroughly testing your project. Make sure every event works as intended. When done trying out this project, stop it (click the Visual C# Express toolbar **Stop** button).

Other Things to Try

For each project in this course, we will offer suggestions for changes you can make and try. Modify the **Shrink Form** and **Grow Form** buttons to make them also move the form around the screen (use the Left and Top properties). Change the form color using other color values. Change the **Hide Buttons** button so that it just sets the buttons' Enabled property to false, not the Visible property. Similarly, modify the **Show Buttons** button.

Congratulations! You have now completed a fairly detailed (at least there's more than one control) Visual C# Express project. You learned about project design, saving projects, details of the form and button controls, and how to build a complete project. You should now be comfortable with the three steps of building a project: placing controls, setting properties, and writing event methods. We will continue to use these steps in future classes to build other projects using new controls and more of the C# language.

5

Labels, Text Boxes, Variables

Review and Preview

We continue our look at the Visual C# Express environment and learn some new controls and new C# statements. As you work through this class, remember the three steps for building a Visual C# Express project: (1) place controls on form, (2) assign properties to controls, and (3) write event methods.

In this class, you will examine how to find and eliminate errors in your projects, learn about the label and text box controls, and about C# variables. You will build a project that helps you plan your savings.

Debugging a Visual C# Express Project

No matter how well you plan your project and no matter how careful you are in implementing your ideas in the controls and event methods, you will make mistakes. Errors, or what computer programmers call **bugs**, do creep into your project. You, as a programmer, need to have a strategy for finding and eliminating those bugs. The process of eliminating bugs in a project is called **debugging**. Unfortunately, there are not a lot of hard, fast rules for finding bugs in a program. Each programmer has his or her own way of attacking bugs. You will develop your ways. We can come up with some general strategies, though, and that's what we'll give you here.

Project errors, or bugs, can be divided into three types:

- **Syntax** errors
- **Run-time** errors
- **Logic** errors

Syntax errors occur when you make an error setting a property in design mode or when typing a line of C# code. Something is misspelled or something is left out that needs to be there. Your project won't run if there are any syntax errors. **Run-time errors** occur when you try to run your project. It will stop abruptly because something has happened beyond its control. **Logic errors** are the toughest to find. Your project will run OK, but the results it gives are not what you expected. Let's examine each error type and address possible debugging methods.

Syntax Errors

Syntax errors are the easiest to identify and eliminate. The Visual C# Express program is a big help in finding syntax errors. Syntax errors will most likely occur as you're setting properties for the controls or writing C# code for event methods.

Start a new project in Visual C# Express. Go to the project window and try to set the form **Width** property to the word **Junk**. (Click the plus sign next to the **Size** property to see **Width**.) What happened? You should see a little window like this:

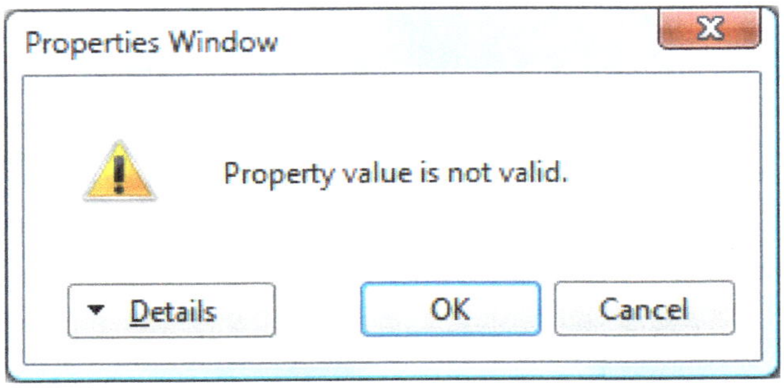

Click **Details** and you will see an explanation of the problem. Remember that property values must be the proper type. Assigning an improper type to a property is a **syntax** error. But, we see Visual C# Express won't let us make that mistake. Click **Cancel** to restore the **Width** to what it was before you tried to change it.

What happens if you cause a syntax error while writing code. Let's try it. Establish a **Form1_Load** event method using the properties window (recall: choose **Events** button in properties window, scroll down to **Load** event and double-click the event name). When the code window opens, under the left curly brace following the header line, type this line, then press <**Enter**>:

```
this.BackColor 0 Color.Red;
```

This would happen if you typed **0** instead of **=** in the assignment statement. What happened? In the code window, part of the line will appear underlined with a squiggle, similar to what Microsoft Word does when you misspell a word:

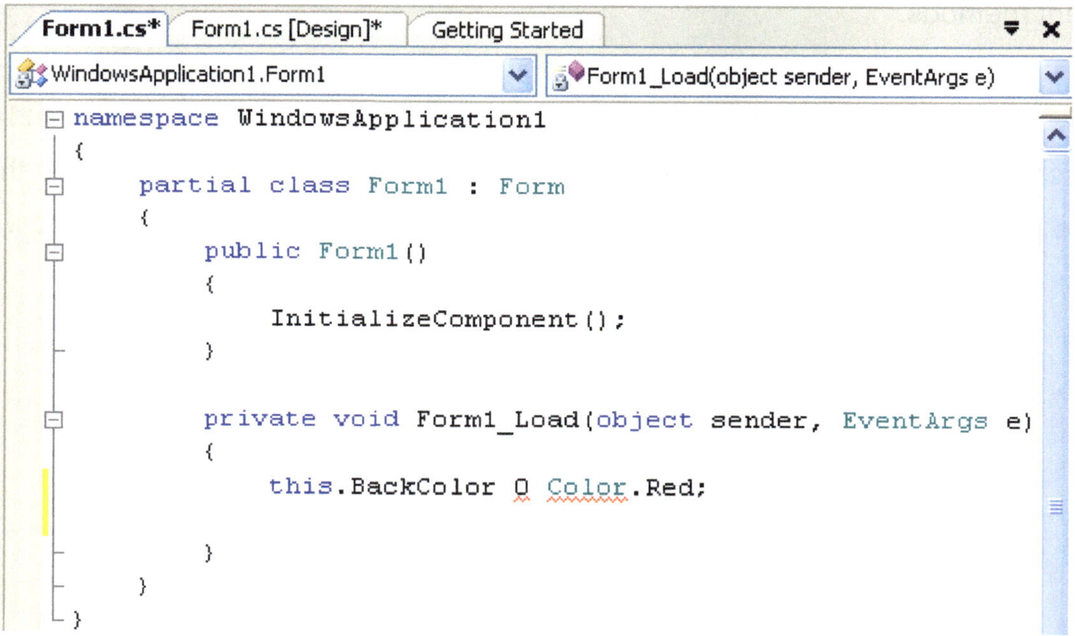

Visual C# Express has recognized that something is wrong with this statement. You should be able to see what. Any line with an error will be 'squiggled' in places. Placing the cursor over a squiggled line will give some indication of your error.

So, if you make a syntax error, Visual C# Express will usually know you've done something wrong and make you aware of your mistake. The on-line help system is a good resource for debugging your syntax errors. Note that syntax errors usually result because of incorrect typing - another great reason to improve your typing skills, if they need it.

Run-Time Errors

Once you successfully set control properties and write event methods, eliminating all identified syntax errors, you try to run your project. If the project runs, great! But, many times, your project may stop and tell you it found an error - this is a run-time error. You need to figure out why it stopped and fix the problem. Again, Visual C# Express and on-line help will usually give you enough information to eliminate run-time errors. Let's look at examples.

Working with the same example as above, try to run the project with the incorrect line of code. After you click the **Start** button on the toolbar, the following window should appear:

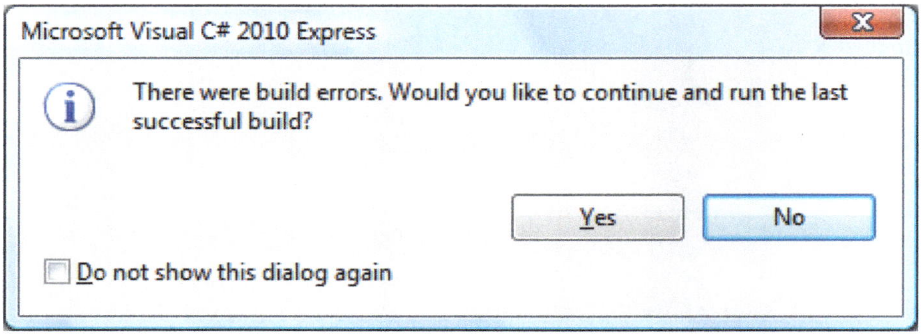

This tell us an error has occurred in trying to 'build' the project. Click **No** – we don't want to continue. We want to find the error. If 'build errors' occur, they are listed in another Visual C# Express window – the **Error List**. This list shows you all errors detected in trying to run your program. Go to that window now (if it's not there already, choose **View** in menu, select **Error List**. Error List appears in the Design window. Yours might be floating or docked somewhere.

My Error List window is:

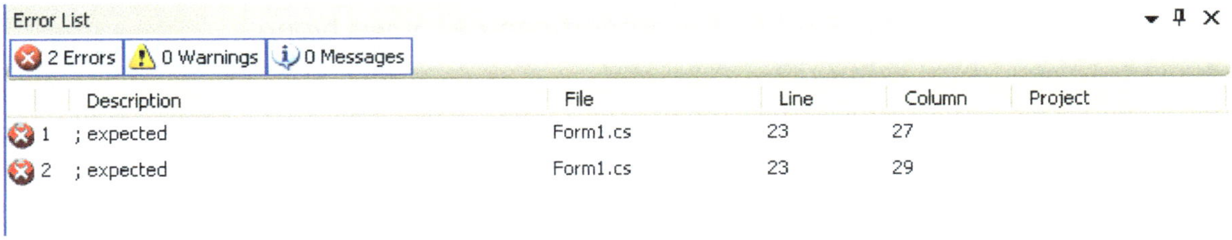

It has two errors that must be cleared before the program will run. Note each error refers to Line 23 on Form1, pointing to the offending line. Double-click the first error to move to the corresponding line – the error should be highlighted:

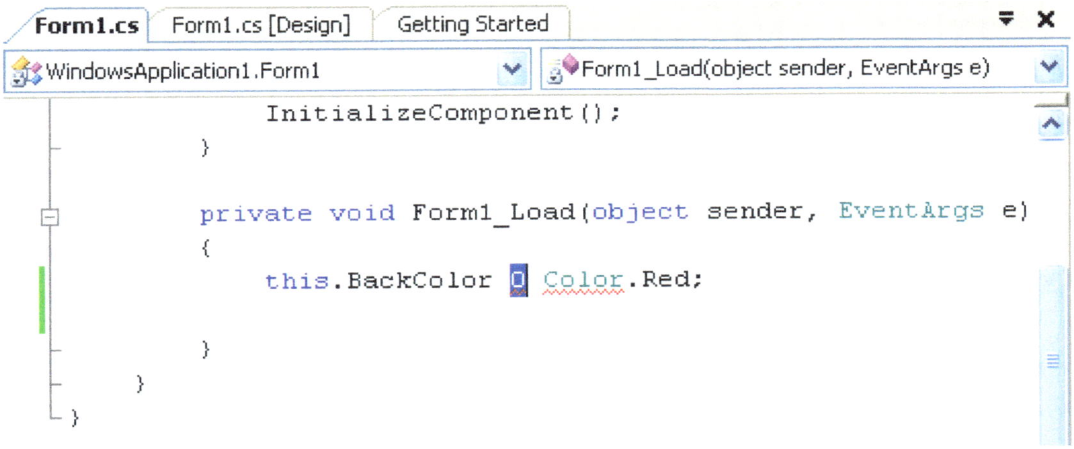

Visual C# Express is telling you that there is something wrong with how you used the **0**. Using the hints from the task list (the code expected an end-of-line indicator), you should be able to see that the assignment operator (**=**) is missing. If you don't see the problem, clicking **<F1>** might give you more help.

Let's say we corrected our error by adding the **=** sign, but we accidentally left out the letter '**k**' in the **BackColor** property name, or we typed:

```
this.BacColor = Color.Red;
```

Try running the project and you'll see another 'build error' window. Choose not to continue and go to the Error List:

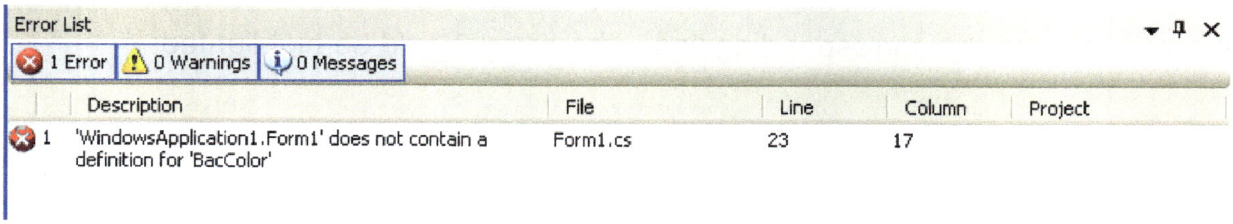

The message again points to Line 23, saying '**BacColor**' is not defined by the form. Again, go to Line 23 (double-click the error message) in the code window and you should see:

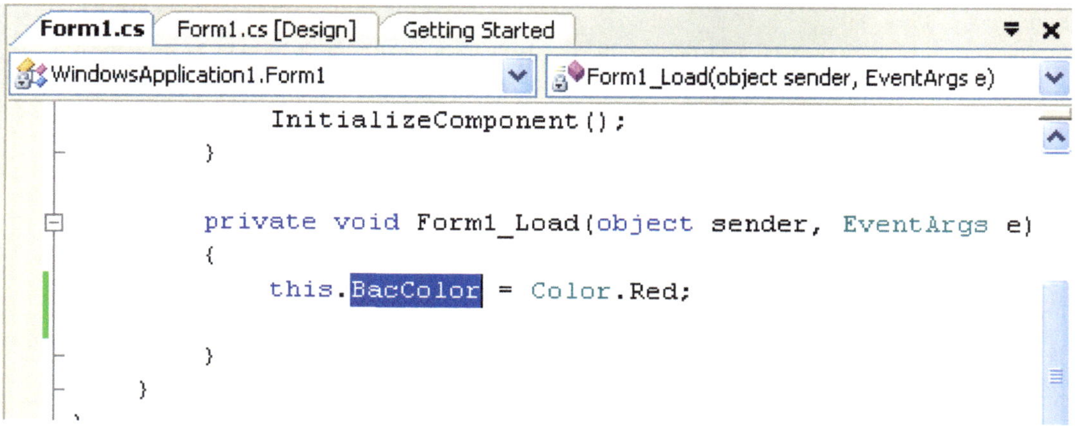

The word **BacColor** will be highlighted. Visual C# Express is telling you it can't find this property for the particular control (the form). You should note the misspelling and correct it.

Now, let's say you correct the property name, but mess up again and type **thiss** instead of **this** when referring to the form:

```
thiss.BackColor = Color.Red;
```

Run the project. You will get another build error, choose not to continue and view the Task list:

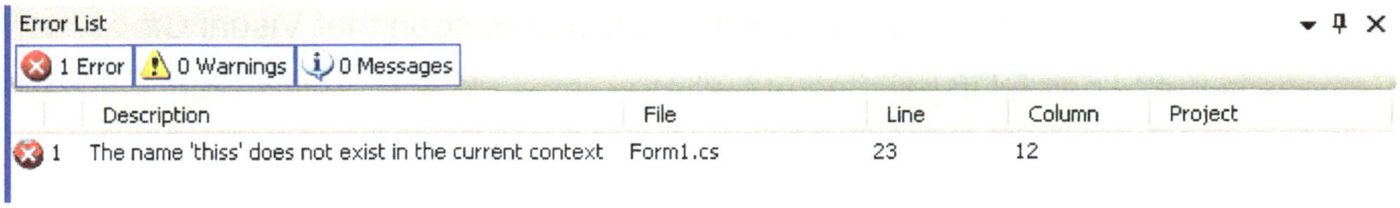

The key message here is 'thiss does not exist ...' This usually appears when you have misspelled the assigned name of a control in C# code. Visual C# Express is trying to assign a property to something using the 'dot notation':

```
controlName.PropertyName = Value;
```

But, it can't find a control with the given name (**thiss** in this case). Go to the code window, correct the error and run the application. You should finally get a red form!!

The errors we've caused here are three of the most common run-time errors: misspelling an assigned Name property, misspelling a property name, or leaving something out of an assignment statement. Notice each run-time error seen was detected prior to running, resulting in a build error. There are other run-time errors that may occur while your application is actually running.

Visual C# Express refers to some run-time errors as **exceptions**. If a window appears saying you have some kind of exception, the line with the detected error will be shown with suggestions for fixing the error. Be sure to stop the program before trying to fix the error.

We've seen a few typical run-time errors. There are others and you'll see lots of them as you start building projects. But, you've seen that Visual C# Express is pretty helpful in pointing out where errors are and on-line help is always available to explain them. One last thing about run-time errors. Visual C# Express will not find all errors at once. It will stop at the first run-time error it encounters. After you fix that error, there may be more. You have to fix run-time errors one at a time.

Logic Errors

Logic errors are the most difficult to find and eliminate. These are errors that don't keep your project from running, but cause incorrect or unexpected results. The only thing you can do at this point, if you suspect logic errors exist, is to dive into your project (primarily, the event methods) and make sure everything is coded exactly as you want it. Finding logic errors is a time-consuming art, not a science. There are no general rules for finding logic errors. Each programmer has his or her own particular way of searching for logic errors.

With the example we have been using, a logic error would be setting the form background color to blue, when you expected red. You would then go into the code to see why this is happening. You would see the color **Color.Blue** instead of the desired value **Color.Red**. Making the change would eliminate the logic error and the form will be red.

Unfortunately, eliminating logic errors is not as easy as this example. But, there is help. Visual C# Express has something called a **debugger** that helps you in the identification of logic errors. Using the debugger, you can print out properties and other values, stop your code wherever and whenever you want, and run your project line-by-line. Use of the debugger is an advanced topic and will not be talked about in this course. If you want to improve your Visual C# Express skills, you are encouraged to eventually learn how to use the debugger.

Now, let's improve your skills regarding Visual C# Express controls. We'll look at two new controls: the **label** and the **text box**.

Label Control

A **label** is a control that displays information the user cannot edit directly. It is most often used to provide titles for other controls. Or, it is used to display the results of some computer operation. The label control is selected from the toolbox. It appears as:

In Toolbox:

On Form (default properties):

Properties

A few useful properties for the label are:

<u>**Property**</u>	<u>**Description**</u>
Name	Name used to identify label. Three letter prefix for label names is **lbl**.
Text	Text (string type) that appears in the label.
TextAlign	Specifies how the label text is positioned.
Font	Sets style, size, and type of Text text.
BackColor	Sets label background color.
ForeColor	Sets color of Text text.
Left	Distance from left side of form to left side of label (referred to by X in properties window).
Top	Distance from top side of form to top side of label (referred to by Y in properties window).

Width	Width of the label in pixels.
Height	Height of label in pixels.
BorderStyle	Determines type of label border.
Visible	Determines whether the label appears on the form (in run mode).
AutoSize	If **True** (default value), label adjusts to size of text. If **False**, label can be resized.

Note, by default, the label control has no resizing handles. To resize the label, set AutoSize to False.

Example

Make sure Visual C# Express is running and start a new project. Put a label on the form. Resize it and move it, if desired. Set the Text property. Try different Fonts. See the difference among the BorderStyle possibilities; notice the default value (**None**) makes the button match with the form, **Fixed Single** places a box around the label, and **Fixed3D** gives the label a three-dimensional inset look. Change the BackColor and ForeColor properties. You may find certain color combinations that don't do a very good job of displaying the Text when in color. Make sure you are aware of combinations that do and don't work. You want your user to be able to read what is displayed.

The most used label property is Text. It holds the information that is displayed in the label control. There are two things you need to be aware of. First, by default, the label will 'grow' to hold any Text you might provide for it. If the label size is not acceptable, you can try things like changing **Font** or **AutoSize**. If the label is made to be larger than the text it holds (by setting AutoSize to False), you will also want to set the TextAlign property. Try different values of the

TextAlign property; there are nine different alignments selected from a 'graphical' menu:

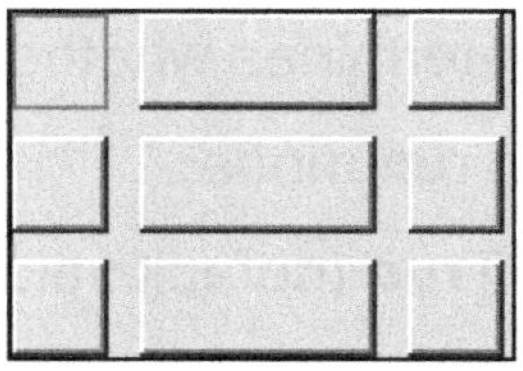

Vertical choices are: top, middle, and bottom justification. Horizontal choices are: left, center, and right justification.

The second thing you need to know is that Text is a string type property. It can only hold string values. When setting the Text property in run mode, the Text information must be in quotes. For example, if you have a label control named **lblExample** and you want to set the **Text** property to **My Label Box**, you would use the C# code (note the dot notation):

```
lblExample.Text = "My Label Box";
```

You don't have to worry about the quotes when setting the Text in design mode. Visual C# Express knows this is a string value.

Events

There is only one label event of interest:

Event	Description
Click	Event executed when user clicks on the label with the mouse.

With this event, you could allow your user to choose among a set of displayed label boxes. Why would you want to do this? Example applications include multiple choice answers in a test or color choices.

Typical Use of Label Control

The usual design steps for the label control to display unchanging text (for example, to provide titling information) are:

- Set the **Name** (though not really necessary since you rarely write code for a label control) and **Text** property.
- You may also want to change the **Font**, **Backcolor** and **Forecolor** properties.

To use the label control for changing text, for example, to show some computed results, use these steps:

- Set the **Name** property. Initialize **Text** to desired string.
- Set **AutoSize** to **False**, resize control and select desired value for **TextAlign**.
- Assign **Text** property (String type) in code where needed.
- You may also want to change the **Font**, **Backcolor** and **Forecolor** properties.

Text Box Control

The **text box** control is used to display information entered in design mode, by a user in run mode, or assigned within an event method. Just think of a text box as a label whose contents your user can (or may not be able to) change. The text box is selected from the Visual C# Express toolbox. It appears as:

In Toolbox:

On Form (default properties):

Properties

The text box has a wealth of useful properties:

Property	Description
Name	Name used to identify text box. Three letter prefix for text box names is **txt**.
Text	Text (string value) that appears in text box.
TextAlign	Sets whether Text is left-justified, right-justified, or centered in text box.
Font	Sets style, size, and type of Text.
MultiLine	Specifies whether text box displays one line or multiple lines.
ScrollBars	Specifies type of displayed scroll bar(s).
MaxLength	Maximum length of displayed Text. If **0**, length is unlimited.
BackColor	Sets text box background color.
ForeColor	Sets color of Text.

Left	Distance from left side of form to left side of text box (X in the properties window).
Top	Distance from top side of form to top side of text box (Y in the properties window).
Width	Width of the text box in pixels.
Height	Height of text box in pixels.
ReadOnly	If **True**, user can't change contents of text box (run mode only).
TabStop	If **False**, the control cannot be 'tabbed' to.
BorderStyle	Determines type of text box border.
Visible	Determines whether the text box appears on the form (in run mode).

Example

Start a new Visual C# Express project. Put a text box on the form. Resize it and move it, if desired. Set the Text property. Try different Fonts. Try different values of the TextAlign property. See the difference among the BorderStyle possibilities. The label box used **None** as default, the text box uses **Fixed3D**. Change the BackColor and ForeColor properties. Set MultiLine to **True** and try different ScrollBars values. I think you can see the text box is very flexible in how it appears on your form.

Like the Text property of the label control, the Text property of a text box is a string value. So, when setting the Text property in run mode, we must enclose the value in quotes (") to provide a proper assignment. Setting the Text property in design mode does not require (and you shouldn't use) quotes.

Events

The most important property of the text box is the Text property. As a programmer, you need to know when this property has changed in order to make use of the new value. There are two events you can use to do this:

Event	Description
TextChanged	Event executed whenever **Text** changes.
Leave	Event executed when the user leaves the text box and causes an event on another control.

The **TextChanged** event is executed a lot - every time a user presses a key while typing in the text box, the TextChanged event method is called. Looking at the Text property in this event method will give you its current value.

The **Leave** event is the more useful event for examining Text. Remember in placing controls on the form in design mode, you can make one control 'active' by clicking on it. There is a similar concept while an application is in run mode. A user can have interaction with only one control at a time. The control the user is interacting with (causing events) is said to have **focus**. While a user is typing in a text box, that box has focus. The Leave event is executed when you leave the text box and another control gets focus. At that point, we know the user is done typing in the text box and is done changing the Text property. That's why this event method is a good place to find the value of the Text property.

Typical Use of Text Box Control

There are two primary ways to use a text box – as an input control or as a display control. If the text box is used to accept some input from the user, the usual design steps:

- Set the **Name** property. Initialize **Text** property to desired string.
- If it is possible to input multiple lines, set **MultiLine** property to **True**. Also, set **ScrollBars** property, if desired.
- You may also want to change the **Font**, **Backcolor** and **Forecolor** properties.

If using the control just to display some information (no user modification possible), follow these usual design steps:

- Set the **Name** property. Initialize **Text** property to desired string.
- Set **ReadOnly** property to **True** (once you do this, note the background color will change).
- Set **TabStop** to False.
- If displaying more than one line, set **MultiLine** property to **True**.
- Assign **Text** property in code where needed.
- You may also want to change the **Font**, **Backcolor** and **Forecolor** properties.

C# - The Second Lesson

In this class, you will learn some new C# concepts. We will discuss variables (name, type, declaring), arithmetic operations, and some functions and techniques for working with strings.

Variables

All computer programs work with information of one kind or another. Numbers, text, colors and pictures are typical types of information they work with. Computer programs need places to store this information while working with it. We have seen one type of storage used by Visual C# Express projects - control properties. Control properties store information like control size, control appearance, control position on the form, and control colors.

But, control properties are not sufficient to store all information a project might need. What if we need to know how much ten bananas cost if they are 25 cents each? We would need a place to store the number of bananas, the cost of each banana, and the result of multiplying these two numbers together. To store information other than control properties in Visual C# Express projects, we use something called **variables**. They are called variables because the information stored there can change, or vary, during program execution. Variables are the primary method for moving information around in a Visual C# Express project. And, certain rules must be followed in the use of variables. These rules are very similar to those we have already established for control properties.

Variable Names

You must **name** every variable you use in your project. Rules for naming variables are:

- No more than 40 characters.
- Can only use letters, numbers, and the underscore (_) character.
- The first character must be a letter. It is customary, though not required, in Visual C# Express that this first letter be lower case.
- You cannot use a word reserved by Visual C# Express (for example, you can't have a variable named Form or one named Beep).

The most important rule is to use variable names that are meaningful. You should be able to identify the information stored in a variable by looking at its name. As an example, in our banana buying example, good names would be:

Quantity	**Variable Name**
Cost of each banana	bananaCost
Number of bananas purchased	bananas
Cost of all bananas	totalBananaCost

As mentioned in an earlier class, the Visual C# language is case sensitive. This means the names **BananaCost** and **bananacost** refer to <u>different</u> variables. Make sure you assign unique, easily identified, names to each variable. As with control names, we suggest mixing upper and lower case letters for improved readability. You will notice, as you type code, that the Visual C# Express editor will adjust the case of control names, variables and reserved C# keywords, as necessary.

Variable Types

We need to know the **type** of information stored by each variable. The same types used for properties can be applied to variables: **int** (integer), **bool** (Boolean) and **string**. There are other types too - consult on-line help for types you might want to use.

Here, we look at one more type we will use with variables: the **double** type. Up to now, all the projects we've worked with have used integer (or whole number) values. But, we know most 'real-world' mathematics involves decimal numbers. The double type is just that - a number that has a decimal point. In computer language, we call it a **floating point number**. The 'point' that is floating (moving around) is the decimal. Examples of double type numbers are:

2.00 -1.2 3.14159

Variables can appear in assignment statements:

```
variableName = NewValue;
```

Only a single variable can be on the left side of the assignment operator (=) while any legal C# expression, using any number of variables, can be on the right side of the operator. Recall that, in this statement, **NewValue** is evaluated first, then assigned to **variableName**. The major thing we need to be concerned with is that NewValue is the same **type** as variableName. That is, we must assign a properly typed value to the variable. This is the same thing we had to do with property values.

Declaring Variables

Once we have named a variable and determined what type we want it to be, we must relay this information to our Visual C# Express project. We need to **declare** our variables. (We don't have to declare control properties since Visual C# Express already knows about them.) The statement used to declare a variable named **variableName** as type **type** is:

```
type variableName;
```

We need a declaration statement like this for every variable in our project. This may seem like a lot of work, but it is worth it. Proper variable declaration makes programming easier, minimizes the possibility of program errors, and makes later program modification easier.

So, where do we put these variable declarations. Start a new Visual C# Express project and bring up the code window. The code window will look like this:

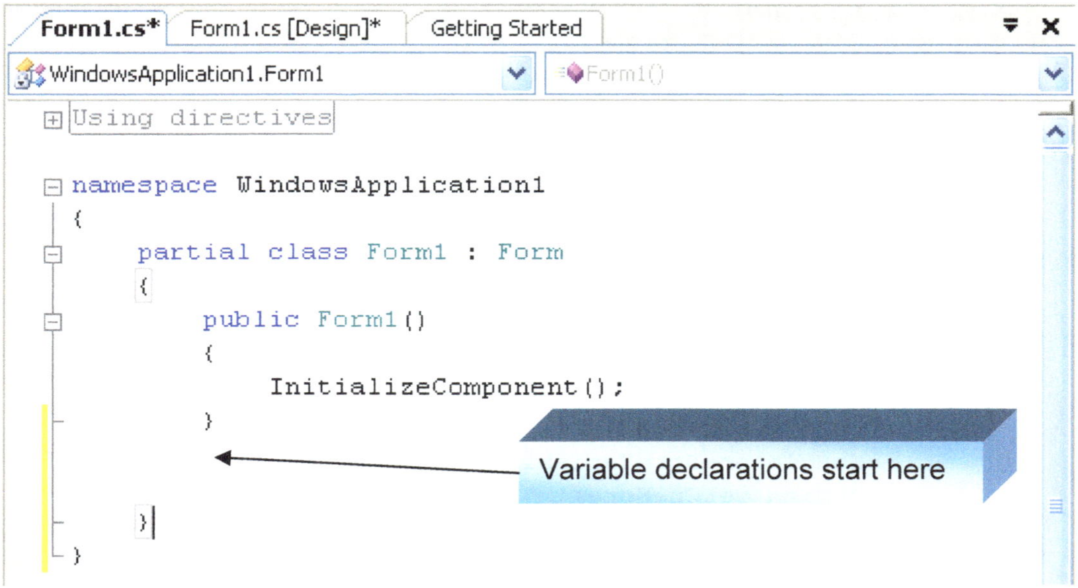

We will put variable declaration statements directly beneath form constructor code (**Public Form1**) and <u>before</u> any event methods. This location in the code window is known as the **general declarations** area and any variables declared here can be used (the value can be accessed and/or changed) in any of the project's event methods.

Try typing some variable declarations in the code window. Here are some examples to try:

Type Casting

In each assignment statement, it is important that the type of data on both sides of the operator (=) is the same. That is, if the variable on the left side of the operator is an int, the result of the expression on the right side should be int. Visual C# (by default) will try to do any conversions for you. When it can't, an error message will be printed. In those cases, you need to explicitly **cast** the result. This means convert the right side to the same side as the left side. Assuming the desired type is **type**, the casting statement is:

```
leftSide = (type) rightSide;
```

You can cast from any basic type (decimal and integer numbers) to any other basic type. For example, in the statement:

```
a = (int) (3.14159);
```

The variable **a** (an **int** type) will be assigned a value of 3.

Be careful when casting from higher precision numbers to lower precision numbers. Problems arise when you are outside the range of numbers.

Arithmetic Operators

One thing computer programs are very good at is doing arithmetic. They can add, subtract, multiply, and divide numbers very quickly. We need to know how to make our Visual C# Express projects do arithmetic. There are five **arithmetic operators** in the C# language.

Addition is done using the plus (**+**) sign and **subtraction** is done using the minus (**-**) sign. Simple examples are:

Operation	**Example**	**Result**
Addition	7 + 2	9
Addition	3 + 8	11
Subtraction	6 - 4	2
Subtraction	11 - 7	4

Multiplication is done using the asterisk (*) and **division** is done using the slash (/). Simple examples are:

Operation	**Example**	
	Result	
Multiplication	8 * 4	32
Multiplication	2 * 12	24
Division	12 / 2	6
Division	42 / 6	7

I'm sure you've done addition, subtraction, multiplication, and division before and understand how each operation works. The other arithmetic operator may not familiar to you, though.

The other arithmetic operator we use is called the remainder operator (**%**). This operator gives you the remainder that results from dividing two whole numbers. It may not be obvious now, but the remainder operator is used a lot in computer programming. Examples:

Example	**Division Result**	**Remainder Result**
7 % 4	1 Remainder 3	3
14 % 3	4 Remainder 2	2
25 % 5	5 Remainder 0	0

Study these examples so you understand how the remainder operator works in C#.

What happens if an assignment statement contains more than one arithmetic operator? Does it make any difference? Look at this example:

7 + 3 * 4

What's the answer? Well, it depends. If you work left to right and add 7 and 3 first, then multiply by 4, the answer is 40. If you multiply 3 times 4 first, then add 7, the answer is 19. Confusing? Well, yes. But, C# takes away the possibility of such confusion by having rules of **precedence**. This means there is a specific order in which arithmetic operations will be performed. That order is:

1. Multiplication (*) and division (/)
2. Remainder (%)
3. Addition (+) and subtraction (-)

So, in an assignment statement, all multiplications and divisions are done first, then remainder operations, and lastly, additions and subtractions. In our example (7 + 3 * 4), we see the multiplication will be done before the addition, so the answer provided by C# would be 19.

If two operators have the same precedence level, for example, multiplication and division, the operations are done left to right in the assignment statement. For example:

```
24 / 2 * 3
```

The division (24 / 2) is done first yielding a 12, then the multiplication (12 * 3), so the answer is 36. But what if we want to do the multiplication before the division - can that be done? Yes - using the C# **grouping operators** - parentheses **()**. By using parentheses in an assignment statement, you force operations within the parentheses to be done first.
So, if we rewrite our example as:

```
24 / (2 * 3)
```

the multiplication (2 * 3) will be done first yielding 6, then the division (24 / 6), yielding the desired result of 4. You can use as many parentheses as you want, but make sure they are always in pairs - every left parenthesis needs a right parenthesis. If you nest parentheses, that is have one set inside another, evaluation will start with the innermost set of parentheses and move outward. For example, look at:

((2 + 4) * 6) + 7

The addition of 2 and 4 is done first, yielding a 6, which is multiplied by 6, yielding 36. This result is then added to 7, with the final answer being 43. You might also want to use parentheses even if they don't change precedence. Many times, they are used just to clarify what is going on in an assignment statement.

As you improve your programming skills, make sure you know how each of the arithmetic operators work, what the precedence order is, and how to use parentheses. Always double-check your assignment statements to make sure they are providing the results you want.

Some examples of C# assignment statements with arithmetic operators:

```
totalBananaCost = numberBananas * bananaCost;
numberOfWeeks = numberOfDays / 7;
averageScore = (score1 + score2 + score3) / 3.0;
```

Notice a couple of things here. First, notice the parentheses in the **averageScore** calculation forces C# to add the three scores <u>before</u> dividing by 3. Also, notice the use of "white space," spaces separating operators from variables. This is a common practice in C# that helps code be more readable. We'll see lots and lots of examples of assignment statements as we build projects in this course.

String/Number Conversion Methods

A common task in any Visual C# Express project is to take numbers input by the user, do some arithmetic operations on those numbers, and output the results of those operations. How do you do this? With the Visual C# Express knowledge you have up to this point, you probably see you could use text box controls to allow the user to input numbers. Then you could use the arithmetic operators to do the math and label controls to display the results of the math. And, that's just what you would do. But, there are two problems:

Problem One: Arithmetic operators can only work with numbers (for example, integer variables and integer properties), but the value provided by a text box control (the Text property) is a string. You can't add and multiply string type variables and properties!

Problem Two: The result of arithmetic operations is a number. But the Text property of a label control (where we want to display these results) is a string type. You can't store numerical data in a string quantity!

We need solutions to these two problems. The solutions lie in the **C# built-in methods**. We need ways to convert strings to numbers and, conversely, numbers to strings. With this ability, we could take the Text property from a text box, convert it to a number, do some math, and convert that numerical result to a string that could be used as a Text property in a label box. This is a very common task in C# and C# has a large set of methods that help us do such common tasks. We will look at these in a bit, but first let's define just what a method is.

A C# method is a built-in procedure that, given some information by us, computes some desired value. The format for using a method is:

```
methodValue = MethodName(ArgumentList);
```

MethodName is the name of the method and **ArgumentList** is a list of values (separated by commas) provided to the function so it can do its work. In this assignment statement, MethodName uses the values in ArgumentList to compute a result and assign that result to the variable we have named **methodValue**. We must insure the variable methodValue has the same type as the value computed by MethodName. How do we know what C# functions exist, what type of information they provide, and what type of **arguments** they require? Use the Visual C# Express on-line help system and search for **Methods**. You'll see that there are lots of them. We'll cover some of them in this class, but you'll have to do a little studying on your own to learn about most of them. Now, let's look at some C# methods that help in converting numbers to strings and vice versa.

There are two C# methods we will use to convert a string type variable (or control property) to a numerical value. The method **Convert.ToInt32** method converts a **string** type to an **int** type (the 32 implies 32 bits are used to store an int type).
The format for using this function is:

```
yourNumber = Convert.ToInt32(yourString);
```

The **Convert.ToInt32** method takes the **yourString** variable (remember this is called an argument of the method), converts it to a numerical value, and assigns it to the variable **yourNumber** (which must be an int type). We could then use yourNumber in any arithmetic statement. Recall strings must be enclosed in quotes. An example using this method:

```
yourNumber = Convert.ToInt32("23");
```

Following this assignment statement, the variable yourNumber has a numerical value of 23.

The corresponding method that converts a **string** to a **double** type is Convert.ToDouble. The format for using this function is:

```
yourNumber = Convert.ToDouble(yourString);
```

The **Convert.ToDouble** method takes the **yourString** variable, converts it to a numerical value, and assigns it to the variable **yourNumber** (which must be a double type). We could then use yourNumber in any arithmetic statement. An example using this method:

```
yourNumber = Convert.ToDouble("3.14159");
```

Following this assignment statement, the variable yourNumber has a numerical value of 3.14159.

The C# **Convert.ToString** method will convert any numerical variable (or control property) to a **string**. The format for using this method is:

```
yourString = Convert.ToString(yourNumber);
```

The **Convert.ToString** method takes the **yourNumber** argument, converts it to a string type value, and assigns it to the string variable named **yourString**. In the example:

```
yourString = Convert.ToString(23);
```

the variable yourString has a string value of “23”. And, with:

```
yourString = Convert.ToString(3.14159);
```

the variable yourString has a string value of “3.14159”.

You should be comfortable with converting numbers to strings and strings to numbers using these methods. As mentioned, this is one of the more common tasks you will use when developing Visual C# Express projects.

String Concatenation

A confession - in the above discussion, you were told a little lie. The statement was made that you couldn't add and multiply strings. Well, you can't multiply them, but you can do something similar to addition. Many times in Visual C# Express projects, you want to take a string variable from one place and 'tack it on the end' of another string. The fancy word for this is **string concatenation**. . The concatenation operator is a plus sign (**+**) and it is easy to use. As an example:

```
newString = "Visual C# Express " + "is Fun!";
```

After this statement, the string variable **newString** will have the value "Visual C# Express is Fun!".

Notice the string concatenation operator is identical to the addition operator. We always need to insure there is no confusion when using both. As you've seen, string variables are a big part of Visual C# Express. As you develop as a programmer, you need to become comfortable with strings and working with them. You're now ready to attack a new project.

Project - Savings Account

Project Design

In this project, we will build a savings account calculator. We will input how much money we can put into an account each week and the number of weeks we put money in the account. The project will then compute how much we saved. We will use text boxes as both the input controls and for output information. A button will be used to do the computation. This project is saved as **Savings** in the course projects folder (**\VCSEKids\VCSEK Projects**).

Place Controls on Form

Start a new project in Visual C# Express. Place three text box controls, three label controls, and two buttons on the form. Your form should resemble this:

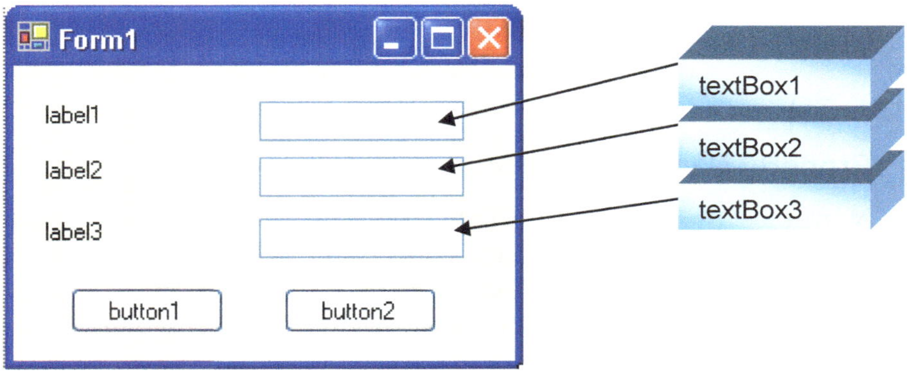

Again, try using copy and paste for the similar controls.

Set Control Properties

Set the control properties using the properties window (remember, controls are listed by their default name):

Form1 Form:

Property Name	Property Value
Text	Savings Account
FormBorderStyle	Fixed Single
StartPosition	CenterScreen

label1 Label:

Property Name	Property Value
Name	lblDepositHeading
Text	Weekly Deposit
Font	Arial
Font Size	10

label2 Label:

Property Name	Property Value
Name	lblWeeksHeading
Text	Number of Weeks
Font	Arial
Font Size	10

label3 Label:

Property Name	Property Value
Name	lblTotalHeading
Text	Total Savings
Font	Arial
Font Size	10

textbox1 Text Box:

Property Name	**Property Value**
Name	txtDeposit
TextAlign	Right
Font	Arial
Font Size	10

textbox2 Text Box:

Property Name	**Property Value**
Name	txtWeeks
TextAlign	Right
Font	Arial
Font Size	10

textbox3 Text Box:

Property Name	**Property Value**
Name	txtTotal
TextAlign	Right
Font	Arial
Font Size	10
ReadOnly	True
BackColor	White
TabStop	False

(Note the background color changes when setting ReadOnly to True. Hence, we set BackColor to White to match the appearance of the other two text boxes.)

button1 Button:

Property Name	**Property Value**
Name	btnCompute
Text	Compute

button2 Button:

Property Name	**Property Value**
Name	btnExit
Text	Exit

Note this is the first time you have been asked to change Font properties. Review the procedure for doing this (Class 4 under Button Control), if necessary. Change any other properties, like colors, if you would like. When you are done, your form should resemble this:

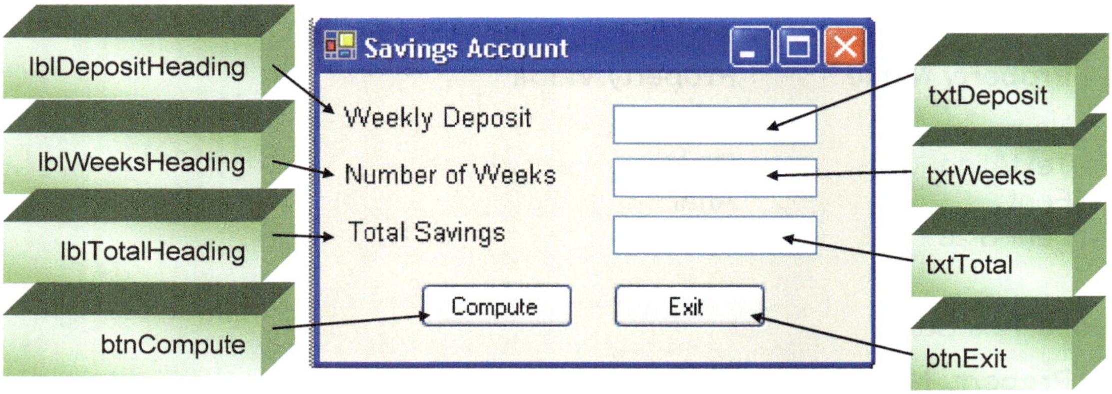

Write Event Procedures

In this project, the user types an amount in the **Weekly Deposit** text box. Then, the user types a value in the **Number of Weeks** text box. Following this, the user clicks the **Compute** button. The project determines the total amount in the savings account and displays it in the lower text box control. Hence, the primary event in this project is the **Click** event on the Compute button. The only other event is the **Click** event on the **Exit** button. It's always good to have an obvious way for the user to exit a project.

We need three variables in this project (we will use **int** types), one to hold the weekly deposit amount (**deposit**), one to store the number of weeks (**weeks**), and one to store the total savings (**total**). Open the code window and find the **general declarations** area (the area right under the form constructor code). Declare these three variables:

```
int deposit;
int weeks;
int total;
```

The code window should appear as:

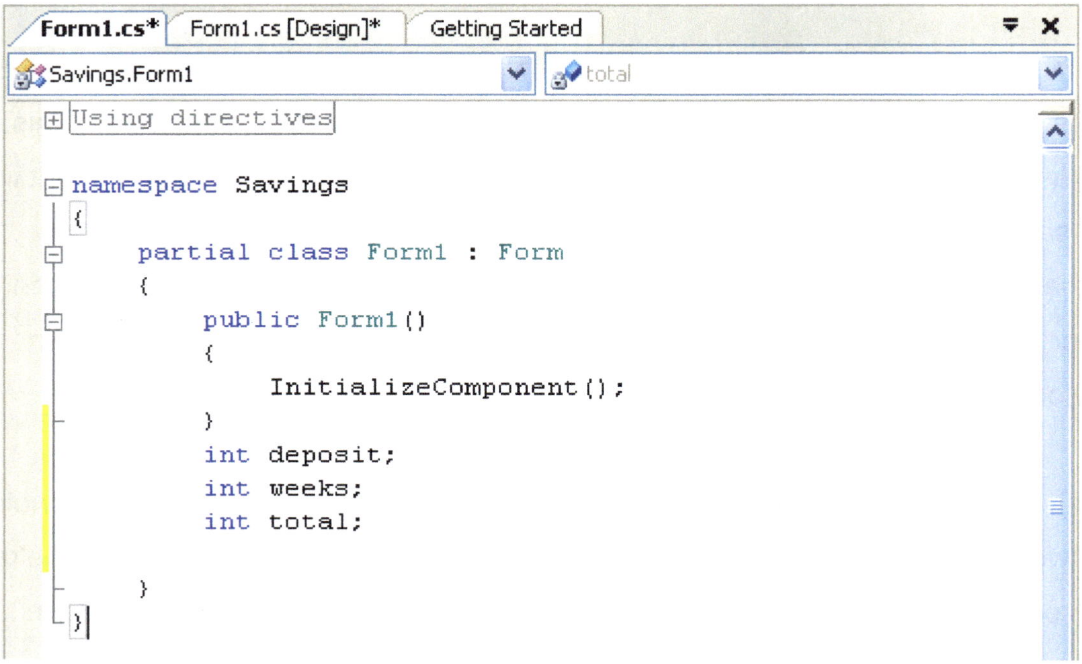

The event methods start after the variable declarations.

The **btnCompute_Click** event implements the following steps:

1. Convert input deposit value (**txtDeposit.Text**) to a number and store it in the variable **deposit**.
2. Convert input number of weeks (**txtWeeks.Text**) to a number and store it in the variable **weeks**.
3. Multiply deposit times weeks and store the result in the variable **total**.
4. Convert the numerical value **total** to a string, concatenate it with a dollar sign ($), and store it in **Text** property of **txtTotal**.

Establish the **btnCompute_Click** event method using the properties window and type this code (which translates the steps above):

```
private void btnCompute_Click(object sender, EventArgs e)
{
    // Get deposit amount
    deposit = Convert.ToInt32(txtDeposit.Text);
    // Get number of weeks
    weeks = Convert.ToInt32(txtWeeks.Text);
    // Compute total savings
    total = deposit * weeks;
    // Display Total
    txtTotal.Text = "$" + Convert.ToString(total);
}
```

Notice how is easy it is to translate the listed steps to actual C# code. It is just paying attention to details. In particular, look at the use of Convert.ToInt32 and Convert.ToString for string-number conversion.

The **btnExit_Click** event method is simply one line of code that stops the program by closing the form:

```
private void btnExit_Click(object sender, EventArgs e)
{
    this.Close();
}
```

Save your project by clicking the **Save All** button.

Run the Project

Run the project. Click in the **Weekly Deposit** text box and type some value. Do the same with **Number of Weeks**. Click the **Compute** button. Your answer should appear in the **Total** text box control. Make sure the answer is correct. Remember, a big step in project design is making sure your project works correctly! If you say you want to save 10 dollars a week for 10 weeks and your computer project says you will have a million dollars by that time, you should know something is wrong somewhere! Click **Exit** to make sure it works. Save your project if you changed anything. Here's a run I made:

This project may not seem all that complicated. And it isn't. After all, we only multiplied two numbers together. But, the project demonstrates steps that are used in every Visual C# Express project. Valuable experience has been gained in recognizing how to read input values, convert them to the proper type, do the math to obtain desired results, and output those results to the user.

Other Things to Try

Most savings accounts yield interest, that is the bank actually pays you for letting them use your money. This savings account project has ignored interest. But, it is fairly easy to make the needed modifications to account for interest - the math is just a little more complicated. We will give you the steps, but not show you how, to change your project. Give it a try if you'd like:

- Define a variable **interest** to store the yearly savings interest rate. Interest rates are decimal numbers, so use the **double** type for this variable (it's the first time we've used decimals!).
- Add another text box to allow the user to input this interest rate. Name it **txtInterest**.
- Add a label control to identify the new text box (set the **Text** to **Interest Rate**).
- Modify the code to use interest in computing **total**. interest is found using:

```
interest = Convert.ToDouble(txtInterest.Text);
```

Then, **total** (get ready - it's messy looking) is computed using:

```
total = (int) (5200 * (deposit * (Math.Pow((1 + interest
/ 5200), weeks) - 1) / interest));
```

Make sure you type this all on one line - the word processor has made it look like it is on two. As we said, this is a pretty messy expression, but it's good practice in using parentheses and arithmetic operators. Note also the use of the **int** keyword to convert (cast) the computed result to an integer number. The number '5200' is used here to convert the interest from a yearly value to a weekly value.

This equation uses a C# method that we haven't seen yet, the **Pow** method, also called the **exponentiation** method. In exponentiation, a number is multiplied times itself a certain number of times. If we multiply a number by itself 4 times, we say we raise that number to the 4th power. The C# method used for exponentiation is:

```
Math.Pow(argument1, argument2)
```

Notice the **Pow** (stands for power) function has two arguments. **argument1** is the number we are multiplying times itself **argument2** times. In other words, this method raises argument1 to the argument2 power. Each argument and the returned value are **double** type numbers. Some examples:

Example	**Result**
`Math.Pow(4.0, 2.0)`	16.0
`Math.Pow(-3.0, 3.0)`	-27.0
`Math.Pow(10.0, 4.0)`	10000.0

In each example here, the arguments have no decimal parts. We have done this to make the examples clear. You are not limited to such values. It is possible to use this function to compute what happens if you multiply 7.654 times itself 3.16 times!! (The answer is 620.99, by the way.)

Now, run the modified project. Type in values for deposit, weeks, and interest. Click the Compute button. Make sure you get reasonable answers. (As a check, if you use a Deposit value of 10, a Weeks value of 20, and an Interest value of 6.5, the Total answer should be $202 - note you'd have $200 without interest, so this makes sense):

The project converts total to an integer (using the cast) even though there is probably a decimal (some cents) involved in the answer. Save your project.

In this class, you have learned a lot of new material. You learned about the label and text box controls. You learned about variables: naming them, their types and how to declare them properly. And, you learned functions that allow you to change from string variables to numbers and from number to strings. You learned how to do arithmetic in C#. Like we said, a lot of new material. In subsequent classes, we will stress new controls and new C# statements more than new features about the Visual C# Express environment. You should be fairly comfortable in that environment, by now.

6

UpDown Control, Decisions, Random Numbers

Review and Preview

You're halfway through the course! You should now feel comfortable with the project building process and the controls you've studied. In the rest of the classes, we will concentrate more on controls and C# and less on the Visual C# Express environment.

In this class, we look at the numeric updown control, at decisions using C#, and at a very fun topic, the random number. You will build a 'Guess the Number' game project.

Numeric UpDown Control

The **Numeric UpDown** control is used to obtain a numeric input. It looks like a text box control with two small arrows. Clicking the arrows changes the displayed value, which ranges from a specified minimum to a specified maximum. The user can even type in a value, if desired. These controls are useful for supplying an integer number, such as a date in a month. The numeric updown control is selected from the Visual C# Express toolbox. It appears as:

In Toolbox:

On Form (default properties):

Properties

The numeric updown properties are:

Property	Description
Name	Name used to identify numeric updown control. Three letter prefix for numeric updown name is **nud**.
Value	Value assigned to the updown control (a **decimal** type).
Increment	Amount to increment (increase) or decrement (decrease) the updown control when the up or down buttons are clicked.
Maximum	Maximum value for the updown control.
Minimum	Minimum value for the updown control.
TextAlign	Sets whether displayed value is left-justified, right-justified or centered.

Font	Sets style, size, and type of displayed value text.
BackColor	Sets updown control background color.
ForeColor	Sets of color of displayed value text.
Left	Distance from left side of form to left side of updown control (X in properties window).
Top	Distance from top side of form to top side of updown control (Y in properties window).
Width	Width of the updown control in pixels.
Height	Height of updown control in pixels.
ReadOnly	Determines whether the text may be changed by the use of the up or down buttons only.
Enabled	Determines whether updown control can respond to user events (in run mode).
Visible	Determines whether the updown control appears on the form (in run mode).

Operation of the numeric updown control is actually quite simple. The **Value** property can be changed by clicking either of the arrows (value will be changed by **Increment** with each click) or, optionally by typing a value (if **ReadOnly** is **False**). If using the arrows, the value will always lie between **Minimum** and **Maximum**. If the user can type in a value, you have no control over what value is typed.

Example

Start Visual C# Express and start a new project. We will create a numeric updown control that provides numbers from 0 to 20. Put a numeric updown control on the form. (Make sure you choose the **numeric updown** control and not the domain updown control.) Resize it and move it, if desired. Set the following properties:

Property	**Value**
Value	10
Increment	1
Minimum	0
Maximum	20
ReadOnly	False

If you like, try changing colors, font and any other properties too. This numeric updown control has an initial Value of 10. The smallest Value can be is 0 (Minimum), the largest it can be is 20 (Maximum). Value will change by 1 (Increment) when an arrow is clicked. The user can type a value (ReadOnly is False) if desired.

Run the project. The numeric updown control will appear and display a value of 10. Click the end arrows and see the value change. Notice the value will not drop below 0 or above 20, the limits established at design time. Click the display area and type in a value of 100. Note that, even though this is higher than the maximum of 20, you can type the value. Try increasing the value, it will not increase. Hit **<Enter>** or try to decrease the value and it is immediately adjusted within the limits you set. So, Visual C# Express makes some attempts to make sure the user doesn't type illegal values. Stop the project.

Events

We will only use a single numeric updown event:

Event	**Description**
ValueChanged	Occurs when the Value property has been changed in some way.

The **ValueChanged** event is executed whenever Value changes. This is where you can use the current value. If the user is allowed to type a value in the control, you might have to check if it is within acceptable limits.

Typical Use of Numeric UpDown Control

The usual design steps for a numeric updown control are:

- Set the **Name, Minimum** and **Maximum** properties. Initialize **Value** property. Decide on value for **ReadOnly**.
- Monitor **ValueChanged** event for changes in Value.
- You may also want to change the **Font**, **Backcolor** and **Forecolor** properties.

Note, for maximum flexibility, **Value** is a **decimal** type, meaning you can have non-integer numbers (you will need to set the **DecimalPlaces** property to some value). If you want an integer value, you need to cast **Value** to an **int** type.

C# - The Third Lesson

In the C# lesson for this class, we learn about one of the more useful functions of a computer program - decision making. We will discuss expressions and operators used in decisions and how decisions can be made. We will also look at a new C# function - the random number. This function is the heart of every computer game.

Logical Expressions

You may think that computers are quite smart. They appear to have the ability to make amazing decisions and choices. Computers can beat masters at chess and help put men and women into space. Well, computers really aren't that smart - the only decision making ability they have is to tell if something is **true** or **false**. But, computers have the ability to make such decisions very quickly and that's why they appear smart (and because, unlike the True or False tests you take in school, computers always get the right answer!). To use C# for decision making, we write all possible decisions in the form of **true or false?** statements, called **logical expressions**. We give the computer a logical expression and the computer will tell us if that expression is true or false. Based on that decision, we can take whatever action we want in our computer program. Note the result of a logical expression is a **bool** type value.

Say in a computer program we need to know if the value of the variable **aValue** is larger than the value of the variable **bValue**. We would ask the computer (by writing some C# code) to provide an answer to the true or false? statement: "aValue is larger than bValue." This is an example of a logical expression. If the computer told us this was true, we could take one set of C# steps. If it was false, we could take another. This is how decisions are done in C#.

To make decisions, we need to know how to build and use logical expressions. The first step in building such expressions is to learn about comparison operators.

Comparison Operators

In the Class 3, we looked at one type of C# operator - arithmetic operators. In this class, we introduce the idea of a **comparison operator**. Comparison operators do exactly what they say - they compare two values, with the output of the comparison being a Boolean value (**bool**). That is, the result of the comparison is either **true** or **false**. Comparison operators allow us to construct logical expressions that can be used in decision making.

There are six comparison operators. The first is the "**equal to**" operator represented by two equal (**==**) signs. This operator tells us if two values are equal to each other. Examples are:

Comparison	Result
6 == 7	false
4 == 4	true

A common error (a logic error) in C# is to only use one equal sign for the "equal to" operator. Using a single equal sign simply assigns a value to the variable making it always true

There is also a “**not equal to**“ operator represented by a symbol consisting of an exclamation point (called the **not** operator) followed by the equal sign (**!=**). Examples of using this operator:

Comparison	**Result**
6 != 7	true
4 != 4	false

There are other operators that let us compare the size of numbers. The “**greater than**“ operator (**>**) tells us if one number (left side of operator) is greater than another (right side of operator). Examples of its usage:

Comparison	**Result**
8 > 3	true
6 > 7	false
4 > 4	false

The “**less than**“ operator (**<**) tells us if one number (left side of operator) is less than another (right side of operator). Some examples are:

Comparison	**Result**
8 < 3	false
6 < 7	true
4 < 4	false

The last two operators are modifications to the "greater than" and "less than" operators. The "**greater than or equal to**" operator (**>=**) compares two numbers. The result is true if the number on the left of the operator is greater than or equal to the number on the right. Otherwise, the result is false. Examples:

Comparison	**Result**
8 >= 3	true
6 >= 7	false
4 >= 4	true

Similarly, the "**less than or equal to**" operator (**<=**) tells us if one number (left side of operator) is less than or equal to another (right side of operator). Examples:

Comparison	**Result**
8 <= 3	false
6 <= 7	true
4 <= 4	true

Comparison operators have equal precedence among themselves, but are lower than the precedence of arithmetic operators. This means comparisons are done after any arithmetic. Comparison operators allow us to make single decisions about the relative size of values and variables. What if we need to make multiple decisions? For example, what if we want to know if a particular variable is smaller than one number, but larger than another? We need ways to combine logical expressions - logical operators can do this.

Logical Operators

Logical operators are used to combine logical expressions built using comparison operators. Using such operators allows you, as the programmer, to make any decision you want. As an example, say you need to know if two variables named **aValue** and **bValue** are both greater than 0. Using the "greater than" comparison operator (>), we know how to see if aValue is greater than zero and we know how to check if bValue is greater than 0, but how do we combine these expressions and obtain one Boolean result (true or false)?

We will look at two logical operators used to combine logical expressions. The first is the **and** operator represented by two ampersands (**&&**). The format for using this operator is (using two logical expressions, **x** and **y,** each with a Boolean (**bool** type) result):

```
x && y
```

This expression is asking the question "are x and y both true?" That's why it is called the and operator. The and operator (&&) will return a true value only if both x and y are true. If either expression is false, the and operator will return a false. The four possibilities for **and** (**&&**) are shown in this **logic table**:

x	**y**	**x && y**
true	true	true
true	false	false
false	true	false
false	false	false

Notice the and operator would be used to solve the problem mentioned in the beginning of this section. That is, to see if the variables aValue and bValue are both greater than zero, we would use the expression:

```
aValue > 0 && bValue > 0
```

The other logical operator we will use is the **or** operator represented by two pipes (||). The pipe symbol is the shift of the backslash key (\) on a standard keyboard. The format for using this operator is:

```
x || y
```

This expression is asking the question "is x or y true?" That's why it is called the or operator. The or (||) operator will return a true value if either x or y is true. If both expressions are false, the or operator will return a false. The four possibilities for **or** (||) are:

x	**y**	**x || y**
true	true	true
true	false	true
false	true	true
false	false	false

The or operator is second in precedence to the and operator (that is, **and** is done before **or**), and all logical operators come after the comparison operators in precedence. Use of comparison operators and logical operators to form logical expressions is key to making proper decisions in C#. Make sure you understand how all the operators (and their precedence) work. Let's look at some examples to help in this understanding.

In these examples, we will have two integer variables **aInteger** and **bInteger**, with values:

```
aInteger = 14
bInteger = 7
```

What if we want to evaluate the logical expression:

```
aInteger > 10 && bInteger > 10
```

Comparisons are done first, left to right since all comparison operators share the same level of precedence. aInteger (14) is greater than 10, so aInteger > 10 is true. bInteger (7) is not greater than 10, so bInteger > 10 is false. Since one expression is not true, the result of the and (&&) operation is false. This expression 'aInteger > 10 && bInteger > 10' is false. What is the result of this expression:

```
aInteger > 10 || bInteger > 10
```

Can you see this expression is true (aInteger > 10 is true, bInteger > 10 is false; true || false is true)?

There is no requirement that a logical expression have just one logical operator. So, let's complicate things a bit. What if the expression is:

```
aInteger > 10 || bInteger > 10 && aInteger + bInteger == 20
```

Precedence tells us the arithmetic is done first (aInteger and bInteger are added), then the comparisons, left to right. We know aInteger > 10 is true, bInteger > 10 is false, aInteger + bInteger == 20 is false. So, this expression, in terms of boolean comparison values, becomes:

```
true || false && false
```

How do we evaluate this? Precedence says the and (&&) is done first, then the or (||). The result of 'false && false' is false, so the expression reduces to:

```
true || false
```

which has a result of true. Hence, we say the expression 'aInteger > 10 || B > 10 && aInteger + bInteger = 20' is true.

Parentheses can be used in logical expressions to force precedence in evaluations. What if, in the above example, we wanted to do the or (||) operation first? This is done by rewriting using parentheses:

```
(aInteger > 10 || bInteger > 10) && aInteger + bInteger == 20
```

You should be able to show this evaluates to false [do the or (||) first]. Before, without parentheses, it was true. The addition of parentheses has changed the value of this logical expression! It's always best to clearly indicate how you want a logical expression to be evaluated. Parentheses are a good way to do this. Use parentheses even if precedence is not affected.

If we moved the parentheses in this example and wrote:

```
aInteger > 10 || (bInteger > 10 && aInteger + bInteger == 20)
```

the result (true) is the same as if the parentheses were not there since the and (&&) is done first anyway. The parentheses do, however, clearly indicate the and is performed first. Such clarity is good in programming.

Comparison and logical operators are keys to making decisions in C#. Make sure you are comfortable with their meaning and use. Always double-check any logical expression you form to make sure it truly represents the decision logic you intend. Use parentheses to add clarity, if needed.

Decisions - The if Statement

We've spent a lot of time covering comparison operators and logical operators and discussed how they are used to form logical expressions. But, just how is all this used in computer decision making? We'll address that now by looking at the C# **if** statement. Actually, the if statement is not a single statement, but rather a group of statements that implements some decision logic. It is conceptually simple.

The if statement checks a particular logical expression with a Boolean (**bool** type) result. It executes different groups of C# statements, depending on whether that expression is true or false. The C# structure for this logic is:

```
if (expression)
{
        [C# code block to be executed if expression is true]
}
else
{
        [C# code block to be executed if expression is false]
}
```

Let's see what goes on here. We have some logical **expression** which is formed from comparison operators and logical operators. **if** expression is true, then the first block of C# statements (marked by a pair of left and right curly braces) is executed. **else** (meaning expression is not true, or it is false), the second block of C# statements is executed. Each block of code contains standard C# statements, indented by some amount. Whether expression is true or false, program execution continues with the first line of C# code after the last right curly brace (**}**).

The else keyword and the block of statements following the else are optional. If there is no C# code to be executed if expression is false, the if structure would simply be:

```
if (expression)
{

        [C# code block to be executed if expression is true]

}
```

Let's try some examples.

Pretend you just opened a lemonade stand and you want to let the computer decide how much you should charge for each cup you sell. Define an **int** type variable **cost** (cost per cup in cents - our foreign friends can use some other unit here) and another **int** variable **temperature** (outside temperature in degrees F - our foreign friends would, of course, use degrees C). We will write an if structure that implements a decision process that establishes a value for cost, depending on the value of temperature.

Look at the C# code:

```
if (temperature > 90)
{
  cost = 50;
}
else
{
  cost = 25;
}
```

We see that if temperature > 90 (a warm day, hence we can charge more), a logical expression, is true, the cost will be 50, else (meaning temperature is not greater than 90) the cost will be 25. Not too difficult. Notice that we have indented the lines of C# code in the two blocks (one line of code in each block here). This is common practice in writing C# code. It clearly indicates what is done in each case and allows us to see where an if structure begins and ends. The Visual C# Express environment will actually handle the indenting for you.

We could rewrite this (and get the same result) without the else statement. Notice, this code is equivalent to the above code:

```
cost = 25;
if (temperature > 90)
{
  cost = 50
}
```

Here, before the if structure, cost is 25. Only if temperature is greater than 90 is cost changed to 50. Otherwise, cost remains at 25. Even though, in these examples, we only have one line of C# code that is executed for each decision possibility, we are not limited to a single line. We may have as many lines of C# code as needed in the code blocks of if structures.

What if, in our lemonade stand example, we want to divide our pricing structure into several different cost values, based on several different temperature values? The if structure can modified to include an **else if** statement to consider multiple logical expressions. Such a structure is:

```
if (expression1)
{
        [C# code block to be executed if expression1 is true]
}
else if (expression2)
{
        [C# code block to be executed if expression2 is true]
}
else if (expression3)
{
        [C# code block to be executed if expression3 is true]
}
else
{
        [C# code block to be executed if expression1, expression 2, and
expression3 are all false]

}
```

Can you see what happens here? It's pretty straightforward - just work down through the code. If expression1 is true, the first block of C# code is executed. If expression1 is false, the program checks to see if expression2 (using the else if) is true. If expression2 is true, that block of code is executed. If expression2 is false, expression3 is evaluated. If expression3 is true, the corresponding code block is executed. If expression3 is false, and note by this time, expression1, expression2, <u>and</u> expression3 have all been found to be false, the code in the else block (and this is optional) is executed.

You can have as many else if statements as you want. You must realize, however, that only one block of C# code in an if structure will be executed. This means that once C# has found a logical expression that is true, it will execute that block of code then leave the structure and execute the first line of code following the last right curly brace (**}**). For example, if in the above example, both expression1 and expression3 are true, only the C# statements associated with expression1 being true will be executed. The rule for if structures is: only the code block associated with the first true expression will be executed.

How can we use this in our lemonade example? A more detailed pricing structure is reflected in this code:

```
if (temperature > 90)
{
  cost = 50;
}
else if (temperature > 80)
{
  cost = 40;
}
else if (temperature > 70)
{
  cost = 30;
}
Else
{
  cost = 25;
}
```

What would the cost be if temperature is 85? temperature is not greater than 90, but is greater than 80, so cost is 40.

What if this code was rewritten as:

```
if (temperature > 70)
{
  cost = 30;
}
else if (temperature > 80)
{
  cost = 40;
}
else if (temperature > 90)
{
  cost = 50;
}
Else
{
  cost = 25;
}
```

This doesn't look that different - we've just reordered some statements. But, notice what happens if we try to find cost for temperature equal to 85 again. The first if expression is true (temperature is greater than 70), so cost is 30. This is not the result we wanted and will decrease profits for our lemonade stand! Here's a case where the "first true" rule gave us an incorrect answer - a logic error.

This example points out the necessity to always carefully check any if structures you write. Make sure the decision logic you want to implement is working properly. Make sure you try cases that execute all possible decisions and that you get the correct results. The examples used here are relatively simple. Obviously, the if structure can be more far more complicated. Using multiple variables, multiple comparisons and multiple operators, you can develop very detailed decision making processes. In the remaining class projects, you will see examples of such processes.

Random Number Generator

Let's leave decisions for now and look at a fun C# concept - the random number. Have you ever played the Windows solitaire card game or Minesweeper or some similar game? Did you notice that every time you play the game, you get different results? How does this happen? How can you make a computer program unpredictable or introduce the idea of "randomness?" The key is the C# random number generator. This generator simply produces a different number every time it is referenced.

Why do you need random numbers? In the Windows solitaire card game, the computer needs to shuffle a deck of cards. It needs to "randomly" sort fifty-two cards. It uses random numbers to do this. If you have a game that rolls a die, you need to randomly generate a number between 1 and 6. Random numbers can be used to do this. If you need to flip a coin, you need to generate Heads or Tails randomly. Yes, random numbers are used to do this too.

Visual C# Express has several methods for generating random numbers. We will use just one of them – a random generator of integers (whole numbers). The generator uses what is called the **Random** object. Don't worry too much about what this means –just think of it as another variable type. Follow these few steps to use it. First create a **Random** object (we'll name it **myRandom**) using the **constructor**:

```
Random myRandom = new Random();
```

This statement is placed with the variable declaration statements.

Now, whenever you need a random integer value, use the **Next** method of this Random object we created:

```
myRandom.Next(limit)
```

This statement generates a random integer value that is greater than or equal to 0 and less than **limit**. Note it is less than limit, not equal to. For example, the method:

```
myRandom.Next(5)
```

will generate random numbers from 0 to 4. The possible values will be 0, 1, 2, 3 and 4.

Let's try it. Start Visual C# Express and start a new project. Put a button (default name **button1**) and label control (default name **label1**) on the form. We won't worry about properties or names here - we're just playing around, not building a real project. In fact, that's one neat thing about Visual C# Express, it is easy to play around with. Open the code window and add this line under the form constructor to create the random number object:

```
Random myRandom = new Random();
```

Then, put this code in the **button1_Click** event method:

```
private void button1_Click(object sender, EventArgs e)
{
    label1.Text = Convert.ToString(myRandom.Next(10));
}
```

This code simply generates a random integer between 0 and 9 (**Next** uses a limit of 10) and displays its value in the label control (after converting it to a string type). Run the project. Click the button. A number should appear in the label control. Click the button again and again. Notice the displayed number changes with each click and there is no predictability to the number - it is random. The number printed should always be between 0 and 9. Try other limit values if you'd like to understand how the random object works.

So, the random number generator object can be used to introduce randomness in a project. This opens up a lot of possibilities to you as a programmer. Every computer game, video game, and computer simulation, like sports games and flight simulators, use random numbers. A roll of a die can produce a number from 1 to 6. To use our **myRandom** object to roll a die, we would write:

```
dieNumber = myRandom.Next(6) + 1;
```

For a deck of cards, the random integers would range from 1 to 52 since there are 52 cards in a standard playing deck. Code to do this:

```
cardNumber = myRandom.Next(52) + 1;
```

If we want a number between 0 and 100, we would use:

```
yourNumber = myRandom.Next(101);
```

Check the examples above to make sure you see how the random number generator produces the desired range of integers. Now, let's move on to a project that will use this generator.

Project - Guess the Number Game

Back in the early 1980's, the first computers intended for home use appeared. Brands like Atari, Coleco, Texas Instruments, and Commodore were sold in stores like Sears and Toys R Us (sorry, I can't type the needed 'backwards' R). These computers didn't have much memory, couldn't do real fancy graphics, and, compared to today's computers, cost a lot of money. But, these computers introduced a lot of people to the world of computer programming. Many games (usually written in the BASIC language) appeared at that time and the project you will build here is one of those classics.

Project Design

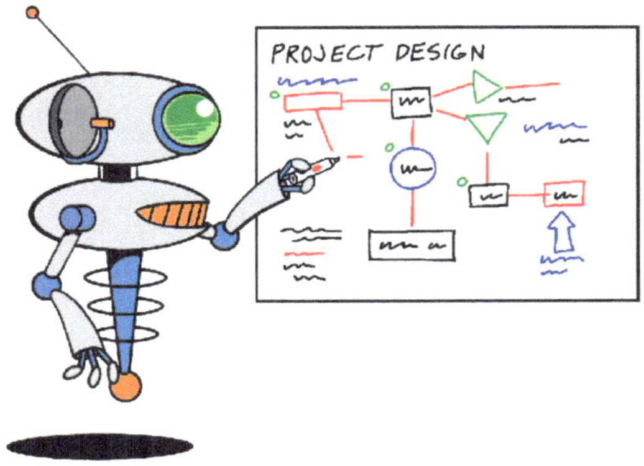

You've all played the game where someone said "I'm thinking of a number between 1 and 10" (or some other limits). Then, you try to guess the number. The person thinking of the number tells you if you're low or high and you guess again. You continue guessing until you finally guess the number they were thinking of. We will develop a computer version of this game here. The computer will pick a number between 0 and 100 (using the random number generator). You will try to guess the number. Based on your guess, the computer will tell you if you are Too Low or Too High.

Several controls will be needed. Buttons will control game play (one to tell the computer to pick a number, one to tell the computer to check your guess, and one to exit the program). We will use a numeric updown control to set and display your guess. A label control will display the computer's messages to you. This project is saved as **GuessNumber** in the course projects folder (**\VCSEKids\VCSEK Projects**).

Place Controls on Form

Start a new project in Visual C# Express. Place three buttons, a text box, and a numeric updown control on the form. Move and size controls until your form should look something like this:

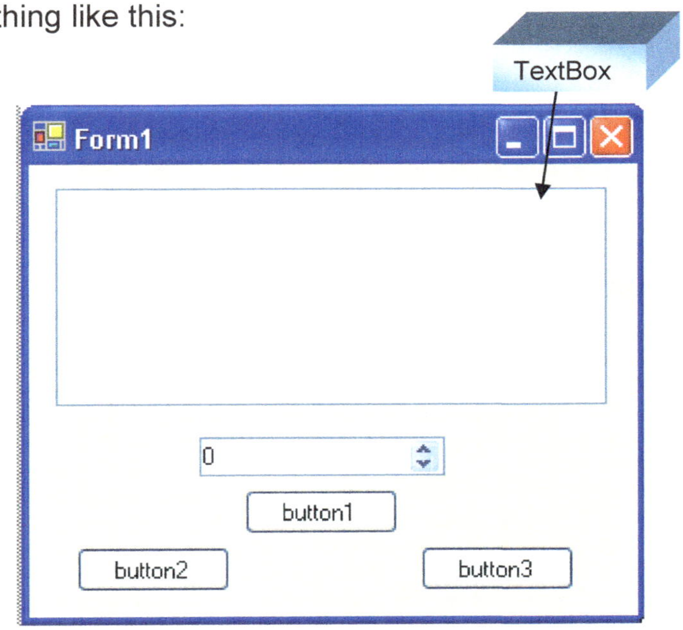

Set Control Properties

Set the control properties using the properties window:

Form1 Form:

Property Name	Property Value
Text	Guess the Number
FormBorderStyle	Fixed Single
StartPosition	CenterScreen

textBox1 Text Box:

Property Name	Property Value
Name	txtMessage
TextAlign	Center
Font	Arial
Font Size	16
BackColor	White
ForeColor	Blue
ReadOnly	True
TabStop	False

numericUpDown1 Numeric UpDown:

Property Name	Property Value
Name	nudGuess
Font	Arial
Font Size	16
BackColor	White
ForeColor	Red
TextAlign	Center
Value	50
Minimum	0
Maximum	100
Increment	1
ReadOnly	True
Enabled	False

button1 Button:

Property Name	**Property Value**
Name	btnCheck
Text	Check Guess
Enabled	False

button2 Button:

Property Name	**Property Value**
Name	btnPick
Text	Pick Number

button3 Button:

Property Name	**Property Value**
Name	btnExit
Text	Exit

When done, your form should look something like this (you may have to move and resize a few controls around to get things to fit):

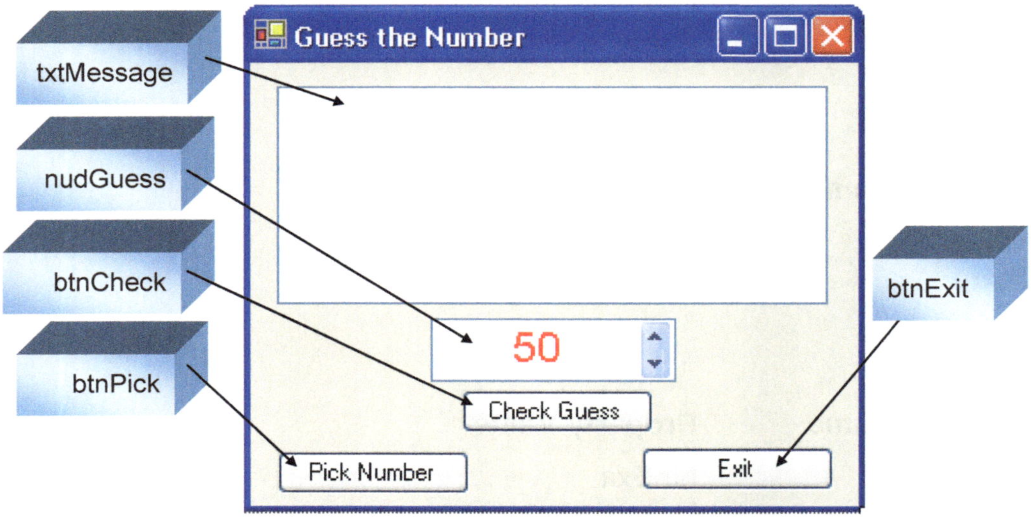

We have set the **Enabled** properties of **btnCheck** and **nudGuess** to **False** initially. We do not want to allow guesses until the **Pick Number** button is clicked.

Write Event Methods

How does this project work? You click **Pick Number** to have the computer pick a number to guess. This click event will 'enable' the numeric updown control and **Check Guess** button (remember we set their Enabled properties initially at

False). Input your guess using the numeric updown control, then click Check Guess. The computer will tell you if your guess is too low, too high, or correct by using the message box (**txtMessage**). So, we need a **Click** event method for each button.

Two variables are needed in this project, both **int** types. One variable will store the number selected by the computer (the number you are trying to guess). We call this variable **theNumber**. Your current guess will be saved in the variable **myGuess**. You will also need a Random object named **myRandom**. Open the code window and declare these variables in the **general declarations** area under the form constructor method:

```
int theNumber;
int myGuess;
Random myRandom = new Random();
```

After typing these lines, the code window should appear as:

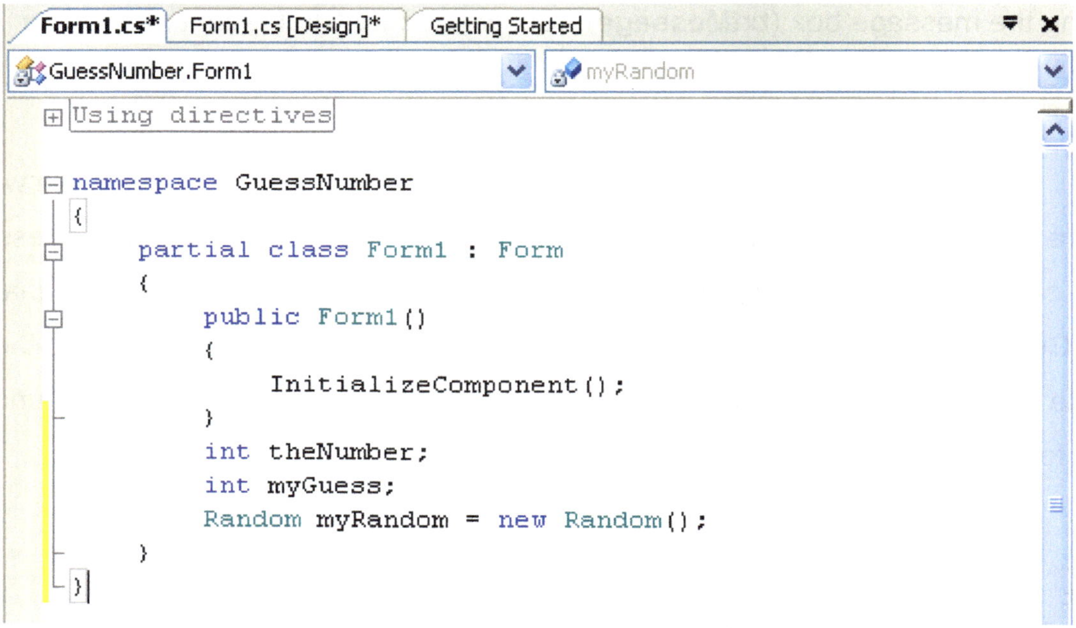

When you click **Pick Number**, the computer needs to perform the following steps:

- Pick a random integer number between 0 and 100.
- Display a message to the user.
- Enable the numeric updown control to allow guesses.
- Enable the Check Guess button to allow guesses.

And, we will add one more step. Many times in Visual C# Express, you might want to change the function of a particular control while the program is running. In this game, once we click Pick Number, that button has no further use until the number has been guessed. But, we need a button to tell us the answer if we choose to give up before guessing it. We will use **btnPick** to do this. We will change the Text property and add decision logic to see which 'state' the button is in. If the button says "Pick Number" when it is clicked (the initial state), the above steps will be followed. If the button says "Show Answer" when it is clicked (the 'playing' state), the answer will be shown and the form controls returned to their initial state. This is a common thing to do in Visual C# Express.

Here's the **btnPick_Click** code that does everything:

```
private void btnPick_Click(object sender, EventArgs e)
{
    if (btnPick.Text == "Pick Number")
    {
        // Get new number and set controls
        theNumber = myRandom.Next(101);
        txtMessage.Text = "I'm thinking of a number between 0
and 100";
        nudGuess.Value = 50;
        nudGuess.Enabled = true;
        btnCheck.Enabled = true;
        btnPick.Text = "Show Answer";
    }
    else
    {
        // Just show the answer and re-set controls
        txtMessage.Text = "The answer is" +
Convert.ToString(theNumber);
        nudGuess.Value = theNumber;
        nudGuess.Enabled = false;
        btnCheck.Enabled = false;
        btnPick.Text = "Pick Number";
    }
}
```

Study this so you see what is going on. Notice the use of indentation in the if structure. Notice in the lines where we set the txtMessage.Text, it looks like two lines of C# code. Type this all on one line - the word processor is making it look like two. In fact, keep an eye out for such things in these notes. It's obvious where a so-called "word wrap" occurs.

When you click **Check Answer**, the computer should see if your current guess (myGuess) is correct (the **Value** returned by the numeric updown control needs to be converted to an **int** type before doing the comparison with myGuess). If so, a message telling you so will appear and the form controls return to their initial state, ready for another game. If not, the computer will display a message telling you if you are too low or too high. You can then make another guess. The **btnCheck_Click** event that implements this logic is:

```
private void btnCheck_Click(object sender, EventArgs e)
{
    // Guess is the updown control value
    myGuess = (int) nudGuess.Value;
    if (myGuess == theNumber)
    {
        // Correct guess
        txtMessage.Text = "That's it!!";
        nudGuess.Enabled = false;
        btnCheck.Enabled = false;
        btnPick.Text = "Pick Number";
    }
    else if (myGuess < theNumber)
    {
        // Guess is too low
        txtMessage.Text = "Too low!";
    }
    else
    {
        // Guess is too high
        txtMessage.Text = "Too high!";
    }
}
```

The last button click event is **btnExit_Click**:

```
private void btnExit_Click(object sender, EventArgs e)
{
    this.Close();
}
```

Save the project by clicking the **Save All** button in the toolbar.

Run the Project

Run the project. Click **Pick Number** to have the computer to pick a number to guess. Use the arrows on the numeric updown control to input your guess. Click **Check Guess**. Continue adjusting your guess (using the computer clues) until you get the correct answer. Make sure the proper messages display at the proper times. Do you see how the text displayed on btnPick changes as the game 'state' changes? Make sure the **Show Answer** button works properly. Again, always thoroughly test your project to make sure all options work. Save your project if you needed to make any changes.

Here's what the form should look like in the middle of a game:

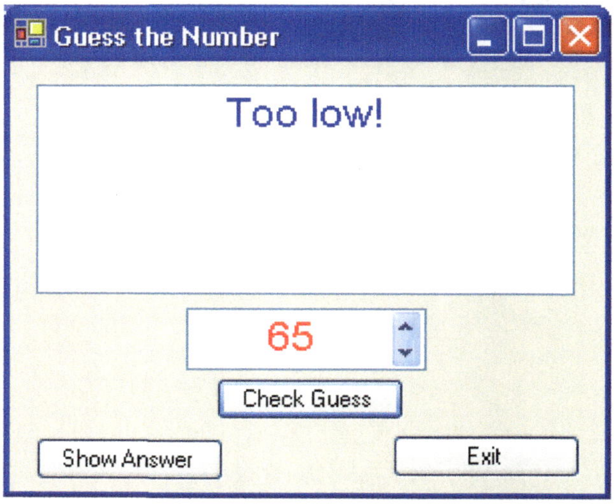

Other Things to Try

You can add other features to this game. One suggestion is to add a text box where the user can input the upper range of numbers that can be guessed. That way, the game could be played by a wide variety of players. Use a maximum value of 10 for little kids, 1000 for older kids.

Another good modification would be to offer more informative messages following a guess. Have you ever played the game where you try to find something and the person who hid the item tells you, as you move around the room, that you are freezing (far away), cold (closer), warm (closer yet), hot (very close), or burning up (right on top of the hidden item)? Try to modify the Guess the Number game to give these kind of clues. That is, the closer you are to the correct number, the warmer you get. To make this change, you will probably need the C# **absolute value** method, **Math.Abs**. This function returns the value of a number while ignoring its sign (positive or negative). The format for using Math.Abs is:

```
yourValue = Math.Abs(inputValue);
```

If inputValue is a positive number (greater than zero), yourValue is assigned inputValue. If inputValue is a negative number (less than zero), yourValue is assigned the numerical value of inputValue, without the minus sign. A few examples:

value	**Math.Abs(value)**
6	6
-6	6
0	0
-1.1	1.1

In our number guessing game, we can use Math.Abs to see how close a guess is to the actual number. One possible decision logic is:

```
if (myGuess == theNumber)
{
        [C# code block for correct answer]
}
else if (Math.Abs(myGuess - theNumber) <= 1)
{
        [C# code block when burning up - within 1 of correct answer]
}
else if (Math.Abs(myGuess - theNumber) <= 2)
{
        [C# code block when hot - within 2 of correct answer]
}
else if (Math.Abs(myGuess - theNumber) <= 3)
{
        [C# code block when warm - within 3 of correct answer]
}
else
{
        [C# code block when freezing - more than 3 away]

}
```

A last possible change would be the make the project into a math game, and tell the guesser “how far away” the guess is. I’m sure you can think of other ways to change this game. Have fun doing it.

In this class, you learned about a useful input control for numbers, the numeric updown control. You'll learn about other input controls in the next class. And, you learned about a key part of C# programming - decision making. You learned about logical expressions, comparison operators, logical operators, and if structures. And, you will see that the random number object is a fun part of many games. You are well on your way to being a Visual C# Express programmer.

7

Icons, Group Boxes, Check Boxes, Radio Buttons

Review and Preview

You should feel very comfortable working within the Visual C# Express environment by now and know the three steps of building a project.

In this class, we learn about three more controls relating to making choices in Visual C# Express: group boxes, check boxes, and radio buttons. We will look at another way to make decisions using the switch structure. We'll have some fun making icons for our projects. And, you will build a sandwich making project.

Icons

Have you noticed that whenever you design or run a Visual C# Express project, a little picture appears in the upper left hand corner of the form. This picture is called an **icon**. Icons are used throughout the Windows environment. There are probably lots of icons on your Windows desktop - each of these represents some kind of application. Look at files using Windows Explorer. Notice every file has an icon associated with it. Here is a blank Visual C# Express form:

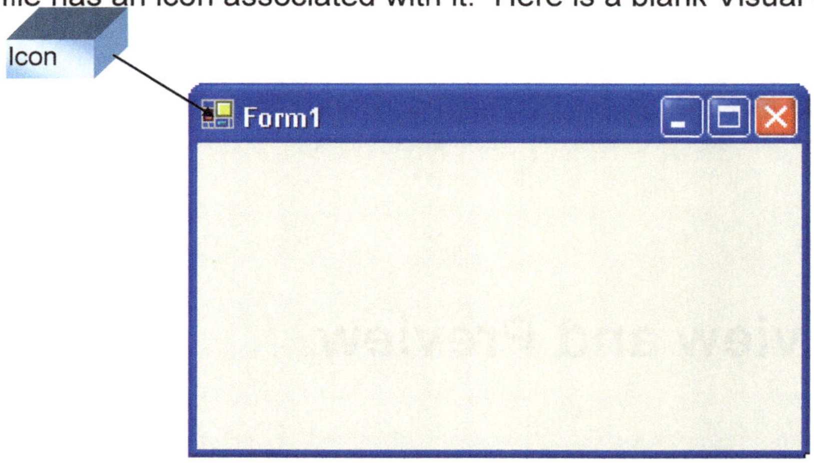

The icon seen is the default Visual C# Express icon for forms. It's really kind of boring. Using the **Icon** property of the form, you can change this displayed icon to something a little flashier. Before seeing how to do this, though, let's see how you can design your own icon.

Designing Your Own Icon with IconEdit

Visual C# Express has a lot of icon files to use for your form's icon. There are also a lot of icons that can be downloaded from the Internet. But, it's more fun to design your own icon to add a personal touch. Several years ago, a computer publication ***PC Magazine*** offered a free program called **IconEdit** that lets you design and save your own icons. Included with these notes is this program and some other files needed by IconEdit (look for the folder named **IconEdit** in the **\VCSEKids\VCSEK Projects** folder). Let's create an icon to see how IconEdit works.

To run IconEdit, click **Start** on the Windows task bar, then click **Run**. Find the **IconEdit** program (use **Browse** mode), then click **OK**. When the IconEdit program window appears, click the **File** menu heading, then choose **New** (we are creating a new icon). The following editor window will appear:

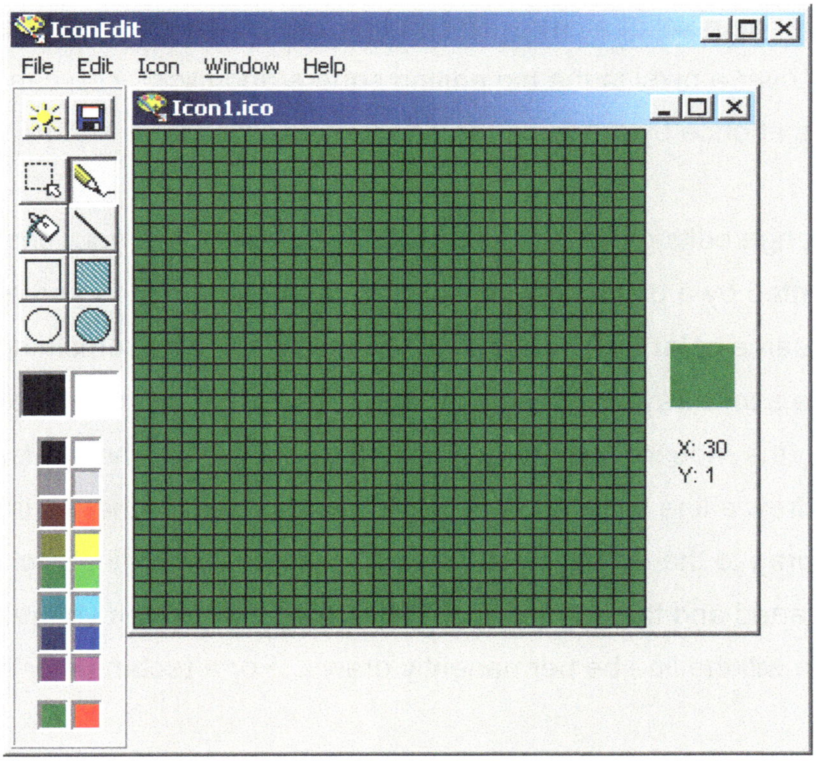

The editor window displays two representations of the icon: a large zoomed-in square (a 32 x 32 grid) that's eight times bigger than the actual icon, and a small square to its right that's actual size. The zoomed square is where the editing takes place. New icons appear as solid green with a black square surrounding each pixel representation. The **pixels** (small squares) are, of course, eight times actual size like the square itself for ease of editing. The green color is not actually the starting color of the icon, but instead represents the transparent "color" (whatever is behind this green color on the screen will be seen).

The basic idea of IconEdit is to draw an icon in the 32 x 32 grid displayed. You can draw single points, lines, open rectangles and ovals, and filled rectangles and ovals. Various colors are available. Once completed, the icon file can be saved for attaching to a form. IconEdit has a tool bar that consists of eight tools: capture (we won't talk about this one), pencil, fill, line, hollow and filled rectangle, and hollow and filled ellipse. These will be familiar to anyone who has used a paint program and on-line help is available. The default tool when you start editing an icon is the pencil, since this is the tool you'll probably use the most. The pencil let's you color one pixel at a time. To change a pixel, simply place the point of the pencil cursor over a pixel in the big editing square and click. You can pencil-draw several pixels at once by dragging the pencil over an area.

To change editing tools, simply click the tool button of your choice. The fill tool (represented by a paint can) will color the pixel you point to and all adjacent pixels of the same color with the color you've selected. The remaining five tools all operate in the same way. You click and hold the mouse button at the starting pixel position, drag the mouse to an ending position, and release the mouse button. For example, to draw a line, click and hold the mouse button on the starting point for the line and drag to the ending point. As you drag, the line will stretch between where you started and the current ending position. Only when you release the mouse button will the line be permanently drawn. For a rectangle or an ellipse, drag from one corner to the opposite corner. You control the color that the tool uses by pressing either the left or right mouse button.

The two large color squares right under the tools are the current colors for the left and right mouse buttons, respectively. When you start IconEdit, the left mouse button color is black and the right mouse button color is white. If you click with the left mouse button on a pixel with the pencil tool, for example, the pixel will turn black. Click with the right mouse button and the pixel will turn white. To change the default colors, click on one of the 16 colors in the palette just below the current color boxes with either the left or right mouse button. Clicking on a palette color with the left button will change the left button color and a right button click will change the right button color. You can pick the transparent “color” at the bottom of the editor if you want a pixel to be transparent.

Try drawing an icon using IconEdit. It's really pretty easy. Here's one I made. It's supposed to be a sandwich with layers of bread, lettuce, tomato, onions and meat (saved as **Sandwich.ico** in the IconEdit folder). I made it using the filled rectangle tool to draw the 'bread' and the pencil tool to draw the other stuff. And, no, I do not claim to be an artist!

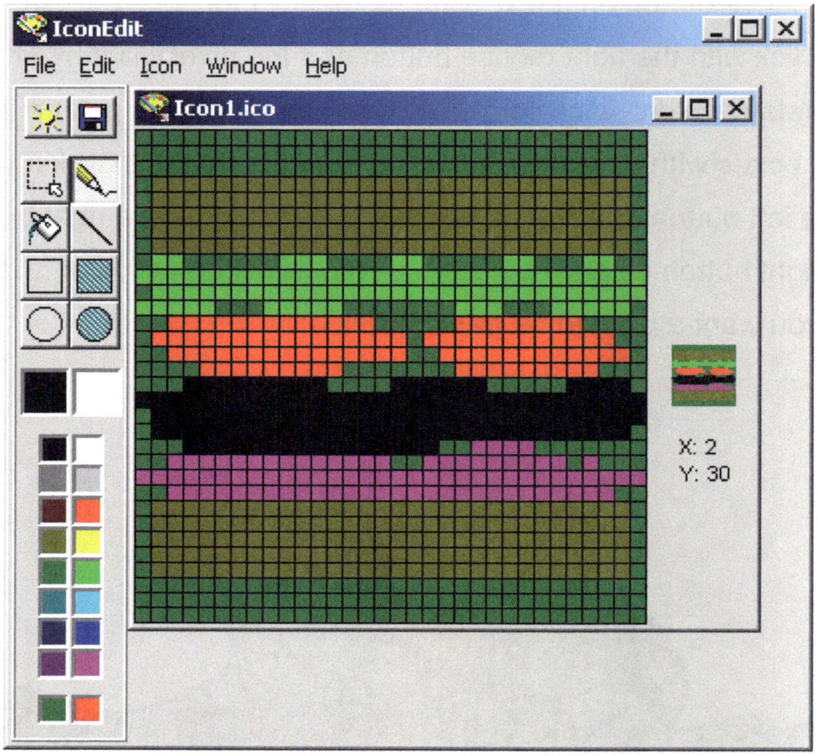

Once you have finished your icon, save it. Click **File**, then **Save**. Icon files are special graphics files saved with an **ico** extension. The save window is just like the window you've used to save files in Visual C# Express and other Windows programs. Remember where you saved your icon.

With IconEdit, you can now customize your projects with your own icons. And, another fun thing to do is load in other icon files you find (click **File**, then **Open**) and see how much artistic talent really goes into creating an icon. You can even modify these other icons and save them for your use.

Assigning Icons to Forms

As mentioned, to assign an icon (either one you designed with IconEdit or one someone else made) to a form, you simply set the form's **Icon** property. Let's try it.

Start Visual C# Express and start a new project. A blank form should appear. Go to the properties window and click on the Icon property. An ellipsis (**...**) button appears. Click that button and a window that allows selection of icon files will appear. Some icon files were probably installed with your copy of Visual C# Express - look for folders in this location (or something similar):

\Program Files\Microsoft Visual Studio 8\Common7\Graphics\Icons

Or, look for the icon you just created and saved (if you did it). Select an icon, click **Open** in the file window and that icon is now 'attached' to your form. Easy, huh? When I attach my sandwich icon, the form looks like this:

You'll have a lot of fun making icons for your projects using IconEdit. It's nice to see a personal touch on your projects.

Group Box Control

A **group box** is simply a control that can hold other controls. Group boxes provide a way to separate and group controls and have an overall enable/disable feature. This means if you disable the group box, all controls in the group box are also disabled. The group box has no events, just properties. The only events of interest are events associated with the controls in the group box. Writing event methods for these controls is the same as if they were not in a group box. The group box is selected from the toolbox. It appears as:

In Toolbox:

On Form (default properties):

Properties

The group box properties are:

Property	Description
Name	Name used to identify group box. Three letter prefix for group box names is **grp**.
Text	Title information at top of group box.
Font	Sets style, size, and type of title text.
BackColor	Sets group box background color.
ForeColor	Sets color of title text.

Left	Distance from left side of form to left side of group box.
Top	Distance from top side of form to top side of group box.
Width	Width of the group box in pixels.
Height	Height of group box in pixels.
Enabled	Determines whether all controls within group box can respond to user events (in run mode).
Visible	Determines whether the group box (and attached controls) appears on the form (in run mode).

Like the Form object, the group box is a **container** control, since it 'holds' other controls. Hence, controls placed in a group box will share **BackColor**, **ForeColor** and **Font** properties. To change this, select the desired control (after it is placed on the group box) and change the desired properties.

Moving the group box control on the form uses a different process than other controls. To move the group box, first select the control. Note a 'built-in' handle (looks like two sets of arrows) for moving the control appears at the upper left corner:

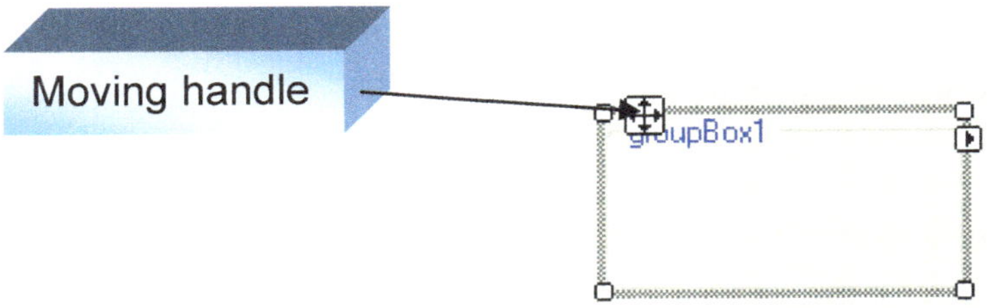

Click on this handle and you can move the control.

Placing Controls in a Group Box

As mentioned, a group box's single task is to hold other controls. To put controls in a group box, you first position and size the group box on the form. Then, the associated controls must be placed in the group box. This allows you to move the group box and controls together. There are several ways to place controls in a group box:

- Place controls directly in the group box using any of the usual methods.
- Draw controls outside the group box and drag them in.
- Copy and paste controls into the group box (prior to the paste operation, make sure the group box is selected).

To insure controls are properly place in a group box, try moving it (use the move handle) and make sure the associated controls move with it. To remove a control from a group box, simply drag it out of the control.

Example

Start Visual C# Express and start a new project. Put a group box on the form and resize it so it is fairly large. Select the button control in the Visual C# Express toolbox. Drag the control until it is over the group box. Drop the control in the group box. Move the group box and the button should move with it. If it doesn't, it is not properly placed in the group box. If you need to delete the control, select it then press the **Del** key on the keyboard. Try moving the button out of the group box onto the form. Move the button back in the group box.

Put a second button in the group box. Put a numeric updown control in the group box. Notice how the controls are associated with the group box. A warning: if you delete the group box, the associated controls will also be deleted! Run the project. Notice you can click on the buttons and use the numeric updown control. Stop the project. Set the group box Enabled property to False. Run the project again. Notice the group box title (set by the Text property) is grayed and all of the controls on the group box are now disabled - you can't click the buttons or updown control. Hence, by simply setting one Enabled property (that of the group box), we can enable or disable a number of individual controls. Stop the project. Reset the group box Enabled property to True. Set the Visible property to False (will remain visible in design mode). Run the project. The group box and all its controls will not appear. You can use the Visible property of the group box control to hide (or make appear) some set of controls (if your project requires such a step). Stop the project.

Change the Visible property back to True. Place a label control in the group box. Change the BackColor property of the group box. Notice the background color of the label control takes on the same value, while the button controls are unaffected. Recall this is because the group box is a 'container' control. Sometimes, this sharing of properties is a nice benefit, especially with label controls. Other times, it is an annoyance. If you don't want controls to share properties (BackColor, ForeColor, Font) with the group box, you must change the properties you don't like individually. Group boxes will come in very handy with the next two controls we look at: the check box and the radio button. You will see this sharing of color properties is a nice effect with these two controls. It saves us the work of changing lots of colors!

Typical Use of Group Box Control

The usual design steps for a group box control are:

- Set **Name** and **Text** property (perhaps changing **Font**, **BackColor** and **ForeColor** properties).
- Place desired controls in group box. Monitor events of controls in group box using usual techniques.

Check Box Control

A **check box** provides a way to make choices from a group of things. When a check box is selected, a check appears in the box. Each check box acts independently. Some, all, or none of the choices in the group may be selected. An example of where check boxes could be used is choosing from a list of ice cream toppings. You might want it plain, you might want a couple of toppings, you might want it with the works - you decide. Check boxes are also used individually to indicate whether a particular project option is active. For example, it might indicate if a control's text is bold (checked) or not bold (unchecked).

Check boxes are usually grouped in a group box control. The check box control is selected from the toolbox. It appears as:

In Toolbox:

On Form (default properties):

Properties

The check box properties are:

Property	Description
Name	Name used to identify check box. Three letter prefix for check box names is **chk**.
Text	Identifying text next to check box.
TextAlign	Specifies how the displayed text is positioned.
Font	Sets style, size, and type of displayed text.
Checked	Indicates if box is checked (**True**) or unchecked (**False**).

BackColor	Sets check box background color.
ForeColor	Sets color of displayed text.
Left	If on form, distance from left side of form to left side of check box. If in group box, distance from left side of group box to left side of check box (X in properties window).
Top	If on form, distance from top side of form to top side of check box. If in group box, distance from top side of group box to top side of check box (Y in properties window).
Width	Width of the check box in pixels.
Height	Height of check box in pixels.
Enabled	Determines whether check box can respond to user events (in run mode).
Visible	Determines whether the check box appears on the form (in run mode).

Pay particular attention to the Left and Top properties. Notice if a check box is in a group box, those two properties give position in the group box, not on the form.

Example

Start Visual C# Express and start a new project. Draw a group box - we will always use group boxes to group check boxes. Place three or four check boxes in the group box using techniques discussed earlier. Move the group box to make sure the check boxes are in the group box. Run the project. Click the check boxes and see how the check marks appear and disappear. Notice you can choose as many, or as few, boxes as you like. In code, we would examine each check box's Checked property to determine which boxes are selected. Stop the project. Change the BackColor of the group box. Notice the check box controls' background color changes to match. This is a nice result of using the group box as a container.

Did you notice we didn't have to write any C# code to make the check marks appear or go away? That is handled by the check box control. There are check box events, however. Let's look at one.

Events

The only check box event of interest is the CheckedChanged event:

Event	Description
CheckedChanged	Event executed when Checked property of a check box changes.

The event occurs each time a user clicks on a check box, either placing a check mark in the box or removing one.

Typical Use of a Check Box Control

Usual design steps for a check box control are:

- Set the **Name** and **Text** property. Initialize the **Checked** property.
- Monitor **CheckChanged** event to determine when control is clicked. At any time, read **Checked** property to determine check box state.
- You may also want to change the **Font**, **Backcolor** and **Forecolor** properties.

Radio Button Control

A **radio button** provides a way to make a "mutually-exclusive" choice from a group of things. This is a fancy way of saying only <u>one</u> item in the group can be selected. When a radio button is selected, a filled circle appears in the button. No other button in the group can be selected, or have a filled circle. There are many places you can use radio buttons - they can be used whenever you want to make only one choice from a group. Say you have a game for one to four players - use radio buttons to select the number of players. Radio buttons can be used to select background colors. Radio buttons can be used to select difficulty levels in arcade type games. As you write more Visual C# Express programs, you will come to rely on the radio button as a device for choice.

Radio buttons always work in groups and each group must be in a separate group box control. Radio buttons in one group box act independently of radio buttons in another group box. So, by using group boxes, you can have as many groups of radio buttons as you want. The radio button control is selected from the toolbox. It appears as:

In Toolbox:

On Form (default properties):

Properties

The radio button properties are:

Property	Description
Name	Name used to identify radio button. Three letter prefix for radio button names is **rdo**.
Text	Identifying text next to radio button.
TextAlign	Specifies how the displayed text is positioned.
Font	Sets style, size, and type of displayed text.
Checked	Indicates if button is selected (**True**) or not selected (**False**). Only one button in a group can have a True value.
BackColor	Sets radio button background color.
ForeColor	Sets color of displayed text.
Left	If on form, distance from left side of form to left side of radio button. If in group box, distance from left side of group box to left side of radio button (X in properties window).
Top	If on form, distance from top side of form to top side of radio button. If in group box, distance from top side of group box to top side of radio button (Y in properties window).
Width	Width of the radio button in pixels.
Height	Height of radio button in pixels.
Enabled	Determines whether <u>all</u> controls within radio button can respond to user events (in run mode).
Visible	Determines whether the radio button appears on the form (in run mode).

One button in each group of radio buttons should always have a Checked property set to True in design mode. And, again, if a radio button is in a group box, the Left and Top properties give position in the group box, not on the form.

Example

Start Visual C# Express and start a new project. Draw a group box. Remember, each individual group of radio buttons (we need one group for each decision we make) has to be in a separate group box. Place three or four radio buttons in the group box using techniques discussed earlier. Set one of the buttons Checked property to True. Run the project. Notice one button has a filled circle (the one you initialized the Checked property for). Click another radio button. That button will be filled while the previously filled button will no longer be filled. Keep clicking buttons to get the idea of how they work. In event methods, we would examine each radio button's Checked property to determine which one is selected. Stop the project. Did you notice that, like for check boxes, we didn't have to write any C# code to make the filled circles appear or go away? That is handled by the control itself. Change the group box BackColor property and notice all the 'contained' radio buttons also change background color.

Draw another group box on the form. Put two or three radio buttons in that group box and set one button's Checked property to True. As always, make sure the buttons are properly placed in the group box. Run the project. Change the selected button in this second group. Notice changing this group of radio buttons has no effect on the earlier group. Remember that radio buttons in one group box do not affect radio buttons in another. Group boxes are used to implement separate choices. Try more group boxes and radio buttons if you want. Stop the project.

Events

The only radio button event of interest is the CheckedChanged event:

Event	Description
CheckedChanged	Event executed when the Checked property changes.

When one radio button acting in a group attains a Checked property of True, the Checked property of all other buttons in its group is set to False. We don't have to write C# code to do this - it is automatic.

Typical Use of a Radio Button Control

Usual design steps for a radio button control are:

- Establish a group of radio buttons by placing them in the same group box control
- For each button in the group, set the **Name** (give each button a similar name to identify them with the group) and **Text** property. You might also change the **Font**, **BackColor** and **Forecolor** properties.
- Initialize the **Checked** property of one button to **True**.
- Monitor the **CheckChanged** event of each radio button in the group to determine when a button is clicked. The 'last clicked' button in the group will always have a **Checked** property of **True**.

C# - The Fourth Lesson

By now, you've learned a lot about the C# language. In this class, we look at just one new idea - another way to make decisions.

Decisions – Switch Structure

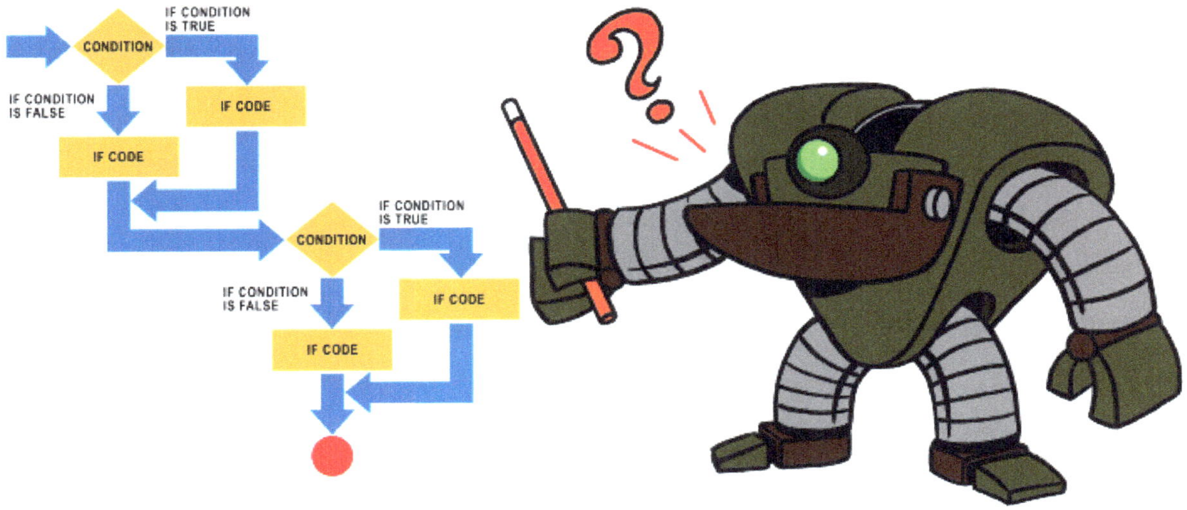

In the previous class, we studied the **if** structure as a way of letting Visual C# Express make decisions using comparison operators and logical operators. We saw that the if structure is very flexible and allows us to implement a variety of decision logics. Many times in making decisions, we simply want to examine the value of just one variable or expression. Based on whatever values that expression might have, we want to take particular actions in our C# code. We could implement such a logic using if and else if statements. C# offers another way to make decisions such as this.

An alternative to a complex **if** structure when simply checking the value of a single variable is the C# **switch** structure. The parts of the switch structure are:

- The **switch** keyword
- A controlling **variable**
- One or more **case** statements followed by an value terminated by a colon (:). After the colon is the code to be executed if the variable equals the corresponding value.
- An optional **break** statement to leave the structure after executing the case code.
- An optional **default** block to execute if none of the preceding case statements have been executed.

The general form for this structure is:

```
switch (variable)
{
case value1:
     [C# code to execute if variable == value1]
     break;
case value2:
     [C# code to execute if variable == value2]
     break;
.
.
default:
     [C# code to execute if no other code has been executed]
     break;
}
```

In this example, if **variable = value1**, the first code block is executed. If **variable = value2**, the second is executed. If no subsequent matches between variable and values are found, the code in the **default** block is executed.

This code is equivalent to the following **if** structure:

```
if (variable == value1)
{
        [C# code to execute if variable = value1]
}
else if (variable == value2)
{
        [C# code to execute if variable = value2]
}
.
.
else
{
        [C# code to execute if no other code has been executed]
}
```

A couple of comments about **switch**. The **break** statements, though optional, will almost always be there. If a break statement is not seen at the end of a particular case, the following case or cases will execute until a break is encountered. This is different behavior than seen in if statements, where only one "case" could be executed. Second, all the execution blocks in a switch structure are enclosed in curly braces, but the blocks within each case do not have to have braces (they are optional). This is different from most code blocks in C#. Look at the use of the switch structure in the next project to see an example of its use.

Project - Sandwich Maker

The local sandwich shop has heard about your fantastic Visual C# Express programming skills and has hired you to make a computer version of their ordering system. What a great place to try out your skills with group boxes, check boxes, and radio buttons!

Project Design

In a project like this, making a computer version of an existing process (ordering a sandwich), the design steps are usually pretty straightforward. We asked the sandwich shop how they do things and this is what they told us:

- Three bread choices (can only pick one): white, wheat, rye
- Five meat choices (pick as many as you want): roast beef, ham, turkey, pastrami, salami
- Three cheese choices (can only pick one): none, American, Swiss
- Six condiment choices (pick as many as you want): mustard, mayonnaise, lettuce, tomato, onion, pickles

It should be obvious what controls are needed.

We will need a group of three radio buttons for bread, a group of five check boxes for meat, a group of three radio buttons for cheese, and six check boxes for condiments. We'll add a button for clearing the menu board, a button to 'build' the sandwich, and a text box, with a label for titling information, where we will print out the sandwich order. This project is saved as **Sandwich** in the course projects folder (**\VCSEKids\VCSEK Projects**).

Place Controls on Form

Start a new project in Visual C# Express. Place and resize four group boxes on the form. Place three radio buttons (for bread choices) in the first group box (remember how to properly place controls in a group box). Place five check boxes (for meat choices) in the second group box. Place three radio buttons (for cheese choices) in the third group box. Place six check boxes (for condiment choices) in the fourth group box. Add two buttons, a label and a text box. My form looks like this:

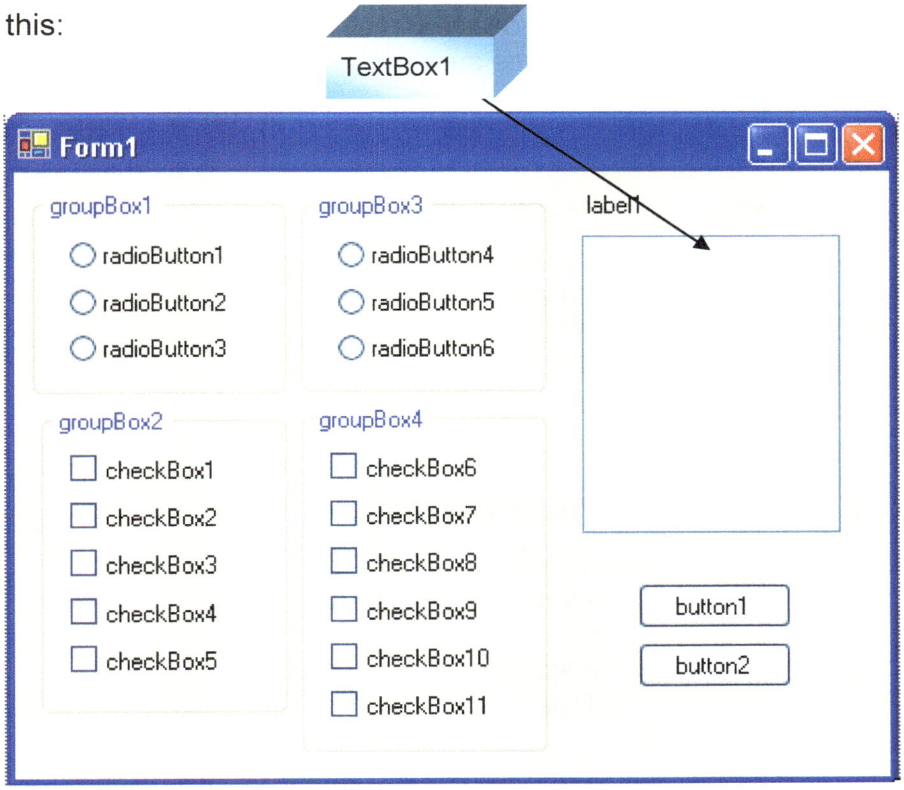

Yes, there are lots of controls involved when working with check boxes and radio buttons, and even more properties. Get ready!

Set Control Properties

Set the control properties using the properties window:

Form1 Form:

Property Name	**Property Value**
Text	Sandwich Maker
FormBorderStyle	Fixed Single
StartPosition	CenterScreen
Icon	[Pick one you make with IconEdit or you can use my little sandwich icon]

groupBox1 Group Box:

Property Name	**Property Value**
Name	grpBread
Text	Bread
Font Size	10
Font Style	Bold

radioButton1 Radio Button:

Property Name	**Property Value**
Name	rdoWhite
Text	White
Font Size	8
Font Style	Regular
Checked	True

radioButton2 Radio Button:

Property Name	**Property Value**
Name	rdoWheat
Text	Wheat
Font Size	8
Font Style	Regular

radioButton3 Radio Button:

Property Name	Property Value
Name	rdoRye
Text	Rye
Font Size	8
Font Style	Regular

groupBox2 Group Box:

Property Name	Property Value
Name	grpMeats
Text	Meats
Font Size	10
Font Style	Bold

checkBox1 Check Box:

Property Name	Property Value
Name	chkRoastBeef
Text	Roast Beef
Font Size	8
Font Style	Regular

checkBox2 Check Box:

Property Name	Property Value
Name	chkHam
Text	Ham
Font Size	8
Font Style	Regular

checkBox3 Check Box:

Property Name	Property Value
Name	chkTurkey
Text	Turkey
Font Size	8
Font Style	Regular

checkBox4 Check Box:

Property Name	Property Value
Name	chkPastrami
Text	Pastrami
Font Size	8
Font Style	Regular

checkBox5 Check Box:

Property Name	Property Value
Name	chkSalami
Text	Salami
Font Size	8
Font Style	Regular

groupBox3 Group Box:

Property Name	Property Value
Name	grpCheese
Text	Cheese
Font Size	10
Font Style	Bold

radioButton4 Radio Button:

Property Name	Property Value
Name	rdoNone
Text	None
Font Size	8
Font Style	Regular
Checked	True

radioButton5 Radio Button:

Property Name	Property Value
Name	rdoAmerican
Text	American
Font Size	8
Font Style	Regular

radioButton6 Radio Button:

Property Name	Property Value
Name	rdoSwiss
Text	Swiss
Font Size	8
Font Style	Regular

groupBox4 Group Box:

Property Name	Property Value
Name	grpCondiments
Text	Condiments
Font Size	10
Font Style	Bold

checkBox6 Check Box:

Property Name	Property Value
Name	chkMustard
Text	Mustard
Font Size	8
Font Style	Regular

checkBox7 Check Box:

Property Name	Property Value
Name	chkMayo
Text	Mayonnaise
Font Size	8
Font Style	Regular

checkBox8 Check Box:

Property Name	Property Value
Name	chkLettuce
Text	Lettuce
Font Size	8
Font Style	Regular

checkBox9 Check Box:

Property Name	**Property Value**
Name	chkTomato
Text	Tomato
Font Size	8
Font Style	Regular

checkBox10 Check Box:

Property Name	**Property Value**
Name	chkOnions
Text	Onions
Font Size	8
Font Style	Regular

checkBox11 Check Box:

Property Name	**Property Value**
Name	chkPickles
Text	Pickles
Font Size	8
Font Style	Regular

label1 Label:

Property Name	**Property Value**
Name	lblOrder
Text	Order:
Font Size	10
Font Style	Bold

textBox1 Text Box:

Property Name	**Property Value**
Name	txtOrder
MultiLine	True
ScrollBars	Vertical

button1 Button:

Property Name	**Property Value**
Name	btnOrder
Text	Order

button2 Button:

Property Name	**Property Value**
Name	btnClear
Text	Clear

When done, turn to the next page to see what my form looks like.

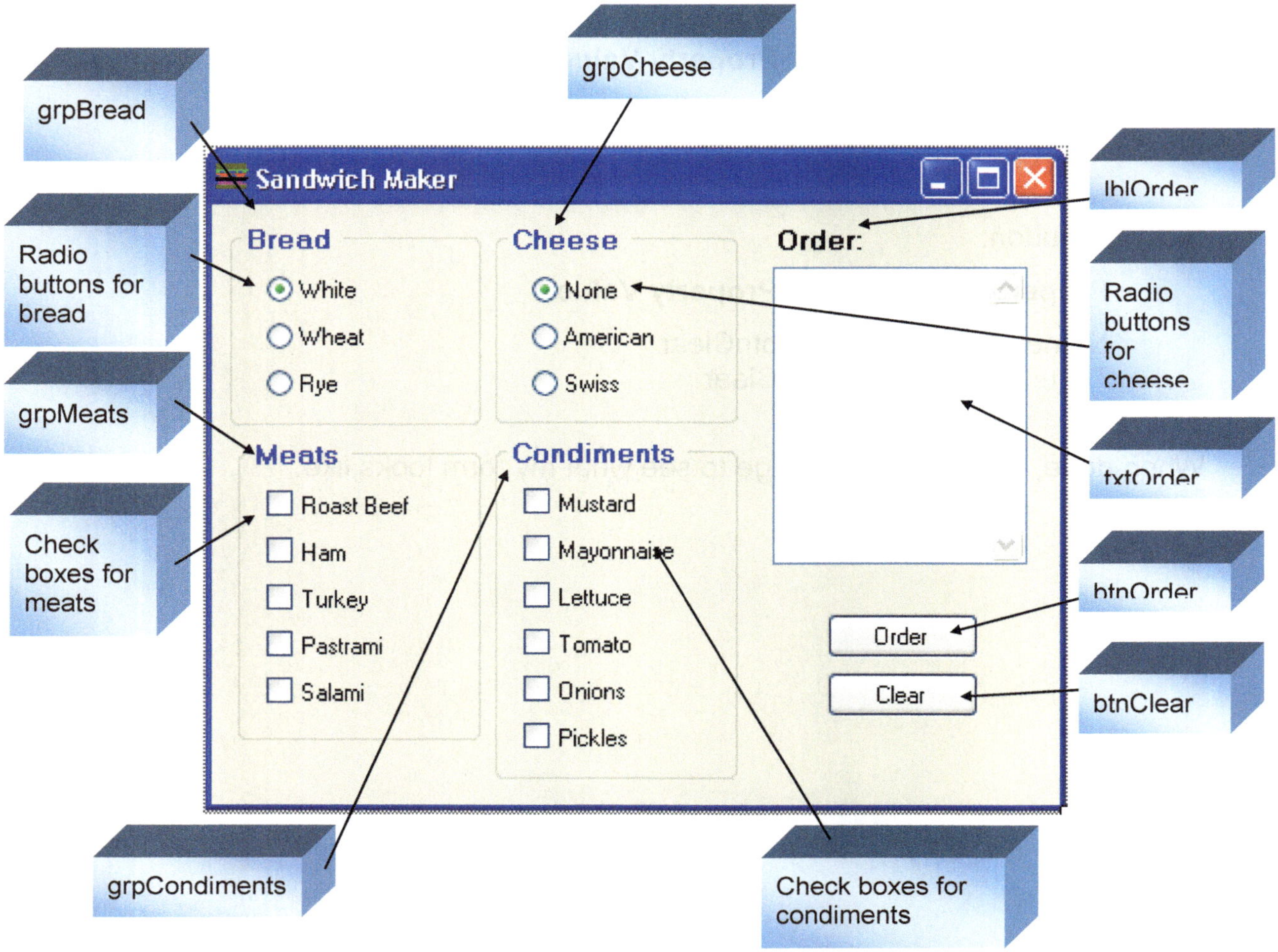

As we said, there is a lot of work involved when working with check boxes and radio buttons - many controls to place in group boxes and many properties to set. This is a part of developing computer applications. Many times, the work is tedious and uninteresting. But, you have the satisfaction of knowing, once complete, your project will have a professional looking interface with controls every user knows how to use. Now, let's write the event methods - they're pretty easy.

Write Event methods

In this project, you use the check boxes and radio buttons in the various group boxes to specify the desired sandwich. When all choices are made, click **Order** and the ingredients for the ordered sandwich will be printed in the text box (for the sandwich makers to read). Clicking **Clear** will return the menu board to its initial state to allow another order. So, we need **Click** events for each button control.

We also need some way to determine which check boxes and which radio buttons have been selected. How do we do this? Notice the final state of each check box is not established until the Order button is clicked. At this point, we can examine each check box Checked property (set automatically by Visual C# Express) to see if it has been selected. So, we don't need really event methods for these boxes.

Radio button value properties are established when one of the buttons in a group is clicked, changing its Checked property. For radio buttons, we will have CheckedChanged events that keep track of which button in a group is currently selected. Two integer variables are needed, one to keep track of which bread (**breadChoice**) is selected and one to keep track of which cheese (**cheeseChoice**) is selected. We will use these values to indicate choices:

breadChoice:

Value	**Selected Bread**
1	White
2	Wheat
3	Rye

cheeseChoice:

Value	**Selected Cheese**
0	None
1	American
2	Swiss

Using variables to indicate radio button choices is common.

We will add two more variables (**numberMeats** and **numberCondiments**) to count how many meats and condiments are selected. Open the code window and declare these variables in the **general declarations** area under the form constructor method:

```
int breadChoice;
int cheeseChoice;
int numberMeats;
int numberCondiments;
```

The code window should look like this:

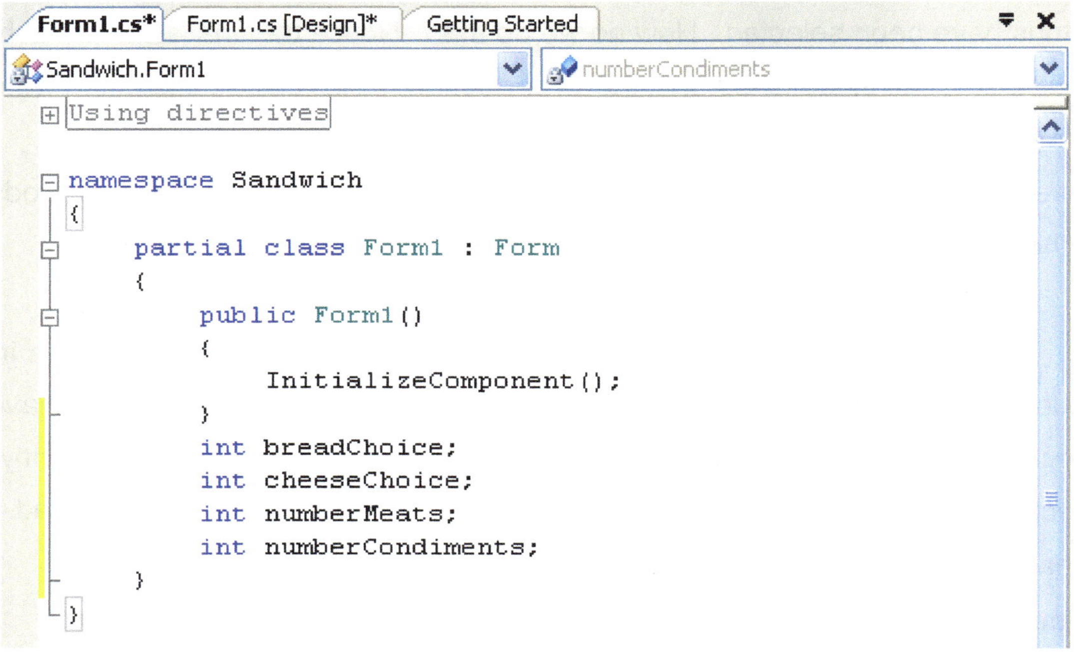

breadChoice and cheeseChoice must be initialized to match the initially selected radio buttons: **rdoWhite** (white bread) has an initial True value (for Checked property) in the bread group, so BreadChoice is initially 1; **rdoNone** (no cheese) has an initial True value (for Checked property) in the cheese group, so CheeseChoice is initially 0. Set these initial values in the **Form1_Load** method (recall this is always a good place to set values the first time you use them):

```
private void Form1_Load(object sender, EventArgs e)
{
    // Initialize bread and cheese choices
    breadChoice = 1;
    cheeseChoice = 0;
}
```

After all choices have been input on the sandwich menu board, you click **Order**. At this point, the computer needs to do the following:

- Decide which bread was selected
- Decide which meats (if any) were selected
- Decide which cheese (if any) was selected
- Decide which condiments (if any) were selected
- Place 'order' in text box

Let's look at how each decision is made.

The bread and cheese decisions are similar - they both use radio buttons. The selected bread is given by the variable breadChoice. breadChoice is established in the CheckedChanged events for each of the three bread radio buttons. It is easy code. First, **rdoWhite_CheckedChanged:**

```
private void rdoWhite_CheckedChanged(object sender, EventArgs
e)
{
    // White bread selected
    breadChoice = 1;
}
```

rdoWheat_CheckedChanged:

```
private void rdoWheat_CheckedChanged(object sender, EventArgs
e)
{
    // Wheat bread selected
    breadChoice = 2;
}
```

rdoRye_CheckedChanged:

```
private void rdoRye_CheckedChanged(object sender, EventArgs
e)
{
    // Rye bread selected
    breadChoice = 3;
}
```

Similar code is used to determine CheeseChoice. The **rdoNone_CheckedChanged** event method:

```
private void rdoNone_CheckedChanged(object sender, EventArgs
e)
{
    // No cheese selected
    cheeseChoice = 0;
}
```

rdoAmerican_CheckedChanged:

```
private void rdoAmerican_CheckedChanged(object sender,
EventArgs e)
{
    // American cheese selected
    cheeseChoice = 1;
}
```

rdoSwiss_CheckedChanged:

```
private void rdoSwiss_CheckedChanged(object sender, EventArgs
e)
{
    // Swiss cheese selected
    cheeseChoice = 2;
}
```

With the above code, we see that by the time Order is clicked, the bread and cheese choices will be known. We do not know the meat and condiment choices, however. The only way to determine these choices is to examine each individual check box Checked property to see if it is checked or not. This is done in the **btnOrder_Click** event method. We also place the complete order in the text box control in this method. Let's see how.

The displayed information in the text box is stored in its **Text** property. We build this multi-line Text property in stages. The stages are:

- Establish bread type in Text property (use switch).
- Replace Text property with previous value plus any added meat(s) (use an if statement for each meat).
- Replace Text property with previous value plus any added cheese (use switch).
- Replace Text property with previous value plus any added condiments(s) (use an if statement for each condiment).
- Text property is complete.

As items are added to the Text property (we'll be using lots of concatenations), we would also like to put each item on a separate line. We use a combination of two Visual C# Express **control characters** to do that – **\r\n**. This is a value (stands for carriage **r**eturn and **n**ew line – a throwback to typewriter days) that tells the Text property to move to a new line – simply append it to a string where you want a new line. Here's the **btnOrder_Click** event method that implements the steps of determining meat and condiments and building the Text property of txtOrder:

```
private void btnOrder_Click(object sender, EventArgs e)
{
    // Start Text with bread type
    txtOrder.Text = "Sandwich Order:\r\n";
    switch (breadChoice)
    {
        case 1:
            txtOrder.Text = txtOrder.Text + "White
Bread\r\n";
            break;
        case 2:
            txtOrder.Text = txtOrder.Text + "Wheat
Bread\r\n";
            break;
        case 3:
            txtOrder.Text = txtOrder.Text + "Rye Bread\r\n";
            break;
```

```
     }
    // Add and count meats
    numberMeats = 0;
    if (chkRoastBeef.Checked)
    {
        numberMeats = numberMeats + 1;
        txtOrder.Text = txtOrder.Text + "Roast Beef\r\n";
    }
    if (chkHam.Checked)
    {
        numberMeats = numberMeats + 1;
        txtOrder.Text = txtOrder.Text + "Ham\r\n";
    }
    if (chkTurkey.Checked)
    {
        numberMeats = numberMeats + 1;
        txtOrder.Text = txtOrder.Text + "Turkey\r\n";
    }
    if (chkPastrami.Checked)
    {
        numberMeats = numberMeats + 1;
        txtOrder.Text = txtOrder.Text + "Pastrami\r\n";
    }
    if (chkSalami.Checked)
    {
        numberMeats = numberMeats + 1;
        txtOrder.Text = txtOrder.Text + "Salami\r\n";
    }
    // If no meats picked, say so
    if (numberMeats == 0)
    {
        txtOrder.Text = txtOrder.Text + "No Meat\r\n";
    }
    // Add cheese type
    switch (cheeseChoice)
    {
        case 0:
            txtOrder.Text = txtOrder.Text + "No Cheese\r\n";
            break;
        case 1:
            txtOrder.Text = txtOrder.Text + "American
Cheese\r\n";
            break;
        case 2:
            txtOrder.Text = txtOrder.Text + "Swiss
Cheese\r\n";
            break;
```

```
    }
    // Finally, add  and count condiments
    numberCondiments = 0;
    if (chkMustard.Checked)
    {
        numberCondiments=numberCondiments+1;
        txtOrder.Text = txtOrder.Text + "Mustard\r\n";
    }
    if (chkMayo.Checked)
    {
        numberCondiments=numberCondiments+1;
        txtOrder.Text = txtOrder.Text + "Mayonnaise\r\n";
    }
    if (chkLettuce.Checked)
    {
        numberCondiments=numberCondiments+1;
        txtOrder.Text = txtOrder.Text + "Lettuce\r\n";
    }
    if (chkTomato.Checked)
    {
        numberCondiments=numberCondiments+1;
        txtOrder.Text = txtOrder.Text + "Tomato\r\n";
    }
    if (chkOnions.Checked)
    {
        numberCondiments=numberCondiments+1;
        txtOrder.Text = txtOrder.Text + "Onions\r\n";
    }
    if (chkPickles.Checked)
    {
        numberCondiments=numberCondiments+1;
        txtOrder.Text = txtOrder.Text + "Pickles\r\n";
    }
    // If no condiments picked, say so
    if (numberCondiments == 0)
    {
        txtOrder.Text = txtOrder.Text + "No Condiments\r\n";
    }
}
```

Wow! That's one long event method. And, after we're done, all we really have is just one very long txtOrder.Text property. But, with your C# knowledge, you should be able to see it's really not that complicated, just long. Each step in the method is very logical.

A few comments. First, as you type in the method from these notes, be aware of places the word processor 'word wraps' a line because it has gone past the right margin. It appears there is a new line, but don't start a new line in your C# code. Type each line of code on just one line in the Visual C# Express code window. Second, this is a great place to practice your copying and pasting skills. Notice how a lot of the code is very similar. Use copy and paste (highlight text, select **Edit** menu, then **Copy** - move to paste location, select **Edit** menu, then **Paste**). Once you paste text, make sure you make needed changes to the pasted text! Third, for long methods like this, I suggest typing in one section of code (for example, the cheese choice), saving the project, and then running the project to make sure this section works. Then, add another section and test it. Then, add another section and test it. Visual C# Express makes such incremental additions very easy. This also lessens the amount of program "debugging" you need to do.

We need one last event method - the **btnClear_Click** event. Clicking Clear will reset the bread and cheese choices, clear all the check boxes, and clear the text box. This event is:

```
private void btnClear_Click(object sender, EventArgs e)
{
    // Set bread to white
    breadChoice = 1;
    rdoWhite.Checked = true;
    // Clear all meat choices
    chkRoastBeef.Checked = false;
    chkHam.Checked = false;
    chkTurkey.Checked = false;
    chkPastrami.Checked = false;
    chkSalami.Checked = false;
    // Set cheese to none
    cheeseChoice = 0;
    rdoNone.Checked = true;
    // Clear all condiment choices
    chkMustard.Checked = false;
    chkMayo.Checked = false;
    chkLettuce.Checked = false;
    chkTomato.Checked = false;
    chkOnions.Checked = false;
    chkPickles.Checked = false;
    // Clear text box
    txtOrder.Text = "";
}
```

You're done! Save your project by clicking the **Save All** button in the toolbar.

Run the Project

Run the project. Make choices on the menu board, then click **Order**. Pretty cool, huh? Here's my favorite sandwich:

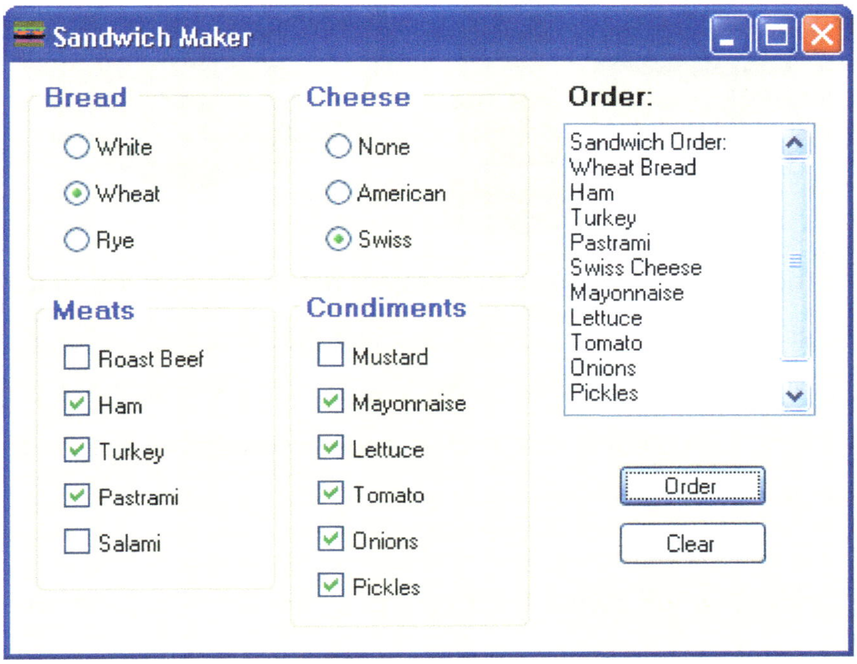

As always, make sure all check boxes and radio buttons work and provide the proper information in the text box. Make sure the **Clear** button works. Notice the text box scroll bar is active only when there is a long sandwich order. If something doesn't work as it should, recheck your control properties and event methods. Save your project if you needed to make any changes.

Other Things to Try

Notice the only ways to stop this project are to click on the Visual C# Express toolbar's Stop button or to click the box that looks like an **X** in the upper right corner of the Sandwich Maker form. We probably should have put an Exit button on the form. Try adding one and its code. Remember the C# **this.Close()** statement stops a project.

The sandwich shop owner liked your program so much, she wants to hook it up to her cash register. She wants you to modify the program so it also prints out (at the bottom) how much the sandwich cost. We'll give the steps - you do the work. The owner says a sandwich costs $3.95. There is an additional $0.75 charge for each extra meat selection (one meat is included in the $3.95 price) and there is an 8% sales tax. Now, the steps: (1) define a double type variable **cost** to compute the sandwich cost and (2) after setting the text box Text property, compute cost using this code segment (place this at the end, right before the final right curly brace in the **btnOrder_Click** event method):

```
// Start with basic cost
cost = 3.95;
// Check for extra meats
if (numberMeats > 1)
{
    cost = cost + (numberMeats - 1) * 0.75;
}
// Add 8 percent sales tax
cost = cost + 0.08 * cost;
// Add cost to text property
txtOrder.Text = txtOrder.Text + Convert.ToString(cost);
```

Can you see how this works? Particularly, look at the if structure used to see if we need to charge for extra meat. Now, run the project and see the cost magically appear (my favorite sandwich costs 5.886). Note the cost value may have more or less than the two decimals we like to see when working with money. Using the **Convert.ToString** method to convert decimal numbers to strings, we have no control on how many (if any) decimals are displayed. There is another C# method that will help us do that - - the C# **Format** function. We'll show you how to use Format to display dollar amounts. To find out more about Format (and it is a very useful function - we just don't use it in this course), consult the Visual C# Express on-line help system. To display two decimals for cost, replace the last line of code with:

```
txtOrder.Text = txtOrder.Text + String.Format("{0:f2}",
cost);
```

One last modification to this project might be to add some way to enter how much money the customer gave you for the sandwich and have the computer tell you how much change the customer gets. Can you think of a way to do this? Try it. You would want to use the Format method here. It's difficult to give $1.2345 in change!

In this class, we learned about three very useful controls for making choices: the group box, check boxes, and radio buttons. And, we looked at another way to make decisions: the switch structure. Using these new tools, you built your biggest project yet - the Sandwich Maker. This project had a lot of controls, a lot of properties to set, and a lot of C# code to write. But, that's how most projects are. But, I think you see that with careful planning and a methodical approach (following the three project steps), building such a complicated project is not really that hard. In the next class, we start looking at a really fun part of Visual C# Express - graphics!

8

Panels, Mouse Events, Colors

Review and Preview

You've seen and learned how to use lots of controls in the Visual C# Express toolbox. In this class, we begin looking at a very fun part of Visual C# Express - adding graphics capabilities to our projects.

A key control for such capabilities is the panel. We will look at this control in detail. We will also look at ways for Visual C# Express to recognize mouse events and have some fun with colors. You will build an electronic blackboard project.

Panel Control

The **Panel** control is another Visual C# Express 'container' control. It is nearly identical to the **GroupBox** control (seen in Class 7) in behavior. Controls are placed in a Panel control in the same manner they are placed in the GroupBox. Radio buttons in a panel work as an independent group. Yet, panel controls can also be used to display graphics (lines, rectangles, ellipses, polygons, text). In this class, we will look at these graphic capabilities of the panel control. The panel is selected from the toolbox. It appears as:

In Toolbox:

On Form (default properties):

Properties

The panel properties are:

Property	Description
Name	Name used to identify panel. Three letter prefix for panel names is **pnl**.
BackColor	Sets panel background color.
Left	Distance from left side of form to left side of panel (X in properties window).
Top	Distance from top side of form to top side of panel (Y in properties window).

Width	Width of the panel in pixels.
Height	Height of panel in pixels.
Enabled	Determines whether all controls within panel can respond to user events (in run mode).
Visible	Determines whether the panel (and attached controls) appears on the form (in run mode).

Like the form and group box objects, the panel is a **container** control, since it 'holds' other controls. Hence, many controls placed in a panel will share the **BackColor** property (notice the panel does not have a Text property). To change this, select the desired control (after it is placed on the group box) and change the background color. Also, note the panel is moved using the displayed 'handle' identical to the process for the group box in the previous class.

Typical Use of Panel Control

The usual design steps for using a panel control are:

- Set **Name** property.
- Place desired controls in panel control.
- Monitor events of controls in panel using usual techniques.

Graphics Using the Panel Control

As mentioned, the panel control looks much like a group box and its use is similar. Panels can be used in place of group box controls, if desired. A powerful feature of the panel control (a feature the group box does not have), however, is its support of graphics. We can use the control as a blank canvas for self-created works of art! There are many new concepts to learn to help us become computer artists. Let's look at those concepts now.

Graphics Methods

To do graphics (drawing) in Visual C# Express, we use the built-in **graphics methods**. A **method** is a procedure or function, similar to the event methods we have been using, that imparts some action to an object or control. Most controls have methods, not just the panel. With the panel, a graphics method can be used to draw something on it. Methods can only be used in run mode. The C# code to use a method is:

```
objectName.MethodName(Arguments);
```

where ObjectName is the object of interest, MethodName is the method being used, and there may be some arguments or parameters (information needed by the method to do its task). Notice this is another form of the dot notation we use to set control properties in code. In this class, we will look at graphics methods that can draw colored lines. As you progress in your programming skills, you are encouraged to study the many other graphics methods that can draw rectangles, ellipses, polygons and virtually any shape, in any color. To use the panel for drawing lines, we need to introduce another concept, that of a **graphics object**.

Graphics Objects

You need to tell Visual C# Express that you will be using graphics methods with the panel control. To do this, you convert the panel control to something called a **graphics object**. Graphics objects provide the "surface" for graphics methods. Creating a graphics object requires two simple steps. We first declare the object using the standard declaration statement. If we name our graphics object **myGraphics**, the form is:

```
Graphics myGraphics;
```

This declaration is placed in the **general declarations** area of the code window, along with our usual variable declarations. Once declared, the object is created using the **CreateGraphics** method:

```
myGraphics = controlName.CreateGraphics();
```

where **controlName** is the name of the control hosting the graphics object (in our work, the **Name** property of the panel control). We will create this object in the form **Load** event of our projects.

Once a graphics object is created, all graphics methods are applied to this newly formed object. Hence, to apply a graphics method named **GraphicsMethod** to the **myGraphics** object, use:

```
myGraphics.GraphicsMethod(Arguments);
```

where **Arguments** are any needed arguments, or information needed by the graphics method.

There are two important graphics methods we introduce now. First, after all of your hard work drawing in a graphics object, there are times you will want to erase or clear the object. This is done with the **Clear** method:

```
myGraphics.Clear(Color);
```

This statement will clear a graphics object (myGraphics) and fill it with the specified **Color**. We will look further at colors next. The usual color argument for clearing a graphics object is the background color of the host control (controlName), or:

```
myGraphics.Clear(controlName.BackColor);
```

Once you are done drawing to an object and need it no longer, it should be properly disposed to clear up system resources. To do this with our example graphics object, use the **Dispose** method:

```
myGraphics.Dispose();
```

This statement is usually placed in the form **FormClosing** event method.

Our drawing will require colors and objects called pens, so let's take a look at those concepts. Doesn't it make sense we need pens to do some drawing?

Colors

Colors play a big part in Visual C# Express applications. We have seen colors in designing some of our previous applications. At design time, we have selected background colors (**BackColor** property) and foreground colors (**ForeColor** property) for different controls. Such choices are made by selecting the desired property in the properties window. Once selected, a palette of customizable colors appears for you to choose from.

Most graphics methods and graphics objects use color. For example, the pen object we study next has a **Color** argument that specifies just what color it draws with. Unlike control color properties, these colors cannot be selected at design time. They must be defined in code. How do we do this? There are two approaches we will take: (1) use built-in colors and (2) create a color.

The colors built into Visual C# Express are specified by the **Color** structure. We have seen a few colors in some our examples and projects. A color is specified using:

```
Color.ColorName
```

where **ColorName** is a reserved color name. There are many, many color names (I counted 141). There are colors like **BlanchedAlmond**, **Linen**, **NavajoWhite, PeachPuff** and **SpringGreen**. You don't have to remember these names. Whenever you type the word **Color**, followed by a dot (.), in the code window, the Intellisense feature of Visual C# Express will pop up a list of color selections. Just choose from the list to complete the color specification. You will have to remember the difference between BlanchedAlmond and Linen though!

If for some reason, the selection provided by the **Color** structure does not fit your needs, there is a method that allows you to create over 16 million different colors. The method (**FromArgb**) works with the **Color** structure. The syntax to specify a color is:

```
Color.FromArgb(Red, Green, Blue)
```

where **Red**, **Green**, and **Blue** are integer measures of intensity of the corresponding primary colors. These measures can range from 0 (least intensity) to 255 (greatest intensity). For example, `Color.FromArgb(255, 255, 0)` will produce yellow. Sorry, but I can't tell you what values to use to create **PeachPuff**.

It is easy to specify colors for graphics methods using the **Color** structure. Any time you need a color, just use one of the built-in colors or the **FromArgb** method. These techniques to represent color are not limited to just providing colors for graphics methods. They can be used anywhere Visual C# Express requires a color; for example, **BackColor** and **ForeColor** properties can also be set (at run-time) using these techniques. For example, to change your form background color to **PeachPuff**, use:

```
this.BackColor = Color.PeachPuff;
```

You can also define variables that take on color values. It is a two step process. Say we want to define a variable named **myRed** to represent the color red. First, in the general declarations area, declare your variable to be of type **Color**:

```
Color myRed;
```

Then, define your color in code using:

```
myRed = Color.Red;
```

From this point on, you can use **myRed** anywhere the red color is desired.

Example

Go the course project folder (**\VCSEKids\VCSEK Projects**) and open a project named **RGBColors**. Run this project. Three numeric updown controls are there: one to control the **Red** (R =) content, one to control the **Green** (G =) content, and one to control the **Blue** (B =) content. Set values for each and see the corresponding color assigned using the **FromArgb** function. Play with this project and look at all the colors available with this function. How long does it take to look at all 16 million combinations? A long time! The running project looks like this:

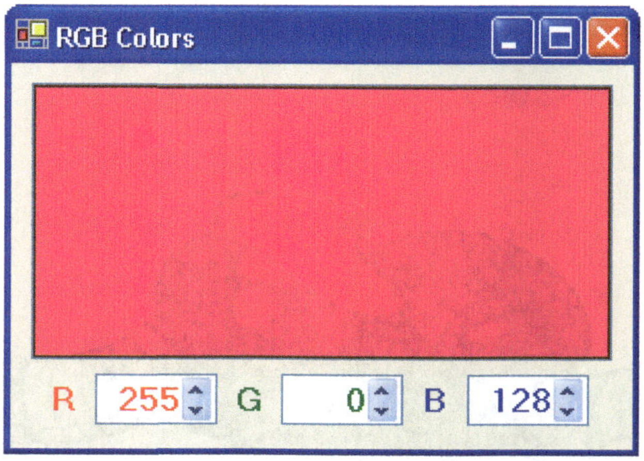

Stop the project when you're done playing with the colors. See if you can figure out how this little project works.

Pen Objects

As mentioned, many of the graphics methods (including the method to draw lines) require a **Pen** object. This virtual pen is just like the pen you use to write and draw. You can choose color and width. You can use pens built into Visual C# Express or create your own pen.

In many cases, the pen objects built into Visual C# Express are sufficient. These pens will draw a line **1** pixel wide in a color you choose (Intellisense will present the list to choose from). If the selected color is **ColorName** (one of the 141 built-in color names), the syntax to refer to such a pen is:

```
Pens.ColorName
```

Creating your own pen is similar to creating a graphics object, but here we create a **Pen** object. To create your own Pen object, you first declare the pen using:

```
Pen myPen;
```

This line goes in the **general declarations** area. The pen is then created using the **Pen constructor** function:

```
myPen = new Pen(Color, Width);
```

where **Color** is the color your new pen will draw in and **Width** is the integer width of the line (in pixels) drawn. The pen is usually created in the form **Load** method. This pen will draw a solid line. The **Color** argument can be one of the built-in colors or one generated with the **FromArgb** function.

Once created, you can change the color and width at any time using the **Color** and **Width** properties of the pen object. The syntax is:

```
myPen.Color = newColor;
myPen.Width = newWidth;
```

Here, **newColor** is a newly specified color and **newWidth** is a new integer pen width.

Like the graphics object, when done using a pen object, it should be disposed using the **Dispose** method:

```
myPen.Dispose();
```

This disposal usually occurs in the form **FormClosing** method.

We're almost ready to draw lines – be patient! Just one more concept and we're on our way.

Graphics Coordinates

We will use Visual C# Express to draw lines using a method called the **DrawLine** method. Before looking at this method, let's look at how we specify the points used to draw and connect lines. All graphics methods use a default **coordinate system**. This means we have a specific way to refer to individual points in the control (a panel in our work) hosting the graphics object. The coordinate system used is:

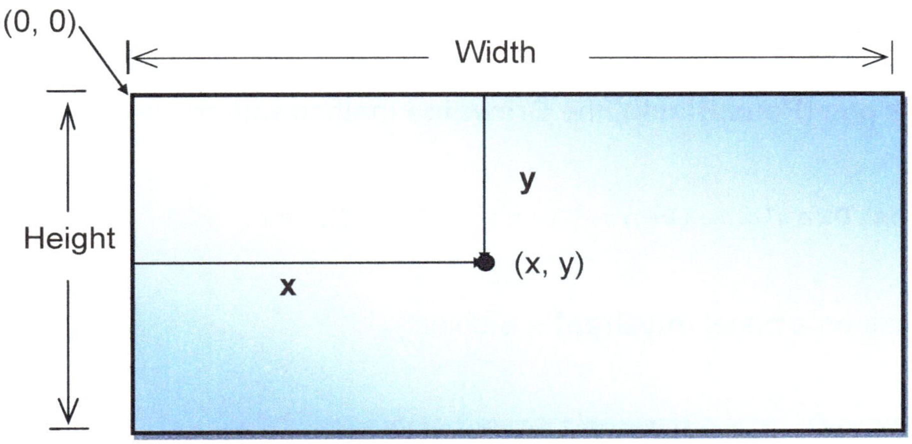

We use two values (coordinates) to identify a single point in the panel. The **x** (horizontal) coordinate increases from left to right, starting at **0**. The **y** (vertical) coordinate increases from top to bottom, also starting at **0**. Points in the panel are referred to by the two coordinates enclosed in parentheses, or **(x, y)**. Notice how x and y, respectively, are similar to the Left and Top control properties. All values shown are in units of **pixels**.

At long last, we're ready to draw some lines.

DrawLine Method

The Visual C# Express **DrawLine** method is used to connect two points with a straight-line segment. It operates on a previously created graphics object. If that object is **myGraphics** and we wish to connect the point (**x1**, **y1**) with (**x2**, **y2**) using a pen object **myPen**, the statement is:

```
myGraphics.DrawLine(myPen, x1, y1, x2, y2);
```

The pen object can be either one of the built-in pens or one you create using the pen constructor just discussed. Each coordinate value is an integer type. Using a built-in black pen (**Pens.Black**), the **DrawLine** method with these points is:

```
myGraphics.DrawLine(Pens.Black, x1, y1, x2, y2);
```

This produces on a panel (**myGraphics** object):

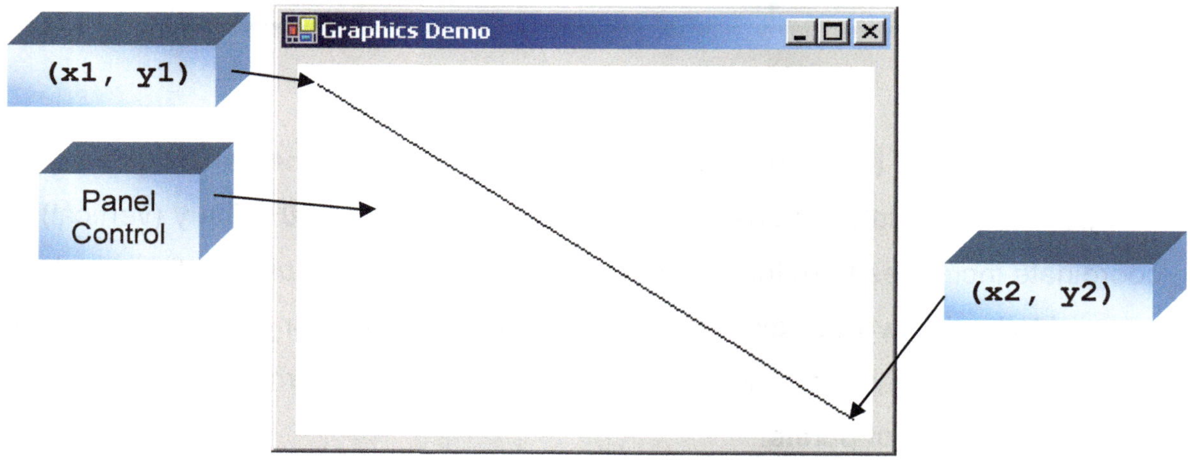

To connect the last point (**x2, y2**) to another point (**x3, y3**), use:

```
myGraphics.DrawLine(Pens.Black, x2, y2, x3, y3);
```

This produces on a panel (**myGraphics** object):

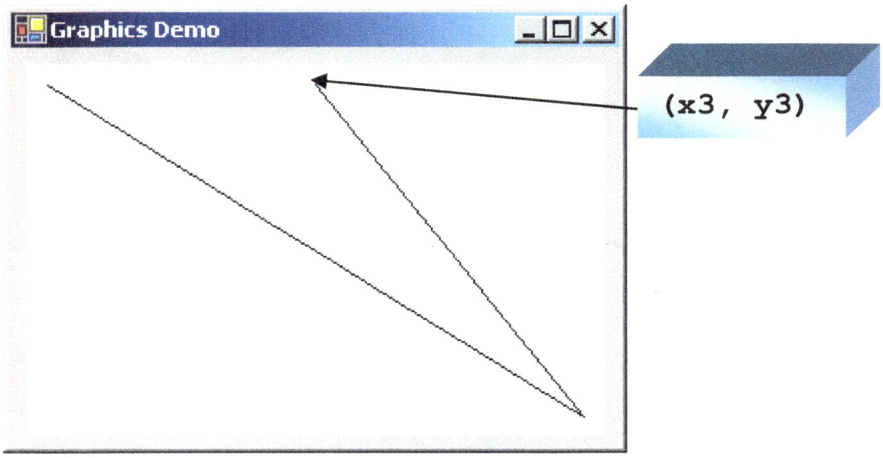

For every line segment you draw, you need a separate **DrawLine** statement. To connect one line segment with another, you need to save the last point drawn to in the first segment (use two integer variables, one for x and one for y). This saved point will become the starting point for the next line segment. You can choose to change the pen color at any time you wish. Using many line segments, with many different colors, you can draw virtually anything you want! We'll do that with the blackboard project in this class.

Graphics Review

We've covered lots of new material here, so it's probably good to review the steps necessary to use the **DrawLine** method to draw line segments:

- **Declare** a **graphics object** in the general declarations area.
- **Create** a **graphics object** in the form Load event method.
- **Select** a **pen object** using the built-in Pens object or **create** your own **pen object**.
- **Draw** to **graphics object** using DrawLine method and specified coordinates.
- **Dispose** of **graphics object** and **pen object** (if created) in the form FormClosing event method.

The process is like drawing on paper. You get your paper (graphics object) and your pens. You do all your drawing and coloring and then put your supplies away!

Example

Start a new project in Visual C# Express. Place a panel control (name **panel1**) on the form. Make it fairly large. Set its **BackColor** property to white. Place a button control (name **button1**) on the form. My form looks like this:

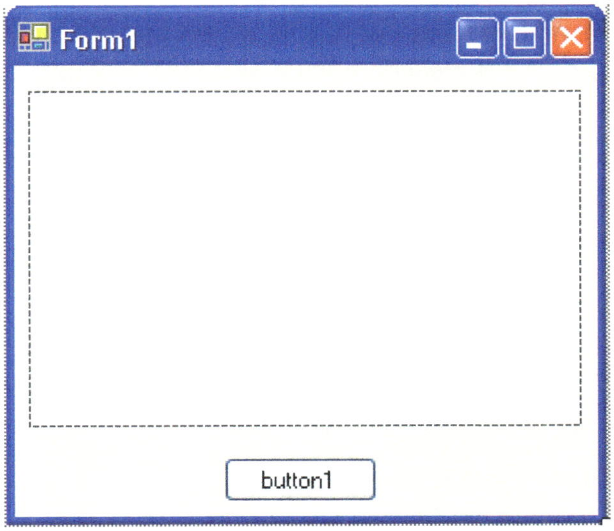

Write down the **Width** and **Height** properties of your panel control (look at the **Size** property; my values are Width = 270 and Height = 170).

In the general declarations area of the code window, declare your graphics object using:

```
Graphics myGraphics;
```

In the **Form1_Load** event, add this line of code to create the graphics object:

```
myGraphics = panel1.CreateGraphics();
```

In the **button1_Click** event, write a line of code that draws a line starting at the point (10, 10) and goes to a point (Width – 10, Height – 10), where Width and Height are the dimensions of your panel control. Using a black pen, this line of code for my panel is:

```
myGraphics.DrawLine(Pens.Black, 10, 10, 260, 160);
```

And, in the **Form1_FormClosing** event, dispose of your graphics object using:

```
myGraphics.Dispose();
```

Make sure your code window looks like this:

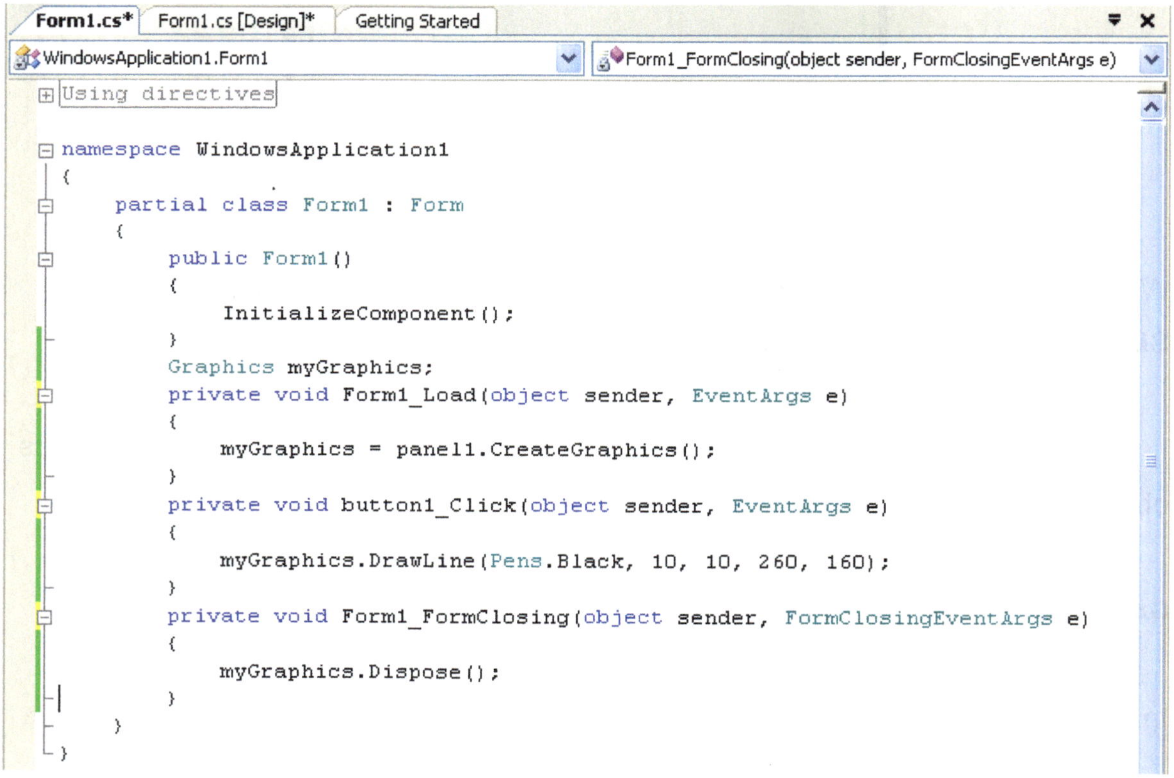

Especially note the placement of the statement declaring the graphics object.

Run the project. Click the button. The code draws a black line from (10, 10), near the upper left corner, to (260, 160), near the lower right corner:

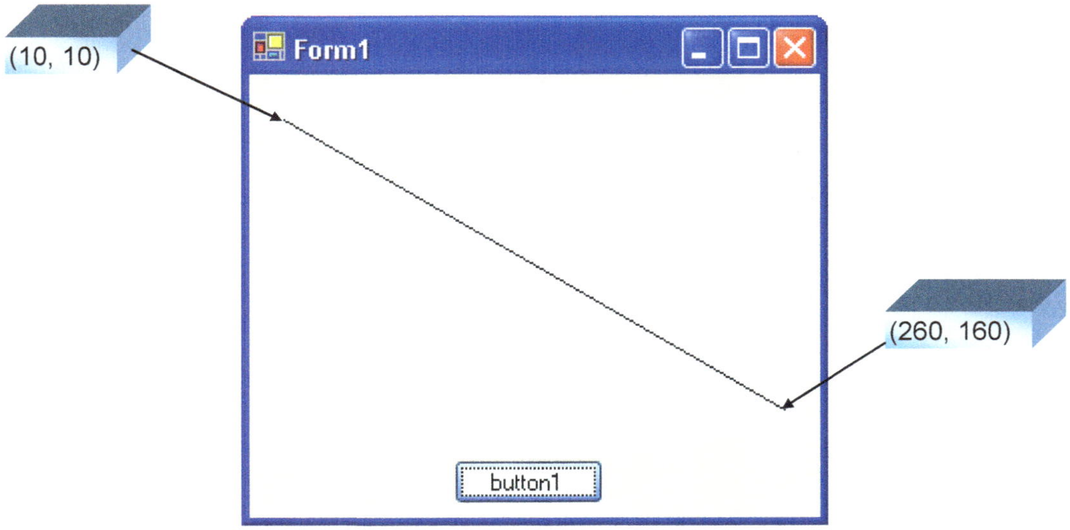

Stop the project and add this line after the current line in the **button1_Click** event:

```
myGraphics.DrawLine(Pens.Red, 260, 160, 260, 10);
```

Run the project again – click the button. A red line, connecting the last point to (260, 10) is added:

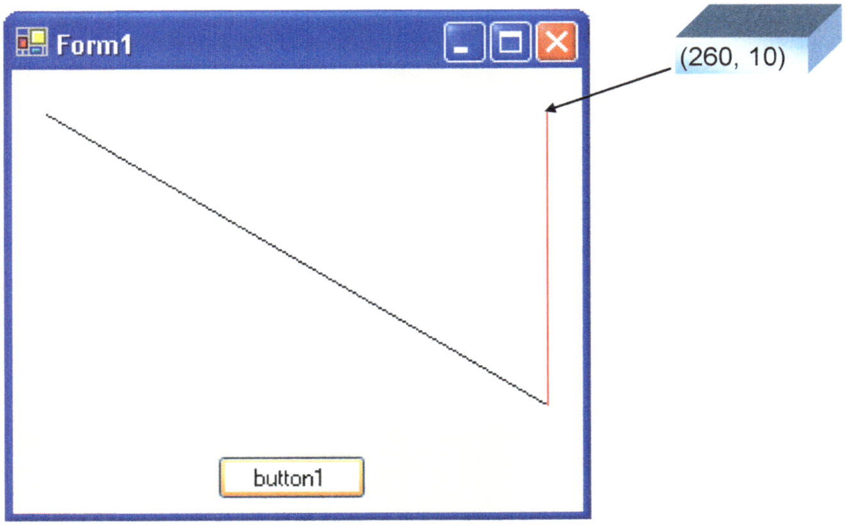

Stop the project. Let's create a wide pen. Add this line in the general declarations area to declare **myPen**:

```
Pen myPen;
```

Add this line of code in the **Form1_Load** event to create myPen as a blue pen with a drawing width of 10:

```
myPen = new Pen(Color.Blue, 10);
```

Add this line of code in the **Form1_FormClosing** event to dispose of myPen:

```
myPen.Dispose();
```

Now add this line after the lines already in the **button1_Click** event to draw a 'wide' blue line that completes a little triangle:

```
myGraphics.DrawLine(myPen, 260, 10, 10, 10);
```

Run the project, click the button and you should see:

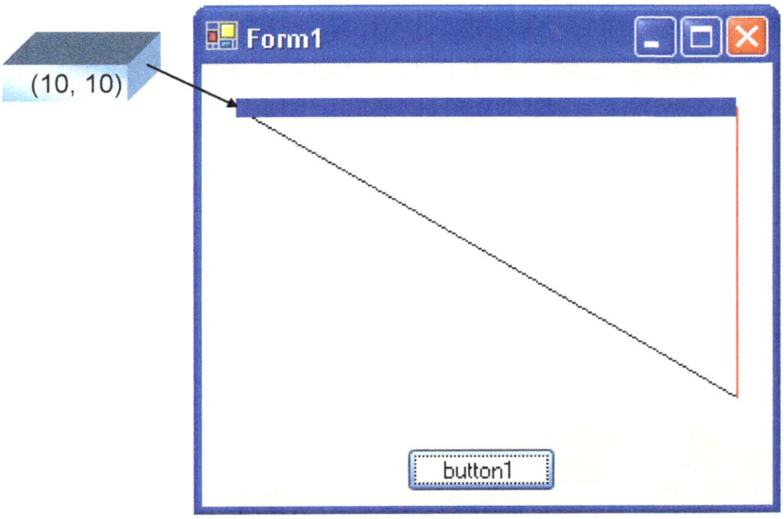

Add more line segments, using other points and colors if you like. Try creating other pens with different colors and drawing widths. Save this project – we'll continue working with it. I think you get the idea of drawing. Just pick some points, pick some colors, and draw some lines. But, it's pretty boring to just specify points and see lines being drawn. It would be nice to have some user interaction, where points could be drawn using the mouse. And, that's just what we are going to do. We will use our newly gained knowledge about graphics methods to build a Visual C# Express drawing program. To do this, though, we need to know how to use the mouse in a project. We do that now.

C# - The Fifth Lesson

In the C# lesson for this class, we examine how to recognize mouse events (clicking and releasing buttons, moving the mouse) to help us build a drawing program with a panel control.

Mouse Events

Related to graphics methods are **mouse events**. The mouse is a primary interface for doing graphics in Visual C# Express. We've already used the mouse to **Click** on controls. Here, we see how to recognize other mouse events in controls. Many controls recognize mouse events - we are learning about them to allow drawing in panel controls.

MouseDown Event

The **MouseDown** event method is triggered whenever a mouse button is pressed while the mouse cursor is over a control. The form of this method is:

```
private void controlName_MouseDown(object sender,
MouseEventArgs e)
{

    [C# code for MouseDown event]

}
```

This is the first time we will use the arguments (information in parentheses) in an event method. This is information C# is supplying, for our use, when this event method is executed. Note this method has two arguments: **sender** and **e**. **sender** is the control that was clicked to cause this event (MouseDown) to occur. In our case, it will be the panel control. The argument **e** is an event handler revealing which button was clicked and the coordinate of the mouse cursor when a button was pressed. We are interested in three properties of the event handler **e**:

Value	Description
e.Button	Mouse button pressed. Possible values are: **MouseButtons.Left**, **MouseButtons.Center**, **MouseButtons.Right**
e.X	X coordinate of mouse cursor in control when mouse was clicked
e.Y	Y coordinate of mouse cursor in control when mouse was clicked

Only one button press can be detected by the MouseDown event - you can't tell if someone pressed the left and right mouse buttons simultaneously. In drawing applications, the **MouseDown** event is used to initialize a drawing process. The point clicked is used to start drawing a line and the button clicked is often used to select line color.

Example

Let's try the MouseDown event with the example we just used with graphics methods. Recall we just have a panel control and a button on a form. Delete the button control from the form. Add two label boxes (one with default Name **label1** and one with default name **label2**) near the bottom of the form- we will use these to tell us which button was clicked and display the mouse click coordinate. My form looks like this:

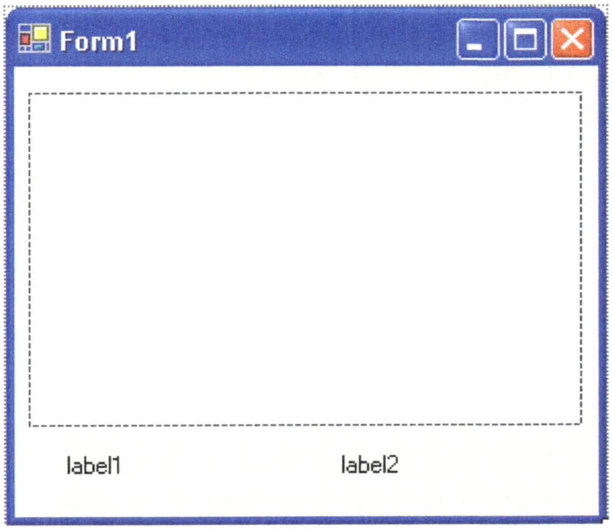

Put these lines of code in the **panel1_MouseDown** event (select the event from the properties window for the panel control):

```
private void panel1_MouseDown(object sender, MouseEventArgs
e)
{
    switch (e.Button)
    {
        case MouseButtons.Left:
            label1.Text = "Left";
            break;
        case MouseButtons.Middle:
            label1.Text = "Middle";
            break;
        case MouseButtons.Right:
            label1.Text = "Right";
            break;
    }
    label2.Text = Convert.ToString(e.X) + "," +
Convert.ToString(e.Y);
}
```

Here, we use a switch structure to specify which button was clicked (displayed in label1 Text property) and we display e.X and e.Y (separated by a comma) in the label2 Text property. Run the project. Click the panel and notice the displayed button and coordinate. Here's an example of a point I clicked:

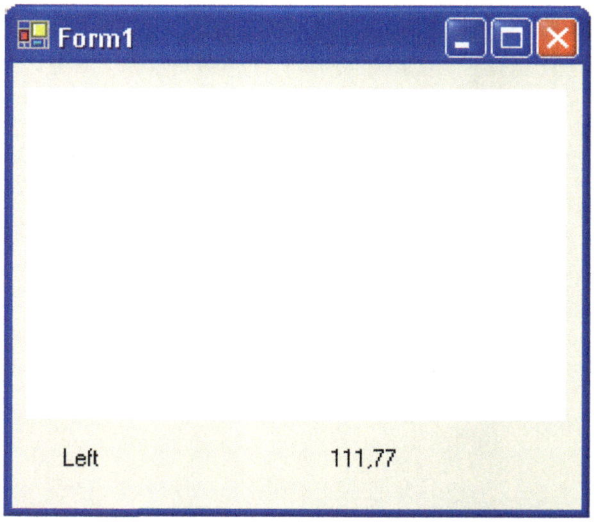

Try different mouse buttons. Click various spots in the panel and see how the coordinates change. Click near the upper left corner. Is (X, Y) close to (0, 0)? It should be. Play with this example until you are comfortable with how the MouseDown event works and what the coordinates mean. Stop and save the project.

MouseUp Event

The **MouseUp** event is the opposite of the MouseDown event. It is triggered whenever a previously pressed mouse button is released. The method format is:

```
private void controlName_MouseUp(object sender,
MouseEventArgs e)
{

        [C# code for MouseUp event]

}
```

Notice the arguments for MouseUp are identical to those for MouseDown. The only difference here is **e.Button** tells us which mouse button was released. In a drawing program, the **MouseUp** event signifies the halting of the current drawing process.

Example

Cut the code from the **panel1_MouseDown** method in our example (highlight the code, click the **Edit** menu, then **Cut**) and paste it in the **panel1_MouseUp** method (click **Edit**, then **Paste**). Make sure you select the correct method from the properties window before pasting. Run the project. Click the panel, move the mouse, then release the mouse. Note the displayed button and coordinates. Become comfortable with how the MouseUp event works and how it differs from the MouseDown event. Stop and save the project.

MouseMove Event

The **MouseMove** event is continuously triggered whenever the mouse is being moved. The event method format is:

```
private void controlName_MouseMove(object sender,
MouseEventArgs e)
{

        [C# code for MouseMove event]

}
```

And, yes, the arguments are the same. **e.Button** tells us which button is being pressed (if any) as the mouse is moving over the control and (e.X, e.Y) tell us the mouse position. In drawing processes, the **MouseMove** event is used to detect the continuation of a previously started line. If drawing is continuing, the current point is connected to the previous point using the current pen.

Example

Cut the code from the **panel1_MouseUp** method in our example and paste it in the **panel1_MouseMove** method. Run the project. Move the mouse over the panel. Notice the coordinates (X, Y) appear and continuously change as the mouse is moving. Click the panel and move the mouse. Notice the label boxes tell you which button was pressed and the current coordinates of the mouse in the panel. Stop the project.

You should now know how the three mouse events work and how they differ. Now let's use the panel control, DrawLine method, mouse events, pens and colors we've studied to build a fun drawing project.

Project - Blackboard Fun

Have you ever drawn on a blackboard with colored chalk? You'll be doing that with the "electronic" blackboard you build in this project. This project is saved as **Blackboard** in the course projects folder (**\VCSEKids\VCSEK Projects**).

Project Design

This is a simple project in concept. Using the mouse, you draw colored lines on a computer blackboard. A panel control will represent the blackboard. Radio buttons will be used to choose "chalk" color. Mouse events will control the drawing process. Two command buttons will be used: one to erase the blackboard and one to exit the program.

Place Controls on Form

Start a new project in Visual C# Express. Place a panel control (make it fairly large), a group box, and two command buttons on the form. Place eight radio buttons (used for color choice) in the group box. When done, my form looks like this:

Set Control Properties

Set the control properties using the properties window:

Form1 Form:

Property Name	Property Value
Text	Blackboard Fun
FormBorderStyle	Fixed Single
StartPosition	CenterScreen

panel1 Panel:

Property Name	Property Value
Name	pnlBlackboard
BorderStyle	Fixed3D
BackColor	Black (Of course! It's a Blackboard!)

groupBox1 Group Box:

Property Name	Property Value
Name	grpColor
Text	Color
BackColor	Black
ForeColor	White
Font Size	10
Font Style	Bold

radioButton1 Radio Button:

Property Name	Property Value
Name	rdoGray
Text	10 to 15 spaces (need some blank space to display color)

radioButton2 Radio Button:

Property Name	**Property Value**
Name	rdoBlue
Text	10 to 15 spaces

radioButton3 Radio Button:

Property Name	**Property Value**
Name	rdoGreen
Text	10 to 15 spaces

radioButton4 Radio Button:

Property Name	**Property Value**
Name	rdoCyan
Text	10 to 15 spaces

radioButton5 Radio Button:

Property Name	**Property Value**
Name	rdoRed
Text	10 to 15 spaces

radioButton6 Radio Button:

Property Name	**Property Value**
Name	rdoMagenta
Text	10 to 15 spaces

radioButton7 Radio Button:

Property Name	**Property Value**
Name	rdoYellow
Text	10 to 15 spaces

radioButton8 Radio Button:

Property Name	Property Value
Name	rdoWhite
Text	10 to 15 spaces

button1 Button:

Property Name	Property Value
Name	btnErase
Text	Erase

button2 Button:

Property Name	Property Value
Name	btnExit
Text	Exit

My form looked like this when I was done:

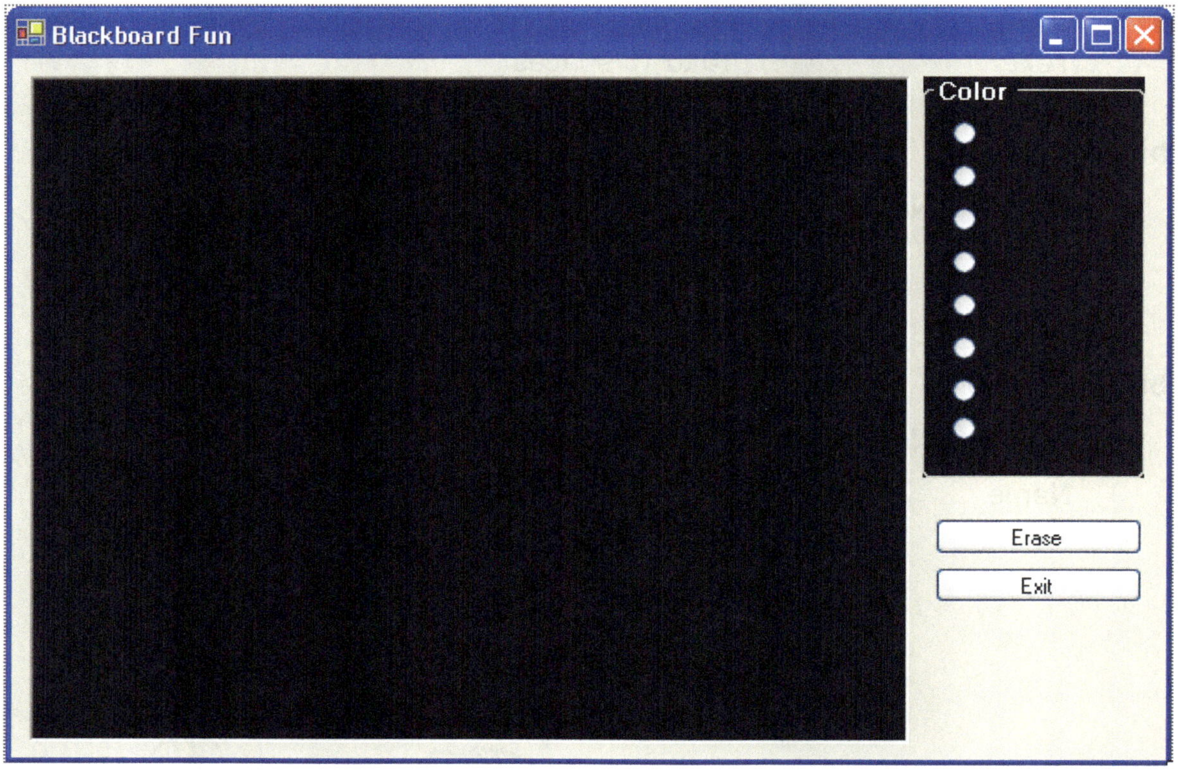

You may be asking – are you crazy? All the radio button Texts are empty spaces - how can these be used for picking colors? Wait a minute and you'll see.

Write Event Methods

This project will work like any paint type program you may have used . Click on a color in the **Color** group box (we'll see colors there soon) to choose a color to draw with. Then, move to the blackboard, left-click to start the drawing process. Drag the mouse to draw lines. Release the mouse button to stop drawing. It's that easy. Clicking **Erase** will clear the blackboard and clicking **Exit** will stop the program. Every step, but initializing a few things and stopping the program, is handled by the panel mouse events.

Three variables are used in this project. We need a Boolean variable (**mousePress**) that tells us whether the left mouse button is being held down. This lets us know if we should be drawing or not. We need two variables (**xLast** and **yLast**) that save the last point drawn in a line (we will always connect the "current" point to the "last" point). We also need a graphics object (**myGraphics**) and a pen object (**myPen**). Open the code window and declare these variables in the **general declarations** area:

```
bool mousePress;
int xLast;
int yLast;
Graphics myGraphics;
Pen myPen;
```

We need to establish some initial values. First, we create the graphics object (**myGraphics**) we will draw on and our pen object (**myPen**). We will set the pen to an initial drawing color of gray. How will we pick colors? Each radio button has a **BackColor** property. We set each BackColor property to its corresponding color using C# code. The user then sees each actual color and not some word describing it. The eight colors we will use are values from the Color structure. These colors were selected to look good on a black background. As seen, the initial color will be Gray, so we set the **rdoGray** radio button **Checked** property to **true**. We also initialize **mousePress** to **false** (we aren't drawing yet). All this is done in the **Form1_Load** method:

```
private void Form1_Load(object sender, EventArgs e)
{
    // Create graphics and pen objects
    myGraphics = pnlBlackboard.CreateGraphics();
    myPen = new Pen(Color.Gray, 1);
    // Initialize the eight radio button colors
    rdoGray.BackColor = Color.Gray;
    rdoBlue.BackColor = Color.Blue;
    rdoGreen.BackColor = Color.LightGreen;
    rdoCyan.BackColor = Color.Cyan;
    rdoRed.BackColor = Color.Red;
    rdoMagenta.BackColor = Color.Magenta;
    rdoYellow.BackColor = Color.Yellow;
    rdoWhite.BackColor = Color.White;
    // Set initial color
    rdoGray.Checked = true;
    mousePress = false;
}
```

You'll see that this is pretty cool in how it works. This is a very common thing to do in Visual C# Express - initialize lots of properties in the form **Load** method instead of using the properties window at design time. It makes project modification much easier.

Each radio button needs a **CheckedChanged** event method to set the corresponding **myPen.Color** values. These eight one-line click events are:

```
private void rdoGray_CheckedChanged(object sender, EventArgs
e)
{
    // Gray
    myPen.Color = rdoGray.BackColor;
}

private void rdoBlue_CheckedChanged(object sender, EventArgs
e)
{
    // Blue
    myPen.Color = rdoBlue.BackColor;
}

private void rdoGreen_CheckedChanged(object sender, EventArgs
e)
{
    // Green
    myPen.Color = rdoGreen.BackColor;
}

private void rdoCyan_CheckedChanged(object sender, EventArgs
e)
{
    // Cyan
    myPen.Color = rdoCyan.BackColor;
}

private void rdoRed_CheckedChanged(object sender, EventArgs
e)
{
    // Red
    myPen.Color = rdoRed.BackColor;
}

private void rdoMagenta_CheckedChanged(object sender,
EventArgs e)
{
    // Magenta
    myPen.Color = rdoMagenta.BackColor;
}
```

```
private void rdoYellow_CheckedChanged(object sender,
EventArgs e)
{
    // Yellow
    myPen.Color = rdoYellow.BackColor;
}

private void rdoWhite_CheckedChanged(object sender, EventArgs
e)
{
    // White
    myPen.Color = rdoWhite.BackColor;
}
```

We'll code the two buttons before tackling the drawing process. The **btnErase** button simply clears the panel. The **btnErase_Click** method is:

```
private void btnErase_Click(object sender, EventArgs e)
{
    // Clear the blackboard
    myGraphics.Clear(pnlBlackboard.BackColor);
}
```

And, the **btnExit_Click** method is, as always:

```
private void btnExit_Click(object sender, EventArgs e)
{
    this.Close();
}
```

Now, let's code the drawing process. There are three events we look for:

- Left mouse button click - starts drawing
- Mouse moving with left mouse button pressed - continues drawing
- Left mouse button release - stops drawing

Each of these is a separate mouse event.

The **pnlBlackboard_MouseDown** event is executed when the left mouse button is clicked. When that happens, we set **mousePress** to **true** (we are drawing) and initialize the "last point" variables, **xLast** and **yLast**. That event method is:

```
private void pnlBlackboard_MouseDown(object sender,
MouseEventArgs e)
{
    // Start drawing if left click
    if (e.Button == MouseButtons.Left)
    {
        mousePress = true;
        xLast = e.X;
        yLast = e.Y;
    }
}
```

The **pnlBlackboard_MouseMove** event is executed when the left mouse button is being pressed (**mousePress** is **true**) and the mouse is moving over the panel. In this event, we connect the last point (**xLast, yLast**) to the current point (**e.X, e.Y**) using the **DrawLine** method with **myPen**. Once done drawing, the "last point" becomes the "current point." This code is:

```
private void pnlBlackboard_MouseMove(object sender,
MouseEventArgs e)
{
    // Draw a line if drawing
    if (mousePress)
    {
        myGraphics.DrawLine(myPen, xLast, yLast, e.X, e.Y);
        xLast = e.X;
        yLast = e.Y;
    }
}
```

The **pnlBlackboard_MouseUp** event is executed when the left mouse button is released. When that happens, we draw the last line segment and set **mousePress** to **false** (we are done drawing). That event method is:

```
private void pnlBlackboard_MouseUp(object sender,
MouseEventArgs e)
{
    // Finish line
    if (e.Button == MouseButtons.Left)
    {
        myGraphics.DrawLine(myPen, xLast, yLast, e.X, e.Y);
        mousePress = false;
    }
}
```

We're almost done. A last step is to dispose of our graphics and pen objects in the **Form1_FormClosing** event:

```
private void Form1_FormClosing(object sender,
FormClosingEventArgs e)
{
    myGraphics.Dispose();
    myPen.Dispose();
}
```

Save the project by clicking the **Save All** button in the toolbar.

Run the Project

Run the project. See how the radio button BackColor property is used to display colors? If the color choice areas are not very wide, make sure you set the Text property of each radio button to some blank space. Choose a color. Draw a line in the panel control. Try other colors. Draw something. Here's my attempt at art (a self-portrait):

I've had students draw perfect pictures of Fred Flintstone and Homer Simpson using this program. Make sure each color works. Make sure **Erase** works. Make sure **Exit** works. As always, thoroughly test your project. Save it if you had to make any changes while running it.

Do you see how simple the drawing part of this program is? Most of the code is used just to set and select colors. The actual drawing portion of the code (MouseDown, MouseMove, MouseUp events) is only a few lines of C#! This shows two things: (1) those drawing programs you use are really not that hard to build and (2) there is a lot of power in the Visual C# Express graphics methods.

Other Things to Try

The Blackboard Fun project offers lots of opportunity for improvement with added options. Have an option to set the pen **Width** property. This way you can draw with very skinny lines or very fat lines. Use a numeric updown control to set the value.

Add the ability to change the background color of the blackboard. Determine and build logic that allows drawing different colored lines depending on whether you press the left or right mouse button. For this, I'd suggest creating a left pen and a right pen. You will also need some way for the user to choose colors for each pen. Then, apply the appropriate pen in the various mouse events depending on what button is pressed.

See if you can figure out ways to get special effects. Here's one possibility to try. Delete (or 'comment out') these lines in the **pnlBlackboard_MouseMove** event:

```
xLast = e.X;
yLast = e.Y;
```

By doing this, the first point clicked (in the MouseDown event) is always the last point and all line drawing originates from this original point. Now, run the project again. Notice the "fanning" effect. Pretty, huh? Play around and see what other effects (change colors randomly, change pen width randomly). Have fun!

There is one effect of the Blackboard Fun project that is annoying. You may have discovered it. You may not have. In the upper right corner of the form is a small button with an "underscore" called the **minimize button**:

When you click this button, your application window disappears (is minimized) and is moved to the Windows task bar at the bottom of the screen. When you click your application name in the task bar, it will return to the screen. Go ahead and try it. Run the project and draw a few lines. Don't draw anything too elaborate – you'll soon find out why. Minimize your application, then restore your application by clicking the appropriate button in the Windows task bar. Where did your lines go?

Why did the lines disappear when the project went away for a bit? Visual C# Express graphics objects have no memory. They only display what has been last drawn on them. If you reduce your form to an icon on the task bar and restore it (as we just did), the graphics object cannot remember what was displayed previously – it will be cleared. Similarly, if you switch from an active Visual C# Express application to some other application, your Visual C# Express form may become partially or fully obscured. When you return to your Visual C# Express application, the obscured part of any graphics object will be erased. Again, there is no memory. Notice in both these cases, however, all controls are automatically restored to the form. Your application remembers these, fortunately! The controls are persistent. We also want **persistent graphics**.

The topic of persistent graphics is beyond the scope of this course. To eliminate this annoyance in the blackboard project, however, we will show you coding changes needed to add persistence. Only a few lines need to be changed. Make the changes if you like. In each case, the modified and/or new code is shown as shaded in gray. The idea is that we create a type of graphics object with memory (maintained in the **BackgroundImage** property of the panel control). The new **Form1_Load** method to do this is:

```
private void Form1_Load(object sender, EventArgs e)
{
    // Create graphics and pen objects
    pnlBlackboard.BackgroundImage = new
Bitmap(pnlBlackboard.Width, pnlBlackboard.Height,
System.Drawing.Imaging.PixelFormat.Format24bppRgb);
    myGraphics =
Graphics.FromImage(pnlBlackboard.BackgroundImage);
    myPen = new Pen(Color.Gray, 1);
    // Initialize the eight radio button colors
    rdoGray.BackColor = Color.Gray;
    rdoBlue.BackColor = Color.Blue;
    rdoGreen.BackColor = Color.LightGreen;
    rdoCyan.BackColor = Color.Cyan;
    rdoRed.BackColor = Color.Red;
    rdoMagenta.BackColor = Color.Magenta;
    rdoYellow.BackColor = Color.Yellow;
    rdoWhite.BackColor = Color.White;
    // Set initial color
    rdoGray.Checked = true;
    mousePress = false;
}
```

We also need to add a single line (shaded) to the **pnlBlackboard_MouseMove** event, **pnlBlackboard_MouseDown** event and **btnErase_Click** event. This line refreshes the added memory after each graphics method. The modified event methods are:

```
private void pnlBlackboard_MouseMove(object sender,
MouseEventArgs e)
{
    // Draw a line if drawing
    if (mousePress)
    {
        myGraphics.DrawLine(myPen, xLast, yLast, e.X, e.Y);
        pnlBlackboard.Refresh();
        xLast = e.X;
        yLast = e.Y;
    }
}

private void pnlBlackboard_MouseUp(object sender,
MouseEventArgs e)
{
    // Finish line
    if (e.Button == MouseButtons.Left)
    {
        myGraphics.DrawLine(myPen, xLast, yLast, e.X, e.Y);
        pnlBlackboard.Refresh();
        mousePress = false;
    }
}

private void btnErase_Click(object sender, EventArgs e)
{
    // Clear the blackboard
    myGraphics.Clear(pnlBlackboard.BackColor);
    pnlBlackboard.Refresh();
}
```

Try running the project again. You should now be able to minimize the project window without fear of losing your lovely work of art!

You've now had your first experience with graphics programming in Visual C# Express using the DrawLine method. You learned about the versatility of the panel control. You learned about three important control events to help in drawing: MouseDown, MouseMove, and MouseUp. And, you learned a lot about colors. In the next class, we'll continue looking at using graphics in projects. And, we'll look at some ways to design computer games.

9

Picture Boxes, Arrays

Review and Preview

In the last class, we introduced the panel control and ways to draw colored lines in a Visual C# Express project. We continue looking at graphics in this class. The picture box control is studied.

In particular, we use that control to display graphics files – photos, drawing, pictures. In our C# lesson, we look at a new way to declare variables and ways to count and loop. And, as a project, we build a version of the card game War.

Picture Box Control

Many times in projects, you want to display pictures or drawings saved as a graphics file on your computer. Maybe you have a little kid's program where if you type an A, an apple appears, B, a ball, and so on. Maybe you want to show a map of the United States (or some other country) for a geography lesson. Maybe you want to see some of the photos you took using a digital camera. The **picture box** is the control for that use. The picture box is selected from the toolbox. It appears as:

In Toolbox:

On Form (default properties):

Properties

The picture box control properties are:

Property	Description
Name	Name used to identify picture box control. Three letter prefix for picture box names is **pic**.
Image	Establishes the graphics file to display in the picture box.
SizeMode	Indicates how the image is displayed.
BorderStyle	Determines type of picture box border.
Left	Distance from left side of form to left side of picture box (X in properties window).
Top	Distance from top side of form to top side of picture box (Y in properties window).

Width	Width of the picture box in pixels.
Height	Height of picture box in pixels.
Enabled	Determines whether picture box can respond to user events (in run mode).
Visible	Determines whether the picture box appears on the form (in run mode).

The **Image** property is used to select the graphic file to display in the picture box and the **SizeMode** property affects how the file is displayed. Let's look at both properties.

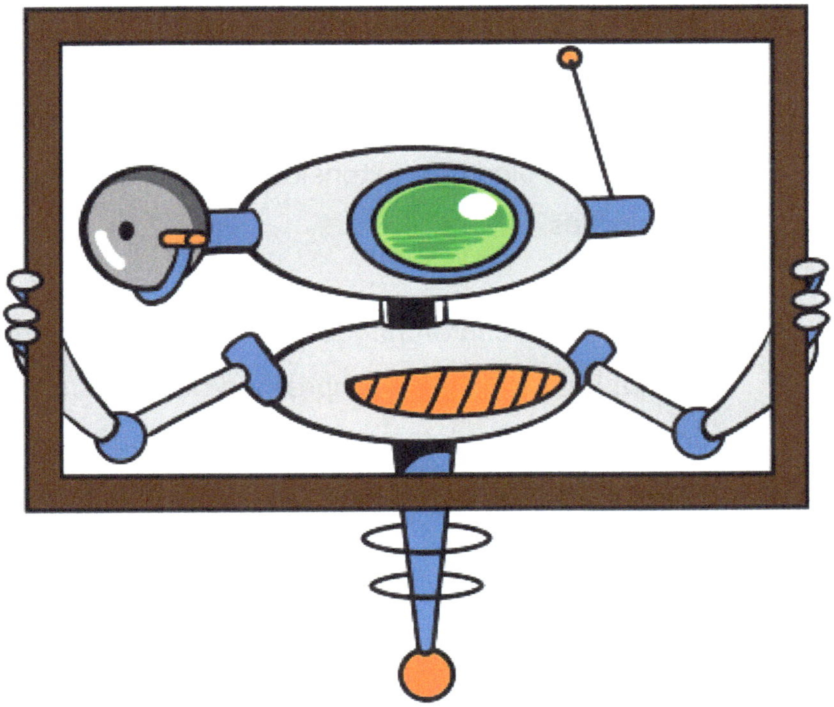

Image Property

The picture box **Image** property specifies the graphics file to display. To set the Image property at design time, simply display the **Properties** window for the picture box control and select the Image property. An ellipsis (…) will appear. Click the ellipsis and a **Select Resource** window will appear. Select **Import** and an **Open File** dialog box will appear. Use that box to locate the graphics file to display. The picture box can display pictures stored in several different **graphics formats**. The formats we study are:

Bitmap A bitmap is an image represented by pixels (screen dots) and stored as a collection of bits in which each bit corresponds to one pixel. It usually has a **bmp** extension. You can also display icon files (**ico** extension) since they are essentially bitmap files.

GIF A GIF (Graphic Interchange Format, pronounce 'jif' like the peanut butter) file is a compressed bitmap format originally developed by the Internet provider CompuServe. Most graphics you see on the Internet are GIF files. A GIF file has a **gif** extension.

JPEG A JPEG (Joint Photographic Experts Group, pronounced 'jay-peg') file is a compressed bitmap format that is popular on the Internet and is the format usually used to store digital photographs. A JPEG file has a **jpg** extension.

These are standard graphics file types and there are other types that can be displayed. There are many programs (Paint Shop Pro by JASC, Eden Prairie, Minnesota is a good one) available that will convert a file from one type to another that you may find useful.

A good place to find sample bitmap and GIF files is on the Internet. To save a displayed Internet graphic as a file, right-click the graphic and choose the **Save Picture As** option (make sure it has a **bmp** or **gif** extension). If you have a digital camera, you probably have hundreds of JPEG files.

In the **\VCSEKids\VCSEK Projects\Graphics** folder, we have included one file of each type for use with our examples:

ball.bmp	Bitmap picture of a ball
kidware.gif	GIF file with the logo our company (KIDware) uses on its website
mexico.jpg	Digital picture from a Mexican vacation

Example

Start Visual C# Express and start a new project. Place a picture box control on the form. Make it fairly large. Click the Image property and the ellipsis (...) button that appears. A **Select Resource** window will appear. Make sure the **Project resource file** radio button is selected and click the button marked **Import** and a file open window will appear. Move (as shown) to the **\VCSEKids\VCSEK Projects\Graphics** folder and you will see our sample files listed:

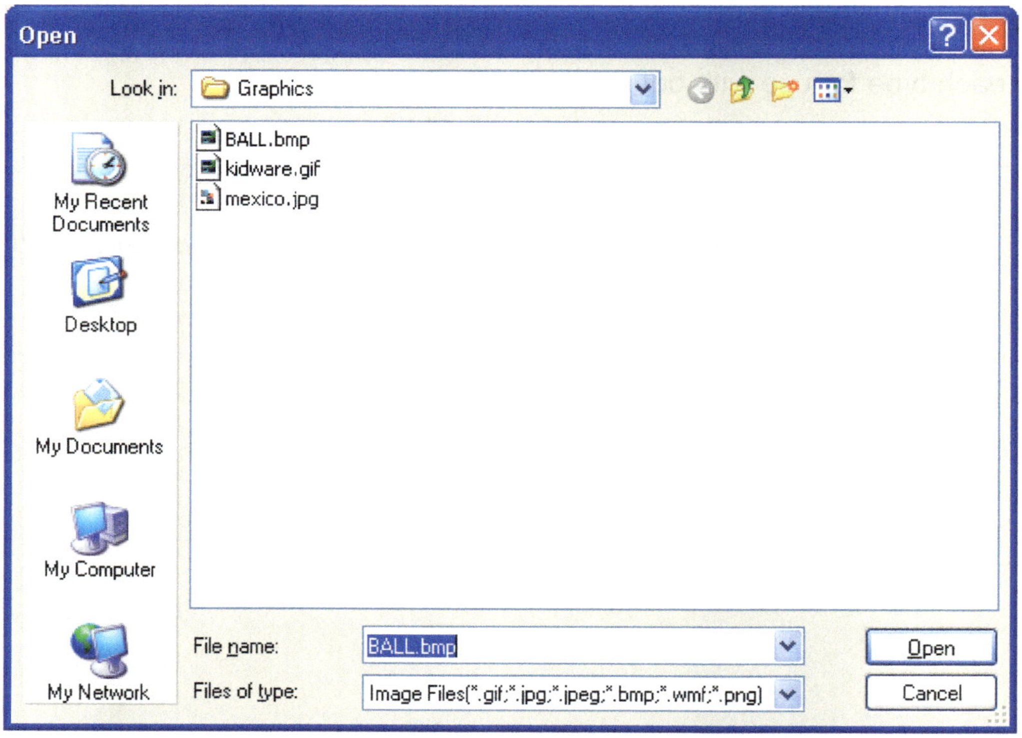

Note six file types are displayed including bitmaps, gifs, and jpegs. Other file types include metafiles (**wmf** extensions) and portable network graphics (**png** extension) – you might like to learn about these other file types on your own. One type not displayed is icon files (ico extension). To see these files, which will display just fine, you need to click **Files of type** and choose **All Files**.

Choose the **ball** bitmap file and click **Open**. You will be returned to the Select Resource window and it should look like this:

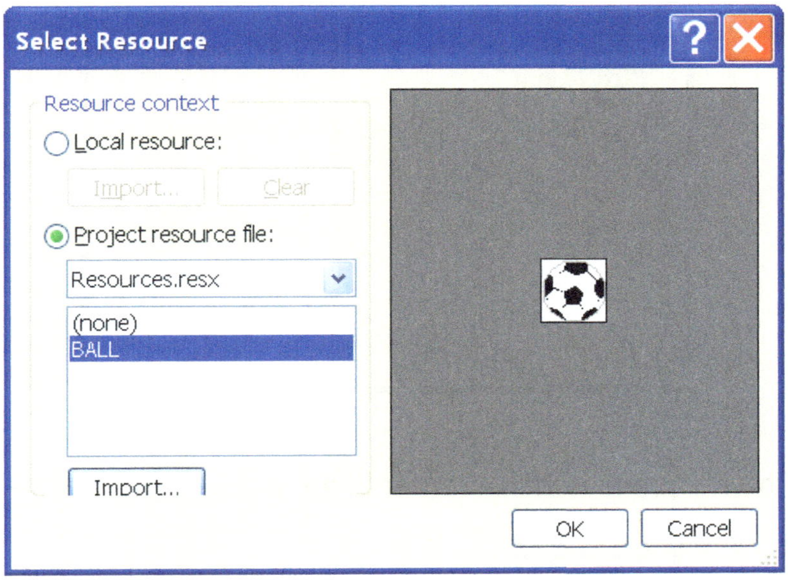

Click the **OK** button.

On your form, you should see something like this (depending on the size of your picture box):

The image is in the upper left hand corner of the picture box. It appears in full-size.

Return to the properties window and choose the **kidware** logo gif file for the picture box Image property (following the same procedure using the Select Resource window):

In this example, the picture box is shorter than the graphic, so the picture is vertically "cropped." It is located in the upper left hand corner and appears in full-size. If the picture is cropped in your example too, you can resize the picture box control to see the entire graphic.

Lastly, load and view the **mexico** JPEG file:

There's not much to see here. The picture box is smaller than the photo, so only the sky is seen. The picture appears in full-size and is seriously cropped.

We see that the bitmap file seems to display satisfactorily. The GIF and JPEG files had cropping problems though. The **SizeMode** property of the picture box control gives us some control on how we want a graphic to display. This will help us solve some of the problems we've seen. We look at that property next, but first a quick look at how to remove a graphic from a picture box.

There are times you may want to delete the graphic displayed in a picture box. To do this, click Image in the properties window. In the right side of the window will be the current file (with a very tiny copy of the graphic). Select this information (double-click to highlight it) and press the keyboard **Del** key. The displayed picture will vanish and the property will read **(None)**.

SizeMode Property

The **SizeMode** property dictates how a particular image will be displayed in a picture box. There are five possible values for this property: **Normal**, **CenterImage, StretchImage**, **AutoSize, Zoom**. The effect of each value is:

SizeMode	Effect
Normal	Image appears in original size. If picture box is larger than image, there will be blank space. If picture box is smaller than image, the image will be cropped.
CenterImage	Image appears in original size, centered in picture box. If picture box is larger than image, there will be blank space. If picture box is smaller than image, image is cropped.
StretchImage	Image will 'fill' picture box. If image is smaller than picture box, it will expand. If image is larger than picture box, it will scale down. Bitmap files do not scale nicely. JPEG and GIF files do scale nicely.
AutoSize	Reverse of StretchImage - picture box will change its dimensions to match the original size of the image. Be forewarned – some files are very large!
Zoom	Similar to StretchImage. The image will adjust to fit within the picture box, however its actual height to width ratio is maintained.

In the previous example, the **SizeMode** property had its default value of **Normal**, so all the images appeared in their original size. In the case of the bitmap file, there was lots of blank space. With the GIF and JPEG files, there was cropping. Similar results would have been seen with the **SizeMode** property changed to **CenterImage**. The most useful (in my opinion) of the **SizeMode** property choices is **StretchImage**. With this property, the image always fills the space you give it.

Example

Continue the previous project. Change the **SizeMode** property of the picture box control to **CenterImage**. Reload each of the three sample graphics files. Note when you click the ellipsis next to Image in the picture box properties window, the Select Resources window will appear as:

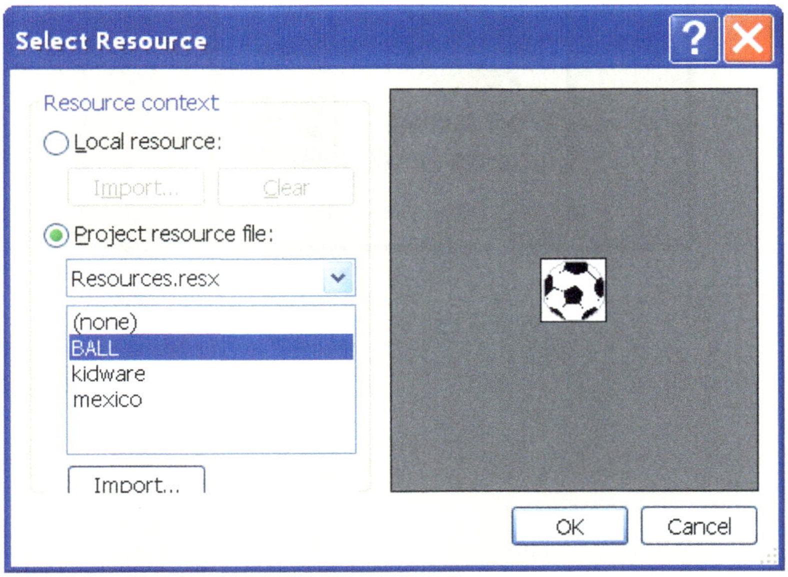

Since each graphic already appears in the Select Resource window (these graphics have become part of the project), there is no need to reload the actual graphics files. You can choose the **Image** property directly from this window. The process is – select the desired graphic (resource) and click **OK**.

With the **CenterImage SizeMode** property, note the difference in how the files are displayed. In particular, the GIF and JPEG files are still cropped, but now they're centered in the control. For example, here is the **kidware** logo graphic with the image centered:

Change the **SizeMode** to **StretchImage**. Reload each of the sample graphics files. Notice how the graphic takes up the entire picture box. Here's the **mexico** graphic:

Try resizing the picture box control. How do the different graphics types resize? After resizing the picture box control, does the picture still look recognizable? You should find that bitmaps (in most cases) scale poorly, while GIF and JPEG graphics scale very nicely. Change the **SizeMode** to **Zoom**. Notice the graphic displays are very similar to those seen with StretchImage. The mexico graphic appears clearer, since the height to width ratio are correct:

Lastly, change the **SizeMode** to **AutoSize**. Load each graphic example and see the results. Watch out! The Mexico photo is very large. **AutoSize** should only be used when you know the size of your images and you allow for that size on your project form. If you like, try finding other graphic files on your computer and view them in the picture box with different SizeMode properties.

Events

The picture box control supports a few events. The important ones are:

Event	Description
Click	Event executed when user clicks on picture box.
MouseDown	Event executed when user presses mouse button while cursor is over picture box.
MouseMove	Event executed when user moves cursor over picture box.
MouseUp	Event executed when user releases mouse button while cursor is over picture box.

You would use the Click event when you are choosing from a group of picture box controls in a multiple choice environment. You would use the mouse events when you need to know which mouse button was pressed or released and/or where the cursor was when a mouse click, move, or release occurred.

Typical Use of Picture Box Control

The usual design steps to use a picture box control for displaying a graphic file are:

- Set the **Name** and **SizeMode** property (most often, **StretchImage**).
- Set **Image** property, either in design mode or at run-time.

C# - The Sixth Lesson

In this C# lesson, we look at ways to store large numbers of variables, a technique for counting, and some code for shuffling a deck of cards (or randomly sorting a list of numbers).

Variable Arrays

Your school principal has recognized your great C# programming skills and has come for your help. Everyone (352 students) in the school has just taken a C# skills test. The principal wants you to write a program that stores each student's name and score. The program should rank (put in order) the scores and compute the average score. The code to do this is not that hard. The problem we want to discuss here is how do we declare all the variables we need? To write this test score program, you need 352 **string** variables to store student names and 352 **int** variables to store student scores. We are required to declare every variable we use. Do you want to type 704 lines of code something like this?:

```
string student1;
string student2;
string student3;
   .
   .
string student352;
int score1;
int score2;
int score3;
   .
   .
int score352;
```

I don't think so.

C# provides a way to store a large number of variables under the same name - **variable arrays**. Each variable in an array, called an **element**, must have the same data type, and they are distinguished from each other by an array **index**. A variable array is declared in a way similar to other variables. To indicate the variable is an array, you use two square brackets (**[ ]**) after the type. Square brackets are used a lot with arrays. At the same time you declare an array, it is good practice to create it using the **new** keyword. For 352 student names and 352 student scores, we declare and create the needed arrays using:

```
string[] student = new string[352];
int[] score = new int[352];
```

The number in brackets is called the array **dimension**. These two lines have the same effect as the 704 declaration lines we might have had to write! And, notice how easy it would be to add 200 more variables if we needed them. You can also declare and create an array in two separate statements if you prefer. For the student name array, that code would be:

```
string[] student;  // the declaration;
student = new string[352];  // the creation
```

We now have 352 **student** variables (**string** type) and 352 **score** variables (**int** type) available for our use. A very important concept to be aware of is that C# uses what are called **zero-based** arrays. This means array indices begin with 0 and end at the dimension value minus 1, in this case 351. Each variable in an array is referred to by its declared name and index. The first student name in the array would be **student[0]** and the last name would be **student[351]**, <u>not</u> student[352]. If you try to refer to student[352], you will get a run-time error saying an array value is out of bounds. This is a common mistake! When working with arrays in C#, always be aware they are zero-based.

As an example of using an array, to assign information to the student with index of 150 (actually, the 151st student in the array because of the zero base), we could write two lines of code like this:

```
student[150] = "Billy Gates";
score[150] = 100;
```

Array variables can be used anywhere regular variables are used. They can be used on the left side of assignment statements or in expressions. To add up the first three test scores, you would write:

```
sum = score[0] + score[1] + score[2];
```

Again, notice the first score in the array is **score[0]**, not **score[1]**. I know this is confusing, but it's something you need to remember. We still need to provide values for each element in each array, but there are also some shortcuts we can take to avoid lots of assignment statements. One such shortcut, the **for** loop, is examined next. You will find variable arrays are very useful when working with large numbers (and sometimes, not so large numbers) of similar variables.

C# for Loops

A common computer programming task is counting. We might like to execute some C# code segment a particular number of times - we would need to count how many times we executed the code. In the school score example from above, we need to go through all 352 scores to compute an average. C# offers a convenient way to do counting: the **for** loop.

The C# **for** loop has this unique structure:

```
for (initialization; expression; update)
{
      [C# code block to execute]
}
```

After the word **for** are three parts separated by semicolons: **initialization**, **expression**, and **update**. The first, **initialization**, is a step executed <u>once</u> and is used to initialize a counter variable (usually an **int** type). A very common initialization would start a counter **i** at zero:

```
i = 0
```

The second part, **expression**, is a step executed <u>before</u> each iteration (repetition) of the code in the loop. If expression is true, the code is executed; if false, program execution continues at the line following the end of the for loop. A common expression would be:

```
i < iMax
```

The final part, **update**, is a step executed after each iteration of the code in the loop; it is used to update the value of the counter variable. A common update would be:

```
i = i + 1
```

Using these example steps, a for loop appears as:

```
for (i = 0; i < iMax; i = i +1)
{
        [C# code block to execute]
}
```

In this example, the counter **i** is initialized at **0** and is then incremented (changed) by **1** each time the program executes the loop. For each execution of the loop, any code between the two curly braces is repeated. The loop is repeated as long as **i** remains smaller than **iMax**. When the loop is completed, program execution continues after the closing brace. To leave the loop before completion, you can use the **break** statement introduced with the switch structure.

A few examples should clear things up. Assume we want to set the value of 10 elements of some array, **myArray[10]**, to 0. The for loop that would accomplish this task is:

```
For (i = 0; i < 10; i = i + 1)
{
    myArray[i] = 0;
}
```

In this loop, the counter variable **i** (declared to be an **int** variable prior to this statement) is initialized at 0. With each iteration, i is incremented by one. The loop is repeated as long as i remains smaller than 10 (remember myArray[9] is the last element of the array).

How about a rocket launch countdown? This loop will do the job:

```
For (i = 10; i <= 0; i = i - 1)
{
        [C# code block for the countdown]
}
```

Here i starts at 10 and goes <u>down</u> by 1 (i = i -1) each time the loop is repeated. Yes, you can decrease the counter. And, you can have counter increments that are not 1. This loop counts from 0 to 200 by 5's:

```
For (i = 0; i <= 200; i = i + 5)
{
        [C# code block to execute]
}
```

In each of these examples, it is assumed that i has been declared prior to these loops.

How about averaging the scores from our student example. This code will do the job:

```
scoreSum = 0;
for (studentNumber = 0; studentNumber < 352; studentNumber =
studentNumber + 1)
{
    scoreSum = scoreSum + score[StudentNumber];
}
average = scoreSum / 300;
```

(Again, it is assumed that all variables have been declared to have the proper type). To find an average of a group of numbers, you add up all the numbers then divide by the number of numbers you have. In this code, scoreSum represents the sum of all the numbers. We set this to zero to start. Then, each time through the loop, we add the next score to that "running" sum. The loop adds up all 352 scores making use of the score array. The first time through it adds in score[0], then score[1], then score[2], and so on, until it finishes by adding in score[351]. Once done, the average is computed by dividing scoreSum by 352. Do you see how the for loop greatly simplifies the task of adding up 352 numbers? This is one of the shortcut methods we can use when working with arrays. Study each of these examples so you have an idea of how the for loop works. Use them when you need to count.

Before leaving the for loop, let's look at one more thing. A very common update to a counter variable is to add one (increment) or subtract one (decrement). C# has special increment and decrement operators that do just that. To add one to a variable named **counterVariable**, you can simply write:

```
counterVariable++;
```

This statement is equivalent to:

```
counterVariable = counterVariable + 1;
```

Similarly, the decrement operator:

```
counterVariable--;
```

Is equivalent to:

```
counterVariable = counterVariable - 1;
```

The increment and decrement operators are not limited to for loops. They can be used anywhere they are needed in a C# program.

Block Level Variables

Let's address another issue. Notice, at a minimum, the for loop requires the declaration of one variable, the loop counter, usually an **int** type variable. This variable is only used in the code block associated with this loop - it's value is usually of no use anywhere else. When we declare a variable in the general declarations area of the code window, as we have been doing, its value is available to all event methods. We say such variables have **form level scope**. Such declarations are not necessary with for loop counters and it becomes a headache if you have lots of for loops. Loop counters can be declared in the initialization part of the for statement. We give these variables **block level scope** - their value is only known within that loop's code block.

As an example of declaring block level variables, look at a modification to the student average example:

```
scoreSum = 0;
for (int studentNumber = 0; studentNumber < 352;
studentNumber++)
{
  scoreSum = scoreSum + score[StudentNumber];
}
average = scoreSum / 300;
```

Notice how the counter (studentNumber) is declared and initialized, all in one step, in the **for** statement. This is perfectly acceptable in C# - whenever, you declare a variable, you can also assign an initial value. Once the for loop is complete, the value of studentNumber is no longer known or available. As you write C# code, you will often give your loop variables such block level scope. Also, notice how we've modified this example to include the increment operator (++).

Method Level Variables

In addition to **block** level and **form** level variables, there is one other level of variable scope we can use – **method** level variables. If a variable only has used within a particular method, there is no need to declare it in the general declarations area. Variables with method level scope are declared immediately following the opening curly brace for a method.

As an example of declaring method level variables, assume we have a button control (named **btnAverage**) on a form that computes the student average score in our example. The **btnAverage_Click** method procedure would look like this:

```
private void btnAverage_Click(object sender, EventArgs e)
{
    int scoreSum;
    scoreSum = 0;
    for (int studentNumber = 0; studentNumber < 352;
studentNumber++)
    {
        scoreSum = scoreSum + score[StudentNumber];
    }
    average = scoreSum / 300;
}
```

In this example, **scoreSum** is only used and needed in this method, hence is declared as a method level variable. The variable **average** should be declared in the general declarations area so it has form level scope and is available everywhere in your project. As you write C# code, decide whether you want your variables to have **block** level, **method** level or **form** level scope and declare them in the proper area in the code window.

Shuffle Routine

Let's use our new knowledge of arrays and for loops to write a very useful method. A common task in any computer program is to randomly sort a list of consecutive integer values. Why would you want to do this? Say you have four answers in a multiple choice quiz. Randomly sort the integers 1, 2, 3, and 4, so the answers are presented in random order. Or, you have a quiz with 30 questions. Randomly sort the questions for printing out as a worksheet. Or, the classic application is shuffling a deck of standard playing cards (there are 52 cards in such a deck). In that case, you can randomly sort the integers from 0 to 51 to "simulate" the shuffling process. Let's build a "shuffle" routine. We call it a shuffle routine, recognizing it can do more than shuffle a card deck. Our routine will sort any number of consecutive integers.

Usually when we need a computer version of something we can do without a computer, it is fairly easy to write down the steps taken and duplicate them in C# code. We've done that with the projects built so far in this course. Other times, the computer version of a process is easy to do on a computer, but hard or tedious to do off the computer. When we shuffle a deck of cards, we separate the deck in two parts, then interleaf the cards as we fan each part. I don't know how you could write C# code to do this. There is a way, however, to write C# code to do a shuffle in a more tedious way (tedious to a human, easy for a computer).

We will perform what could be called a "one card shuffle." In a one card shuffle, you pull a single card (at random) out of the deck and lay it aside on a pile. Repeat this 52 times and the cards are shuffled. Try it! I think you see this idea is simple, but doing a one card shuffle with a real deck of cards would be awfully time-consuming. We'll use the idea of a one card shuffle here, with a slight twist. Rather than lay the selected card on a pile, we will swap it with the bottom card in the stack of cards remaining to be shuffled. This takes the selected card out of the deck and replaces it with the remaining bottom card. The result is the same as if we lay it aside.

Here's how the shuffle works with n numbers:

- Start with a list of n consecutive integers.
- Randomly pick one item from the list. Swap that item with the last item. You now have one fewer items in the list to be sorted (called the remaining list), or n is now n - 1.
- Randomly pick one item from the remaining list. Swap it with the item on the bottom of the remaining list. Again, your remaining list now has one fewer items.
- Repeatedly remove one item from the remaining list and swap it with the item on the bottom of the remaining list until you have run out of items. When done, the list will have been replaced with the original list in random order.

Confusing? Let's show a simple example with n = 5 (a very small deck of cards).

The starting list is (with 5 remaining items):

1 2 3 4 5

Remaining List

We want to pick one item, at random, from this list. Using the C# random number generator, we would choose a random number from 1 to 5. Say it was 3. We take the third item in the list (the 3) and swap it with the last item in the list (the 5). We now have:

1 2 5 4 **3**

Remaining List

There are 4 items in the remaining list. Pick a random number from 1 to 4 - say it's 4. The fourth item in the remaining list is 4. Swap it with the last item in the remaining list. Wait a minute! The last item in the remaining list is the 4. In this case, we swap it with itself, or it stays put. If the random number was something other than 4, there really would have been a swap here. We now have:

1 2 5 **4 3**

Remaining List

There are 3 items in the remaining list. Pick a random number from 1 to 3 - say it's 1. The first item in the list is 1. Swap the 1 with the last item in the remaining list (the 5), giving us:

5 2 **1 4 3**

Remaining List

There are 2 items in the remaining list. Pick a random number from 1 to 2 - say it's 1. The first item in the list is 5. Swap the 5 with the last item in the remaining list (the 2), giving us the final result, the numbers 1 to 5 randomly sorted:

2 5 1 4 3

Pretty neat how this works, huh?

We want to describe the one card shuffle with C# code. Most of the code is straightforward. The only question is how to do the swap involved in each step. This swap is easy on paper. How do we do a swap in C#? Actually, this is a common C# task and is relatively simple. At first thought, to swap variable aVariable with variable bVariable, you might write:

```
aVariable = bVariable;
bVariable = aVariable;
```

The problem with this code is that when you replace aVariable with bVariable in the first statement, you have destroyed the original value of aVariable. The second statement just puts the newly assigned aVariable value (bVariable) back in bVariable. Both aVariable and bVariable now have the original bVariable value! Actually, swapping two variables is a three step process. First, put aVariable in a temporary storage variable (make it the same type as aVariable and bVariable). Then, replace aVariable by bVariable. Then, replace bVariable by the temporary variable (which holds the original aVariable value). If tVariable is the temporary variable, a swap of aVariable and bVariable is done using:

```
tVariable = aVariable;
aVariable = bVariable;
bVariable = tVariable;
```

You use swaps like this in all kinds of C# applications.

Now, we'll see the C# code that uses a one card shuffle to randomly sort N consecutive integer values. When done the random list of integers is in the array **numberList**, which should be declared in the general declarations area of your project with the proper dimension. Also declare the variable, **numberOfItems**, which is the length of the list. For a deck of cards, these declarations would be:

```
int[] numberList = new int[52];
int numberOfItems;
```

You need to make sure to assign a value (52) to **numberOfItems** somewhere, most likely in the form **Load** procedure. We need a random number object (**myRandom**) with method level scope to do all the random number generation. And four variables will have block level scope within the particular for loops implementing the shuffle:

loopCounter - integer loop counter variable
remaining - integer loop variable giving number of items in remaining list
itemPicked - integer variable giving item picked in remaining list
tempValue - temporary integer variable used for swapping

One note – recall arrays in C# are zero-based. In this code, if you ask it to shuffle n consecutive integers, the indices on the returned array range from 0 to n – 1 and the randomized integers will also range from 0 to n – 1, not 1 to n. If you need integers from 1 to n, just simply add 1 to each value in the returned array! The code is:

```
// Variable declarations (put at top of method)
Random myRandom = new Random();

// One card shuffle code
// initialize NumberList
for (int loopCounter = 0; loopCounter < numberOfItems;
loopCounter++)
{
    numberList[loopCounter] = loopCounter;
}
// Work through remaining values
// Start at numberOfItems and swap one value
// at each for loop step
// After each step, remaining is decreased by 1
for (int remaining = numberOfItems; remaining >= 1;
remaining--)
{
    // Pick item at random
    int itemPicked = myRandom.Next(remaining);
    // Swap picked item with bottom item
    int tempValue = numberList[itemPicked];
    numberList[itemPicked] = numberList[remaining - 1];
    numberList[remaining - 1] = tempValue;
}
```

Study this code and see how it implements the procedure followed in the simple five number example. It's not that hard to see. Understanding how such code works is a first step to becoming a good C# programmer. Notice this bit of code uses everything we talked about in this class' C# lesson: arrays, for loops, and block and method level variables.

Project - Card Wars

In this project, we create a simplified version of the kid's card game - War. You play against the computer. You each get half a deck of cards (26 cards). Each player turns over one card at a time. The one with the higher card wins the other player's card. The one with the most cards at the end wins. Obviously, the shuffle routine will come in handy here. We call this project Card Wars! This project is saved as **CardWars** in the projects folder **(\VCSEKids\VCSEK Projects**).

Project Design

We will use a panel control to represent the outline of each player's card. A label control will show the card's value and a picture box control will display the card's suit (hearts, diamonds, clubs, spades). A button will control starting a new game or drawing a new card, depending on game state. Another button will control stopping the game, if playing, or stopping the program, if not playing. The current score (number of cards each player has) will be displayed in a labeled text box control.

Place Controls on Form

Start a new project in Visual C# Express. Place two panel controls on the form. Size them to represent the two displayed cards. Place a label and picture box control in each panel. Add two buttons to the form. Add two labels and two text boxes that will be used for the scoring system. Add a large text box to tell us when the game is over. And, add four more picture boxes that will be used to hold the images for each card suit. When done, my form looks like this:

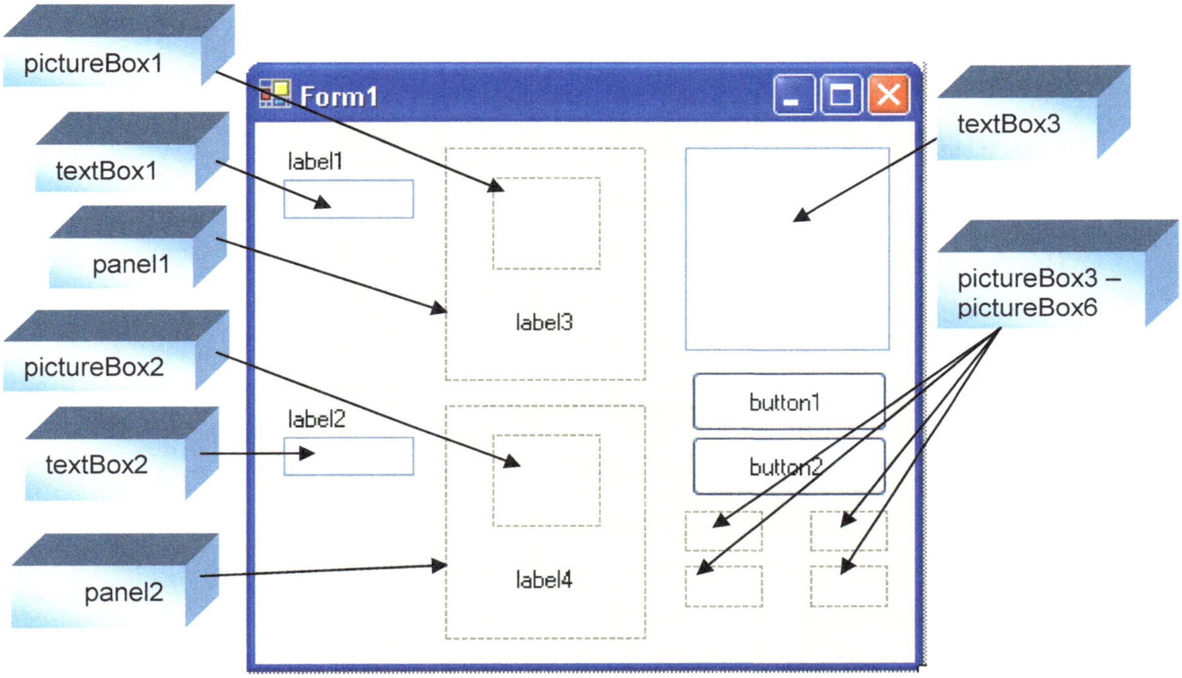

Set Control Properties

Set the control properties using the properties window:

Form1 Form:

Property Name	Property Value
Text	Card Wars
FormBorderStyle	Fixed Single
StartPosition	CenterScreen

panel1 Panel:

Property Name	Property Value
Name	pnlPlayer
BackColor	White
BorderStyle	FixedSingle

panel2 Panel:

Property Name	Property Value
Name	pnlComputer
BackColor	White
BorderStyle	FixedSingle

picture Box1 Picture Box:

Property Name	Property Value
Name	picPlayer
SizeMode	StretchImage

picture Box2 Picture Box:

Property Name	Property Value
Name	picComputer
SizeMode	StretchImage

pictureBox3 Picture Box:

Property Name	Property Value
Name	picHeart
Image	Heart.ico (in **\VCSEKids\VCSEK Projects\CardWars** folder)
SizeMode	AutoSize
Visible	False

pictureBox4 Picture Box:

Property Name	Property Value
Name	picDiamond
Image	Diamond.ico (in **\VCSEKids\VCSEK Projects\CardWars** folder)
SizeMode	AutoSize
Visible	False

pictureBox5 Picture Box:

Property Name	Property Value
Name	picClub
Image	Club.ico (in **\VCSEKids\VCSEK Projects\CardWars** folder)
SizeMode	AutoSize
Visible	False

pictureBox6 Picture Box:

Property Name	Property Value
Name	picSpade
Image	Spade.ico (in **\VCSEKids\VCSEK Projects\CardWars** folder)
SizeMode	AutoSize
Visible	False

The Visible properties for these four picture box controls (picHeart, picDiamond, picClub, picSpade) are purposely False. We don't want them to show up on the form in run mode - we just want to use their stored picture for our card displays. This is done a lot in Visual C# Express. When setting the Image property, in the Open File Dialog, you will need to make sure you view **All Files** and not just the **Image Files**. Icon files will not appear unless you make this change.

label1 Label:

Property Name	Property Value
Name	lblYou
Text	You
Font Size	10

textBox1 Text Box:

Property Name	Property Value
Name	txtYouScore
Text	0
Font Size	12
Font Style	Bold
ReadOnly	True
TextAlign	Center
BackColor	White

label2 Label:

Property Name	Property Value
Name	lblComp
Text	Computer
Font Size	10

textBox2 Text Box:

Property Name	Property Value
Name	txtCompScore
Text	0
Font Size	12
Font Style	Bold
ReadOnly	True
TextAlign	Center
BackColor	White

label3 Label:

Property Name	Property Value

Name	lblPlayer
Text	[Blank]
Font Size	18
Font Style	Bold
TextAlign	MiddleCenter

label4 Label:

Property Name	**Property Value**
Name	lblComputer
Text	[Blank]
Font Size	18
Font Style	Bold
TextAlign	MiddleCenter

textBox3 Text Box:

Property Name	**Property Value**
Name	txtOver
Text	Game Over
Font Size	14
Font Style	Bold
ReadOnly	True
TextAlign	Center
BackColor	White
ForeColor	Red

button1 Button:

Property Name	**Property Value**
Name	btnNew
Text	New Game

button2 Button:

Property Name	**Property Value**
Name	btnExit
Text	Exit

When done, my form looks like this:

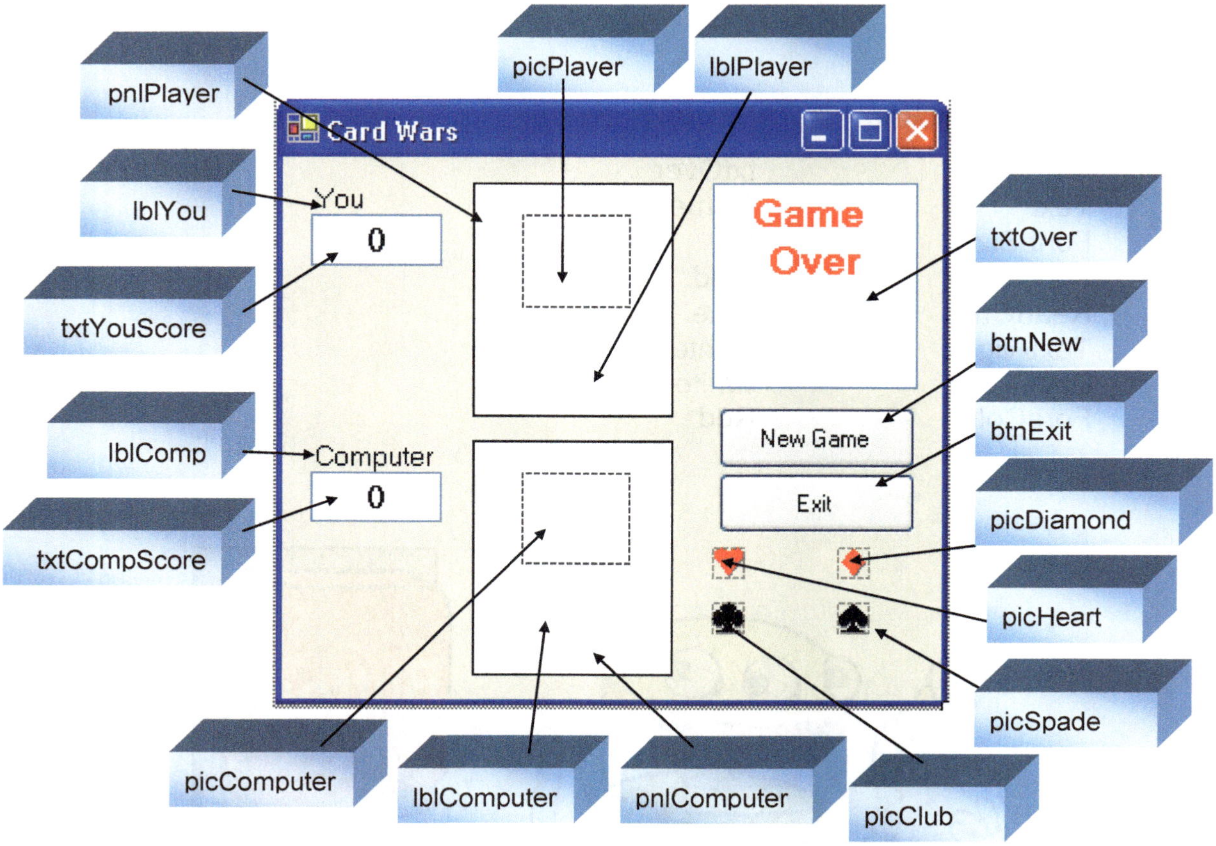

Write Event methods

The idea of this game is quite simple. You click the **New Game** button to start. This shuffles the cards, resets the scores to zero and changes the button's Text to **Next Card**. It also changes the **Exit** button Text to **Stop** (for stopping the current game). A card for you (upper card) and a card for the computer (lower card) are displayed. The computer decides which card is higher. The player with the higher card gets two points. If it's a tie, each player gets one point. Scores are displayed under **You** (txtYouScore has your score) and **Computer** (txtCompScore has computer's score). Click **Next Card**. A new card is displayed for each player and the scores updated. Continue clicking **Next Card** until the game is over (each player has shown 26 cards). At that point, the 'Game Over' message is displayed and the button captions are reset to their original values. By checking the score, a winner can be determined. You can stop the game early by clicking **Stop**. There are only two event methods - one for **btnNew_Click** and one for **btnExit_Click**. Before looking at these events, let's look at needed variables.

We only need two variables (well, really 53, but, arrays help out) for this project. The first is an integer array (**cardNumber**) that has the 52 shuffled numbers representing each card in the deck. The first half (cardNumber[0] – cardNumber[25]) will be your cards while the second half (cardNumber[26] – cardNumber[51]) will be the computer's. The second variable is **cardIndex**, an integer indicating which card to display. Open the code window and declare these variables in the **general declarations** area:

```
int [] cardNumber = new int[52];
int cardIndex;
```

Now, let's outline the steps involved in the **btnNew_Click** event. First, we are letting this command button have two purposes. It either starts a new game (**Text** is **New Game**) and or gets a new card (**Text** is **Next Card**). So, the Click event has two segments. If Text is New Game, the steps are:

- Hide 'Game Over' notice
- Set btnNew Text to "Next Card"
- Set btnExit Text to "Stop"
- Set scores to zero
- Shuffle cards
- Initialize cardIndex to zero
- Display first card for each player
- Compare cards - update score

If Text is Next Card, the steps are:

- Display two new cards
- Compare displayed cards - update scores
- Increment CardIndex
- If there are no cards left, stop game - display 'Game Over' message, change button captions. Otherwise, wait for click on Next Card button.

Most of these steps are easily done now that we know how to shuffle a deck of cards. The only tough part is deciding how to display and compare cards. Let's look at that in some detail.

Displaying a card consists of answering two questions: what is the card suit and what is the card value? The four suits are hearts, diamonds, clubs, and spades. The thirteen card values, from lowest to highest, are: 2, 3, 4, 5, 6, 7, 8, 9, 10, Jack (J), Queen (Q), King (K), Ace (A). We've seen in our shuffle routine that a card number will range from 0 to 51. How do we translate that card number to a card suit and value? (Notice the distinction between card **number** and card **value** - card number ranges from 0 to 51, card value can only range from 2 to Ace.) We need to develop some type of translation rule. This is done all the time in C#. If the number you compute with or work with does not directly translate to information you need, you need to make up rules to do the translation. For example, the numbers 1 to 12 are used to represent the months of the year. But, these numbers tell us nothing about the names of the month. We need a rule to translate each number to a month name.

We know we need 13 of each card suit. Hence, an easy rule to decide suit is: cards numbered 0 - 12 are hearts, cards numbered 13 - 25 are diamonds, cards numbered 26 - 38 are clubs, and cards numbered 39 - 51 are spades. Suit is represented on the displayed card by the two picture boxes: picPlayer (your card) and picComputer (computer's card). For card values, lower numbers should represent lower cards. A rule that does this for each number in each card suit is:

Card Numbers

Hearts	Diamonds	Clubs	Spades	Card Value
0	13	26	39	Two
1	14	27	40	Three
2	15	28	41	Four
3	16	29	42	Five
4	17	30	43	Six
5	18	31	44	Seven
6	19	32	45	Eight
7	20	33	46	Nine
8	21	34	47	Ten
9	22	35	48	Jack
10	23	36	49	Queen
11	24	37	50	King
12	25	38	51	Ace

As examples, notice card 22 is a Jack of Diamonds. Card 30 is a 6 of Clubs. The card values are displayed in the lblPlayer and lblComputer label controls. We now can display cards. How do we compare them?

Card comparisons must be based on a numerical value, not displayed card value - it's difficult to check if K is greater than 7, though it can be done. So, one last rule is needed to relate card value to numerical value. It's a simple one - start with a 2 having a numerical value of 0 (lowest) and go up, with an Ace (A) having a numerical value of 12 (highest). This makes numerical card comparisons easy. Notice hearts card numbers already go from 0 to 12. If we subtract 13 from diamonds numbers, 26 from clubs numbers, and 39 from spades numbers, each of those card numbers will also range from 0 to 12. This gives a common basis for comparing cards. This all may seem complicated, but look at the C# code and you'll see it really isn't.

The C# code that implements the **btnNew_Click** event method is:

```
private void btnNew_Click(object sender, EventArgs e)
{
    // Method level variables
    Random myRandom = new Random();
    int yourNumber = 0; // Your card number
    int computerNumber = 0; // Computer card number
    if (btnNew.Text == "New Game")
    {
        // New game clicked
        txtOver.Visible = false;
        btnNew.Text = "Next Card";
        btnExit.Text = "Stop";
        // Zero out scores
        txtYouScore.Text = "0";
        txtCompScore.Text = "0";
        // Shuffle cards using one card shuffle code
        // Initialize CardNumbers
        for (int loopCounter = 0; loopCounter < 52;
loopCounter++)
        {
            cardNumber[loopCounter] = loopCounter;
        }
        // Work through remaining values
        // Start at 52 and swap one value
        // at each for loop step
        // After each step, remaining is decreased by 1
        for (int remaining = 52; remaining >= 1; remaining--)
        {
            // Pick item at random
            int itemPicked = myRandom.Next(remaining);
            // Swap picked item with bottom item
            int tempValue = cardNumber[itemPicked];
            cardNumber[itemPicked] = cardNumber[remaining -
1];
            cardNumber[remaining - 1] = tempValue;
        }
        // Set CardIndex to zero
        cardIndex = 0;
    }
    // Display cards
    // Display your card's suit
    // Determine your card's number for comparisons
    if (cardNumber[cardIndex] >= 0 && cardNumber[cardIndex]
<= 12)
```

```
    {
        picPlayer.Image = picHeart.Image;
        yourNumber = cardNumber[cardIndex];
    }
    else if (cardNumber[cardIndex] >= 13 &&
cardNumber[cardIndex] <= 25)
    {
        picPlayer.Image = picDiamond.Image;
        yourNumber = cardNumber[cardIndex] - 13;
    }
    else if (cardNumber[cardIndex] >= 26 &&
cardNumber[cardIndex] <= 38)
    {
        picPlayer.Image = picClub.Image;
        yourNumber = cardNumber[cardIndex] - 26;
    }
    else if (cardNumber[cardIndex] >= 39 &&
cardNumber[cardIndex] <= 51)
    {
        picPlayer.Image = picSpade.Image;
        yourNumber = cardNumber[cardIndex] - 39;
    }
    // Display your card's value
    switch (yourNumber)
    {
        case 9:
            lblPlayer.Text = "J";
            break;
        case 10:
            lblPlayer.Text = "Q";
            break;
        case 11:
            lblPlayer.Text = "K";
            break;
        case 12:
            lblPlayer.Text = "A";
            break;
        default:
            lblPlayer.Text = Convert.ToString(yourNumber + 2)
+ " ";
            break;
    }
    // Display computer's card suit
    // Determine computer's number for comparisons
    if (cardNumber[cardIndex + 26] >= 0 &&
cardNumber[cardIndex + 26] <= 12)
    {
```

```
        picComputer.Image = picHeart.Image;
        computerNumber = cardNumber[cardIndex + 26];
    }
    else if (cardNumber[cardIndex + 26] >= 13 &&
cardNumber[cardIndex + 26] <= 25)
    {
        picComputer.Image = picDiamond.Image;
        computerNumber = cardNumber[cardIndex + 26] - 13;
    }
    else if (cardNumber[cardIndex + 26] >= 26 &&
cardNumber[cardIndex + 26] <= 38)
    {
        picComputer.Image = picClub.Image;
        computerNumber = cardNumber[cardIndex + 26] - 26;
    }
    else if (cardNumber[cardIndex + 26] >= 39 &&
cardNumber[cardIndex + 26] <= 51)
    {
        picComputer.Image = picSpade.Image;
        computerNumber = cardNumber[cardIndex + 26] - 39;
    }
    // Display computer card's value
    switch (computerNumber)
    {
        case 9:
            lblComputer.Text = "J";
            break;
        case 10:
            lblComputer.Text = "Q";
            break;
        case 11:
            lblComputer.Text = "K";
            break;
        case 12:
            lblComputer.Text = "A";
            break;
        default:
            lblComputer.Text =
Convert.ToString(computerNumber + 2) + " ";
            break;
    }
    // Compare displayed cards
    if (yourNumber > computerNumber)
    {
        // You win
        txtYouScore.Text =
Convert.ToString(Convert.ToInt32(txtYouScore.Text) + 2);
```

```
    }
    else if (computerNumber > yourNumber)
    {
        // Computer win
        txtCompScore.Text =
Convert.ToString(Convert.ToInt32(txtCompScore.Text) + 2);
    }
    else
    {
        // a tie!
        txtYouScore.Text =
Convert.ToString(Convert.ToInt32(txtYouScore.Text) + 1);
        txtCompScore.Text =
Convert.ToString(Convert.ToInt32(txtCompScore.Text) + 1);
    }
    cardIndex++;
    // Check to see if all cards have been used
    if (cardIndex > 25)
    {
        // Game over
        txtOver.Visible = true;
        btnNew.Text = "New Game";
        btnExit.Text = "Exit";
    }
}
```

You should be able to see each outlined step in this code. Notice particularly the shuffle routine and how **cardIndex** is used with the **cardNumber** array to display your card and the computer card. Remember the computer card is 26 elements ahead of your card in the cardNumber array. Look at how the card numbers are found and how comparisons are made. Check out the tricky way scores are updated without using any variables! Notice, too, how as your programming knowledge expands, there's a lot more happening in the code we write. Remember to use cut and paste where you can - it will make your work easier.

We now need to code the **btnExit_Click** event. Like **btnNew**, It also has two purposes. If the button **Text** property is **Exit**, the program stops. If the **Text** is **Stop**, the current game stops. That code is pretty simple:

```
private void btnExit_Click(object sender, EventArgs e)
{
    if (btnExit.Text == "Exit")
    {
        // Stop program
        this.Close();
    }
    else
    {
        //  Stop game
        txtOver.Visible = true;
        btnExit.Text = "Exit";
        btnNew.Text = "New Game";
    }
}
```

Save the project by clicking the **Save All** button in the toolbar.

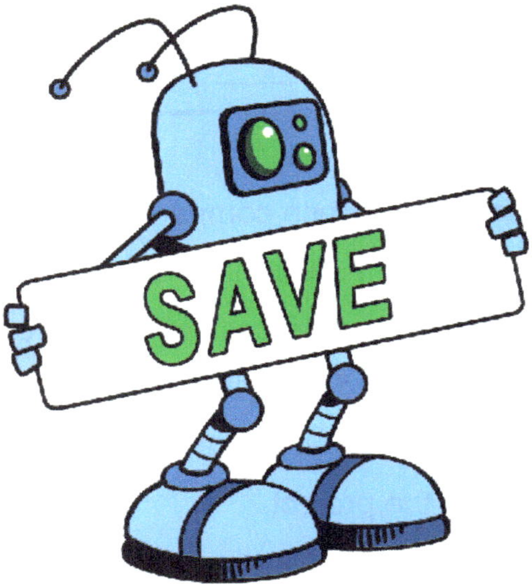

Run the Project

Run the project. Click **New Game** to get started. Click **Next Card** to display each pair of cards. Notice how the different controls are used to make up the cards. Make sure the program works correctly. Here's what my screen looks like in the middle of a game:

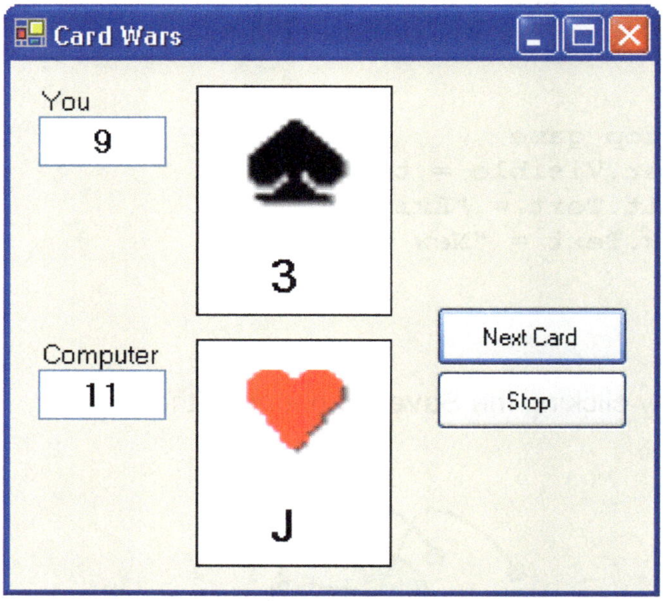

Play through one game and check each comparison to make sure you get the correct result and score with each new card. Make sure the **Stop** and **Exit** buttons work properly. Go through the usual process of making sure the program works as it should. Once you're convinced everything is OK, have fun playing the game. Share your creation with friends. If you made any changes during the running process, make sure you save the project.

Other Things to Try

Possible changes to the Card Wars project are obvious, but not easy. One change would be to have more than two players. Set up three and four player versions. You could also add a message after each comparison to way which player won (or whether it was a tie). You could use the txtOver control that's already there.

In Card Wars, we stop the game after going through the deck one time. In the real card game of War, after the first round, the players pick up the cards they won, shuffle them, and play another round. Every time a player uses all the cards in their "hand," they again pick up their winnings pile, reshuffle and continue playing. This continues until one player has lost all of their cards. Another change to Card Wars would be to write code that plays the game with these rules. As we said, it's not easy. You would need to add code to keep track of which cards each player won, when they ran out of cards to play, how to reshuffle their remaining cards, and new logic to see when a game was over. Such code would use more arrays, more for loops, and more variables. If you want a programming challenge, go for it!

And, while you're tackling challenges, here's another. In the usual War game, when two cards have the same value - War is declared! This means each player takes three cards from their "hand" and lays them face down. Then another card is placed face up. The higher card at that time wins all 10 cards! If it's still a tie, there's another War. Try adding this logic to the game. You might need to change the display to allow more cards. You'll need to figure out how to lay cards "face down" in C#. You'll need to check if a player has enough cards to wage War. Another difficult task, but give it a try if you feel adventurous.

This class presented one of the more challenging projects yet. The code involved in shuffling cards and displaying cards, though straightforward, was quite involved. The use of panel and picture box controls helped in the display. The use of arrays and for loops made the coding a bit easier. If you completely understood the Card Wars project, you are well on your way to being a good Visual C# Express programmer. Now, on to the last class.

10

Timers, Animation, Keyboard Events

Review and Preview

It's the last class. By now, you should have some confidence in your abilities as a Visual C# Express programmer. In this class, we'll look at one more control that's a lot of fun - the timer control.

It's a key control for adding animation (motion) to graphics in projects. We study some animation techniques and we'll examine how to recognize user inputs from the keyboard via keyboard events. Then, you'll build one last project (at least, the last project in this class) - your first video game!

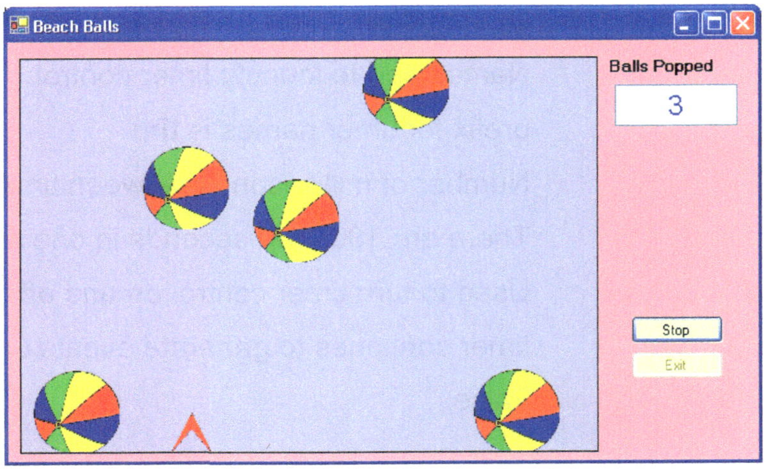

Timer Control

The Visual C# Express **timer** control has an interesting feature. It is the one control that can generate events without any input from the user. Timer controls work in your project's background, generating events at time intervals you specify. This event generation feature comes in handy for graphics animation where screen displays need to be updated at regular intervals. The timer control is selected from the toolbox. It appears as:

In Toolbox:

Below Form (default properties):

There is no user interface (nothing to click or nothing to look at) for the timer control, so it will not appear on the form. Such controls are placed in the "tray area" below the form in the design window.

Properties

The timer control properties are:

Property	Description
Name	Name used to identify timer control. Three letter prefix for timer names is **tim**.
Interval	Number of milliseconds between timer events. There are 1000 milliseconds in one second.
Enabled	Used to turn timer control on and off. When True, timer continues to generate events until set to False.

Events

The timer control has a single event:

Event	Description
Tick	Event method executed every Interval milliseconds when timer control Enabled property is True.

Examples

A few examples should clarify how the timer control works. It's very simple and very powerful. Here's what happens. If a timer control's **Enabled** property is **True** (the timer is on), every **Interval** milliseconds, Visual C# Express will generate an event and execute the corresponding **Tick** event method. No user interaction is needed. If your timer is named **timExample**, the Timer event method has the form:

```
private void timExample_Tick(object sender, EventArgs e)
{
        [C# code to be executed every Interval milliseconds]
}
```

Whatever C# code you want to execute is put in this method.

The Interval property is the most important timer control property. This property is set to the number of milliseconds between timer events. A millisecond is 1/1000th of a second, or there are 1,000 milliseconds in a second. If you want to generate N events per second, set Interval to 1000 / N. For example, if you want a timer event to occur 4 times per second, set Interval to 250. About the lowest practical value for Interval is 50 and values that differ by 5, 10, or even 20 are likely to produce similar results. It all depends on your particular computer.

The only other property to worry about is the Enabled property. It is used to turn the timer on (true) or off (false). In design mode, the timer control Enabled property is given a default value of False. We will always leave this at False. It is good programming practice to control timers programmatically. This simply means turn your timers on and off in C# code. It's a matter of changing the Enabled property. And, always make sure if you turn a timer on that you turn it off when you need to. Now, the first example.

Start Visual C# Express and start a new project. Add a timer control (it will appear below the form) and button to the form. In this example, we will use the timer control to make your computer beep every second. The button will turn the timer on and off. Set the timer control (**timer1** default name) Interval property to 1000 (1000 milliseconds equals one second). Put this code in the **timer1_Tick** event method (it will be one of the few events listed for the timer control in the code window):

```
private void timer1_Tick(object sender, EventArgs e)
{
    System.Media.SystemSounds.Beep.Play();
}
```

Beep is the C# function that makes the computer beep, or is that obvious?

Put this code in the button (default name **Button1**) **Button1_Click** event method:

```
private void button1_Click(object sender, EventArgs e)
{
    if (timer1.Enabled)
    {
        timer1.Enabled = false;
    }
    else
    {
        timer1.Enabled = true;
    }
}
```

What does this code do? If the timer is on (timer1.Enabled = true), it turns it off (timer1.Enabled = false), and vice versa. We say this code "toggles" the timer. Run the project. Click the button. Your computer will beep every second (the Tick event is executed every 1000 milliseconds, the Interval value) until you click the button again. Notice it does this no matter what else is going on. It requires no input (once the timer is on) from you, the user. Click the button. The beeping will stop. Remember to always let your C# code turn timer controls on and off. Stop the project when you get tired of the beeping.

Add the two shaded lines of code to the **timer1_Tick** event, so it now reads:

```
private void timer1_Tick(object sender, EventArgs e)
{
    System.Media.SystemSounds.Beep.Play();
    Random myRandom = new Random();
    this.BackColor = Color.FromArgb(myRandom.Next(256),
myRandom.Next(256), myRandom.Next(256));
}
```

This extra code randomly changes the form (name **this**) background color using the **FromArgb** method (using random red, green and blue values). Run the project. Click the button. Now, every second, the computer beeps and the form changes color. Stop the timer. Stop the project.

What if we want the computer to beep every second, but want the form color to change four times every second? If events require different intervals, each event needs its own timer. Add another timer control to the form (default name **timer2**). We'll use this timer to control the form color. Set timer2's Interval to 250 (Tick event executed every 0.25 seconds, or 4 color changes per second). Cut and paste the lines of code in **timer1_Tick** that sets color into the **timer2_Tick** event. The two timer Tick events are now:

```
private void timer1_Tick(object sender, EventArgs e)
{
    System.Media.SystemSounds.Beep.Play();
}

private void timer2_Tick(object sender, EventArgs e)
{
    Random myRandom = new Random();
    this.BackColor = Color.FromArgb(myRandom.Next(256),
myRandom.Next(256), myRandom.Next(256));
}
```

We also need to add code to the **button1_Click** event to toggle (turn it on and off) this new timer. We could copy and paste the five lines of code there for timer1 and change all the timer1 words to timer2. And, this would work. But, let me show you a quick way to toggle Boolean (bool type) variables, like the Enabled property. We'll be able to replace five lines of code with one!

Way back in Class 6, we studied logical operators - operators that work with Boolean variables. Remember and (**&&**)? Remember or (**||**)? Well, there's another logical operator that comes in handy - the **not** operator, represented by the exclamation point (**!**).. This operator works on a single Boolean variable. If we have a Boolean variable (**bool** type) named x, it can have two values, true or false. **!x** has the opposite value of X as shown in this simple logic table:

x	!x
true	false
false	true

Notice the not operator toggles the Boolean variable x. If x is on (true), the not operator turns x off (false). If x is off (false), the not operator turns x on (true). So, we can use the not operator to turn timer controls on and off. Use this code in the **button1_Click** event method in our example:

```
private void button1_Click(object sender, EventArgs e)
{
    timer1.Enabled = !(timer1.Enabled);
    timer2.Enabled = !(timer2.Enabled);
}
```

Notice how the not operator simplifies using timer controls. Do you see that one line of C# code using not has exactly the same effect as the five lines of code we used earlier to toggle the timer? Run the project. Click the button. Do you see how the two timer events are interacting? You should hear a beep every four times the screen changes color. Stop the project when you're done playing with it.

Let's use the timer to do some flashier stuff. Start a new project. Add a panel control (default name **panel1**). Make the panel fairly big – make it wider than it is tall. Add a button (default name **button1**), and a timer control (default name **timer1**). Set the timer control Interval property to 50. Declare and initialize an int type variable **delta** in the general declarations area:

```
int delta = 0;
```

Toggle the timer in the **Button1_Click** event:

```
private void button1_Click(object sender, EventArgs e)
{
    timer1.Enabled = !(timer1.Enabled);
}
```

Put this code in the **Timer1_Tick** event:

```
private void timer1_Tick(object sender, EventArgs e)
{
    Graphics myGraphics;
    Pen myPen;
    Random myRandom = new Random();
    myGraphics = panel1.CreateGraphics();
    myPen = new Pen(Color.FromArgb(myRandom.Next(256),
myRandom.Next(256), myRandom.Next(256)), 2);
    myGraphics.DrawEllipse(myPen, delta, delta, panel1.Width
- 2 * delta, panel1.Height - 2 * delta);
    delta = delta + (int) myPen.Width;
    if (delta > panel1.Height / 2)
    {
        delta = 0;
        myGraphics.Clear(panel1.BackColor);
    }
    myPen.Dispose();
    myGraphics.Dispose();
}
```

You should recognize most of what's here. We've created a graphics object and pen object (with a random color) to do some drawing. Notice, though, we use a graphics method (**DrawEllipse**) we haven't seen before. You should be able to understand it and you'll see it gives a really neat effect in this example. The **DrawEllipse** method has the form:

```
myGraphics.DrawEllipse(myPen, x, y, width, height);
```

Here, **myGraphics** is the graphics object. This command draws an ellipse, with a width **width** and height **height**, in the graphics object starting at the point (**x**, **y**). A picture shows the result:

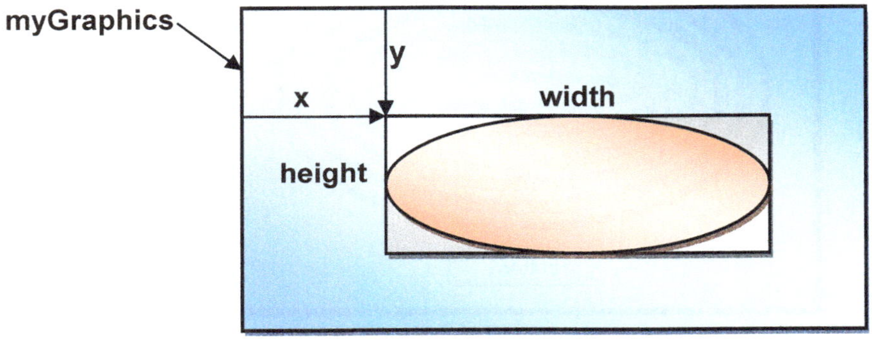

In your work with Visual C# Express, you will often see code you don't recognize. Learn to use the on-line help facilities (try it with **DrawEllipse**) in these cases.

Back to the code, you should see the **DrawEllipse** method draws the first ellipse around the border of the panel control (**x = 0** initially). The surrounding rectangle moves "in" an amount **delta** (in each direction) with each Tick event, resulting in a smaller rectangle (the width and height are decreased by both **2*delta**). Once delta (incremented by the pen width in each step) exceeds half of the panel height, it is reset to 0, the panel is cleared and the process starts all over. Run the project. Click the button. Are you hypnotized? Here's a sample of a run I made:

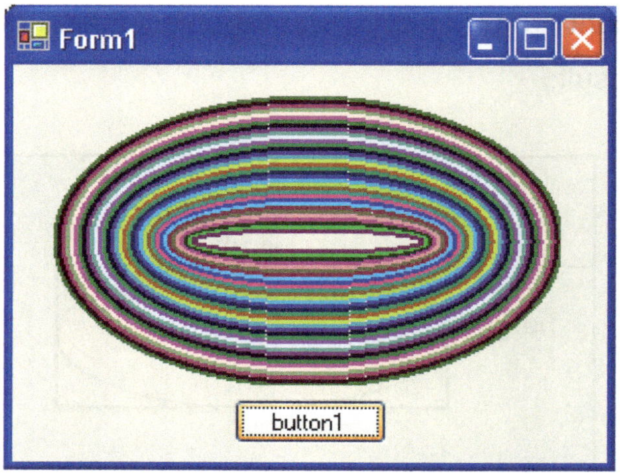

Can you think of other things you could draw using other graphics methods? Look at **DrawRectangle** for example. Try your ideas.

In this last example, the periodic (every 0.050 seconds) changing of the display in the graphics object, imparted by the timer control, gives the appearance of motion – the ellipses seem to be moving inward. This is the basic concept behind a very powerful graphics technique - **animation**. In animation, we have a sequence of pictures, each a little different from the previous one. With the ellipse example, in each picture, we add a new ellipse. By displaying this sequence over time, we can trick the viewer into thinking things are moving. It all has to do with how fast the human eye and brain can process information. That's how cartoons work - 24 different pictures are displayed every second - it makes things look like they are moving, or animated. Obviously, the timer control is a key element to animation, as well as for other Visual C# Express timing tasks. In the C# lesson for this class, we will look at how to do simple animations and some other things.

Typical Use of Timer Control

The usual design steps to use a timer control are:

- Set the **Name** property and **Interval** property.
- Write code in **Tick** event.
- At some point in your application, set **Enabled** to **True** to start timer. Also, have capability to reset **Enabled** to **False**, when desired.

C# - The Final Lesson

In this last C# lesson, we study some simple animation techniques, look at math needed with animations, and learn how to detect keyboard events.

Animation - DrawImage Graphics Method

In the last example, we saw that by using a timer to periodically change the display in a panel control, a sense of motion, or animation, is obtained. We will use that idea here to do a specific kind of animation - moving objects around. This is the basis for nearly every video game ever made. The objects we move will be images contained in Visual C# Express picture box controls.

Moving images in a panel is easy to do. First, establish an image (set the **Image** property) in the picture box. This image is then placed in the panel control using the **DrawImage** graphics method. Like the other graphics methods we've seen (DrawLine and DrawEllipse), before using DrawImage, you need to establish a graphics object to draw to. The graphics object is declared in the usual manner (usually in the **general declarations** area):

```
Graphics myGraphics;
```

We then create the graphics object (assume **myControl** is the host control; we'll use a panel):

```
myGraphics = myControl.CreateGraphics();
```

This creation usually occurs in the form **Load** method. You dispose of the object in the form **FormClosing** method.

Now, assume we have an image in a picture box control named **picExample**. At this point, we can draw **picExample.Image** in **myGraphics**, using **DrawImage**. The **DrawImage** method that does this is:

```
myGraphics.DrawImage(picExample.Image, x, y, w, h);
```

where **x** is the horizontal position of the image within **myGraphics** and **y** is the vertical position. The image will have a width value **w** and a height **h**. The width and height can be the original image size or scaled up or down. It's your choice.

A picture illustrates what's going on with **DrawImage**:

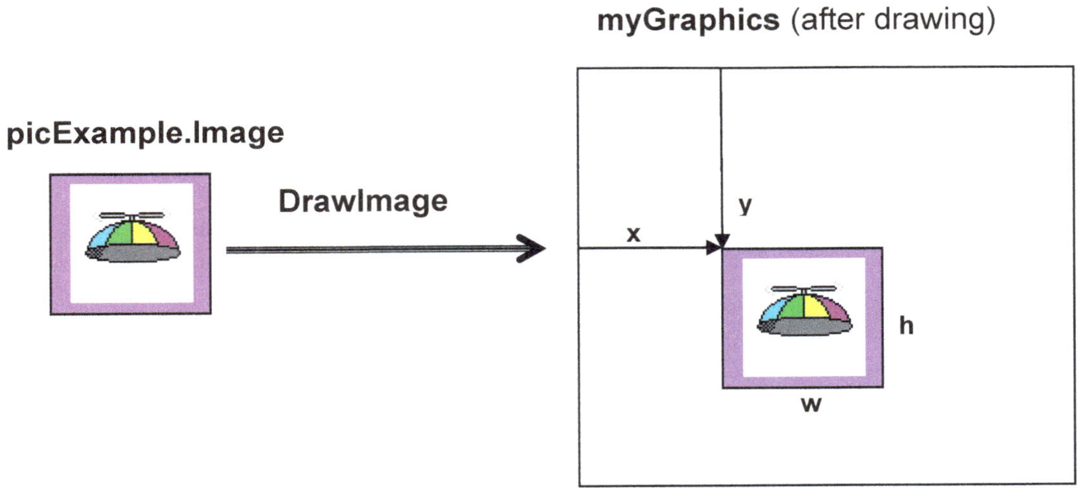

Note how the transfer of the rectangular image occurs. Successive transfers (always erasing the previous position of the image) gives the impression of motion, or animation. Where do we put the DrawImage statement?

Each picture box image to be moved must have an associated timer control. If desired, several images can use the same timer. The DrawImage statement is placed in the corresponding timer control Tick event. Whenever a Tick event is triggered, the image is erased at its old position (by putting a "blank" image in that position), a new image position is computed and the DrawImage method executed. This periodic movement is **animation**. Let's look at an example to see how simple it really is.

Start Visual C# Express and start a new project. Put a panel (default name **panel1**) on the form - make it fairly tall with a white background color. Put a small picture box (name **pictureBox1**) on the form. Set its **Image** property (I used the soccer ball bitmap graphic in the **\VCSEKids\VCSEK Projects\Graphics** folder). Place a timer control (default name **timer1**) on the form. Use an Interval property of 100. Place a button (default name **button1**) on the form for starting and stopping the timer. We will use this example a lot. Try to make it look something like this:

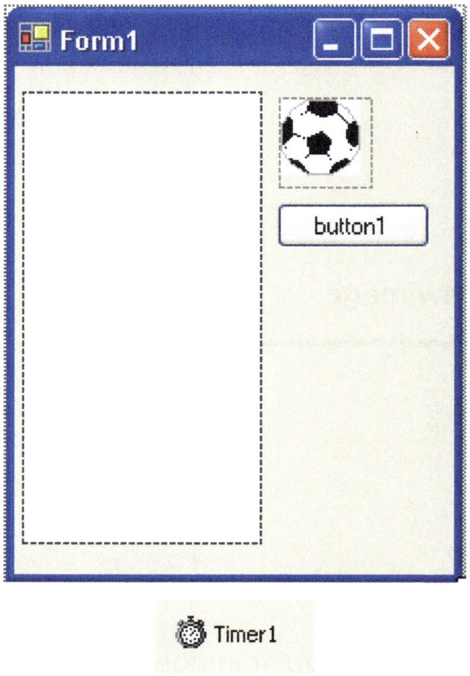

Define the needed graphics object in the **general declarations** area. Also include a variable (**imageY**) to keep track of the vertical position of the image:

```
Graphics myGraphics;
int imageY;
```

And create the object in the **Form1_Load** event method:

```
private void Form1_Load(object sender, EventArgs e)
{
    myGraphics = panel1.CreateGraphics();
}
```

Dispose of the graphics object in the **Form1_FormClosing** event method:

```
private void Form1_FormClosing(object sender,
FormClosingEventArgs e)
{
    myGraphics.Dispose();
}
```

Use **button1_Click** to toggle the timer and initialize the position (**imageY**) of **pictureBox1.Image** at the top of the panel control:

```
private void button1_Click(object sender, EventArgs e)
{
    timer1.Enabled = !(timer1.Enabled);
    imageY = 0;
}
```

Now, move the image in the **timer1_Tick** event:

```
private void timer1_Tick(object sender, EventArgs e)
{
    int imageX = 10;
    int imageW = 30;
    int imageH = 25;
    myGraphics.Clear(panel1.BackColor);
    imageY = imageY + panel1.Height / 40;
    myGraphics.DrawImage(pictureBox1.Image, imageX, imageY,
imageW, imageH);
}
```

In this event, the image width (**imageW**) and height (**imageH**) are given values, as is the horizontal location (**imageX**). Then, the graphics object is cleared to erase the previous image. The vertical position of the image (**ImageY**) is increased by 1/40th of the panel height each time the event is executed (every 0.1 seconds). The picture box image is moving down. It should take 40 executions of this routine, or about 4 seconds, for the image to reach the bottom. Let's try it.

Run the example project. Click the button to start the timer. Watch the image drop. Notice the image is scaled to fit the area defined by the DrawImage method. Pretty easy, wasn't it? How long does it take the image to reach the bottom? What happens when it reaches the bottom? It just keeps on going down through the panel, through the form and out through the bottom of your computer monitor to who knows where! We need to be able to detect this disappearance and do something about it. We'll look at two ways to handle this. First, we'll make the image reappear at the top of the panel, or scroll. Then, we'll make it bounce. Stop the project. Save it too. We'll be using it again.

Image Disappearance

When images are moving in a panel, we need to know when they move out of the panel across a border. Such information is often needed in video type games. We just saw this need with the falling ball example. When an **image disappearance** happens, we can either ignore that image or perhaps make it "scroll" around to other side of the panel control. How do we decide if an image has disappeared? It's basically a case of comparing various positions and dimensions.

We need to detect whether a image has completely moved across one of four panel borders (top, bottom, left, right). Each of these detections can be developed using this diagram of a picture box image (**myImage**) within a panel (**myPanel**):

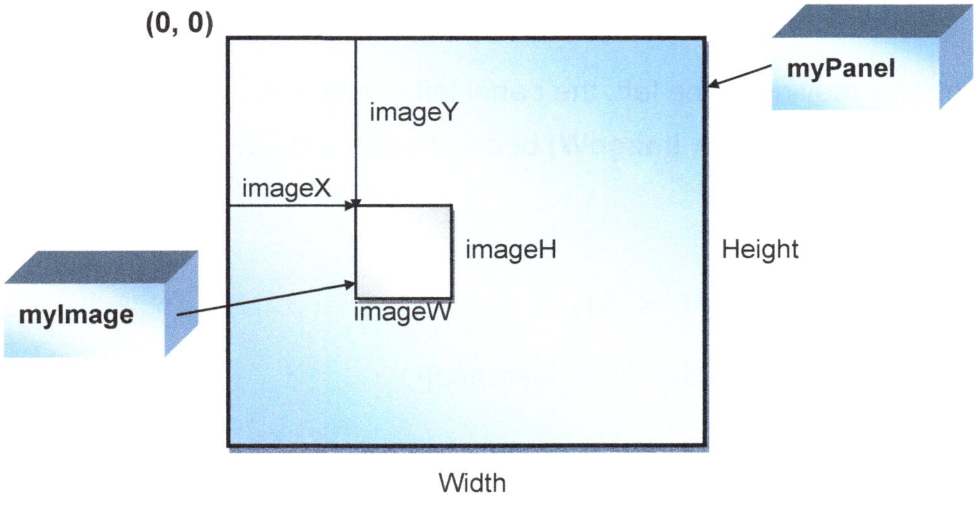

Notice the image is located at (**imageX**, **imageY**), is **imageW** pixels wide and **imageH** pixels high.

If the image is moving down, it completely crosses the panel bottom border when its top (**imageY**) is lower than the bottom border. The bottom of the panel is **myPanel.Height**. C# code for a bottom border disappearance is:

```
if (imageY > myPanel.Height)
{
        [C# code for bottom border disappearance]
}
```

If the image is moving up, the panel top border is completely crossed when the bottom of the image (**imageY + imageH**) becomes less than 0. In C#, this is detected with:

```
if ((imageY + imageH) < 0)
{
        [C# code for top border disappearance]
}
```

If the control is moving to the left, the panel left border is completely crossed when image right side (**imageX + imageW)** becomes less than 0. In C#, this is detected with:

```
if ((imageX + imageW) < 0)
{
        [C# code for left border disappearance]
}
```

If the image is moving to the right, it completely crosses the panel right border when its left side (**imageX**) passes the border. The right side of the panel is **myPanel.Width**. C# code for a right border disappearance is:

```
if (imageX > myPanel.Width)
{
    [C# code for right border disappearance]
}
```

Let's add disappearance detection to our "falling soccer ball" example. Return to that project. Say, instead of having the image disappear when it reaches the bottom, we have it magically reappear at the top of the panel. We say the image is scrolling. Modify the **timer1_Tick** event to this (new lines are shaded):

```
private void timer1_Tick(object sender, EventArgs e)
{
    int imageX = 10;
    int imageW = 30;
    int imageH = 25;
    myGraphics.Clear(panel1.BackColor);
    imageY = imageY + panel1.Height / 40;
    myGraphics.DrawImage(pictureBox1.Image, imageX, imageY,
imageW, imageH);
    if (imageY > panel1.Height)
    {
        imageY = -imageH;
    }
}
```

We added the bottom border disappearance logic. Notice when the image disappears, we reset its imageY value so it is repositioned just off the top of the panel. Run the project. Watch the image scroll. Pretty easy, wasn't it? Stop and save the project.

Border Crossing

What if, in the falling image example, instead of scrolling, we want the image to bounce back up when it reaches the bottom border? This is another common animation task - detecting the initiation of **border crossings**. Such crossings are used to change the direction of moving images, that is, make them bounce. How do we detect border crossings?

The same diagram used for image disappearances can be used here. Checking to see if an image has crossed a panel border is like checking for image disappearance, except the image has not moved quite as far. For top and bottom checks, the image movement is less by an amount equal to its height value (imageH). For left and right checks, the control movement is less by an amount equal to its width value (imageW). Look back at that diagram and you should see these code segments accomplish the respective border crossing directions:

```
if (imageY < 0)
{
        [C# code for top border crossing]
}
```

```
if ((imageY + imageH) > myPanel.Height)
{
        [C# code for bottom border crossing]
}


if (imageX < 0)
{
        [C# code for left border crossing]
}


if ((imageX + imageW) > myPanel.Width)
{
        [C# code for right border crossing]
}
```

Let's modify the falling image example to have it bounce when it reaches the bottom of the panel. Declare an integer variable **imageDir** in the **general declarations** area:

```
int imageDir;
```

imageDir is used to indicate which way the image is moving. When imageDir is 1, the image is moving down (imageY is increasing). When imageDir is -1, the image is moving up (imageY is decreasing). Change the **button1_Click** event to (new line is shaded):

```
private void button1_Click(object sender, EventArgs e)
{
    timer1.Enabled = !(timer1.Enabled);
    imageY = 0;
    imageDir = 1;
}
```

We added a single line to initialize imageDir to 1 (moving down).

Change the **timer1_Tick** event to this (again, changed and/or new lines are shaded):

```
private void timer1_Tick(object sender, EventArgs e)
{
    int imageX = 10;
    int imageW = 30;
    int imageH = 25;
    myGraphics.Clear(panel1.BackColor);
    imageY = imageY + imageDir * panel1.Height / 40;
    myGraphics.DrawImage(pictureBox1.Image, imageX, imageY,
imageW, imageH);
    if (imageY + imageH > panel1.Height)
    {
        imageY = panel1.Height - imageH;
        imageDir = -1;
    }
}
```

We modified the calculation of imageY to account for the imageDir variable. Notice how it is used to impart the proper direction to the image motion (down when imageDir is 1, up when imageDir is –1). We have also replaced the code in the existing if structure for a bottom border crossing. Notice when a crossing is detected, the image is repositioned (by resetting imageY) at the bottom of the panel (**panel1.Height - imageH**) and imageDir is set to -1 (direction is changed so the image will start moving up). Run the project. Now when the image reaches the bottom of the panel, it reverses direction and heads back up. We've made the image bounce! But, once it reaches the top, it's gone again!

Add top border crossing detection, so the **timer1_Tick** event is now (changes are shaded):

```
private void timer1_Tick(object sender, EventArgs e)
{
    int imageX = 10;
    int imageW = 30;
    int imageH = 25;
    myGraphics.Clear(panel1.BackColor);
    imageY = imageY + imageDir * panel1.Height / 40;
    myGraphics.DrawImage(pictureBox1.Image, imageX, imageY,
imageW, imageH);
    if (imageY + imageH > panel1.Height)
    {
        imageY = panel1.Height - imageH;
        imageDir = -1;
    System.Media.SystemSounds.Beep.Play();
    }
    else if (imageY < 0)
    {
        imageY = 0;
        imageDir = 1;
        System.Media.SystemSounds.Beep.Play();
    }
}
```

In the top crossing code (the else if portion), we reset imageY to 0 (the top of the panel) and change imageDir to 1. We've also added a couple of Beep statements so there is some audible feedback when either bounce occurs. Run the project again. Your image will now bounce up and down, beeping with each bounce, until you stop it. Stop and save the project.

The code we've developed here for checking and resetting image positions is a common task in Visual C# Express. As you develop your programming skills, you should make sure you are comfortable with what all these properties and dimensions mean and how they interact. As an example, do you see how we could compute imageX so the image is centered in the panel? Try this in the **timer1_Tick** method:

```
imageX = (int) (0.5 * (panel1.Width - imageW));
```

Make sure you put this line after the line declaring imageW. Note the use of the cast (conversion) of the computation to an **int** type. Save the project one more time.

You've now seen how to do lots of things with animations. You can make images move, make them disappear and reappear, and make them bounce. Do you have some ideas of simple video games you would like to build? You still need two more skills – image erasure and collision detection - which are discussed next.

Image Erasure

In the little example we just did, we had to clear the panel control (using the **Clear** graphics method) prior to each DrawImage method. This was done to erase the image at its previous location before drawing a new image. This "erase, then redraw" process is the secret behind animation. But, what if we are animating many images? The Clear method would clear all images from the panel and require repositioning every image, even ones that haven't moved. This would be a slow, tedious and unnecessary process. It would also result in an animation with lots of flicker.

We will take a more precise approach to erasure. Instead of erasing the entire panel before moving an image, we will only erase the rectangular region previously occupied by the image. To do this, we will use the **FillRectangle** graphics method, a new concept. This method is straightforward and, with your Visual C# Express knowledge, you should easily understand how it is used. If applied to a graphics object named **myGraphics**, the form is:

```
myGraphics.FillRectangle(myBrush, x, y, width, height);
```

This line of code will “paint” a rectangular region located at (**x, y**), **width** wide, and **height** high with a brush object (**myBrush**).

And, yes, there’s another new concept – a **brush** object. A brush is like a “wide” pen. It is used to fill areas with a color. A brush object is declared (assume an object named **myBrush**) using:

```
Brush myBrush;
```

Then, a solid brush (one that paints with a single color) is created using:

```
myBrush = new SolidBrush(Color);
```

where you select the **Color** of the brush. Once done with the brush, dispose of the object using the **Dispose** method.

So, how does this work with the problem at hand? We will create a “blank” brush (we’ll even name it **blankBrush**) with the same color as the BackColor property of the panel (**myPanel**) control. The code to do this (after declaring the brush object) is:

```
blankBrush = new SolidBrush(myPanel.BackColor);
```

Then, to erase an image located in **myGraphics** at (imageX, imageY), imageW pixels wide and imageH pixels high, we use:

```
myGraphics.FillRectangle(blankBrush, imageX, imageY, imageW,
imageH);
```

This will just paint the specified rectangular region with the panel background color, effectively erasing the image that was there.

Open up the "bouncing soccer ball" example one more time. Add this line of code in the **general declarations** area:

```
Brush blankBrush;
```

Add this line in the **Form1_Load** method:

```
blankBrush = new SolidBrush(panel1.BackColor);
```

And, add this line in the **Form1_FormClosing** method:

```
blankBrush.Dispose();
```

These three lines declare, create and dispose of the brush object at the proper times. Finally, in the **Timer1_Tick** method, replace the line using the Clear method with this new line of code (selective erasing):

```
myGraphics.FillRectangle(blankBrush, imageX, imageY, imageW,
imageH);
```

Rerun the project. You probably won't notice much difference since we only have one object moving. But, in more detailed animations, this image erasing approach is superior.

Collision Detection

Another requirement in animation is to determine if two images have collided. This is needed in games to see if a ball hits a paddle, if an alien rocket hits its target, or if a cute little character grabs some reward. Each image is described by a rectangular area, so the **collision detection** problem is to see if two rectangles collide, or overlap. This check is done using each image's position and dimensions.

Here are two images (**image1** and **image2**) in a panel control:

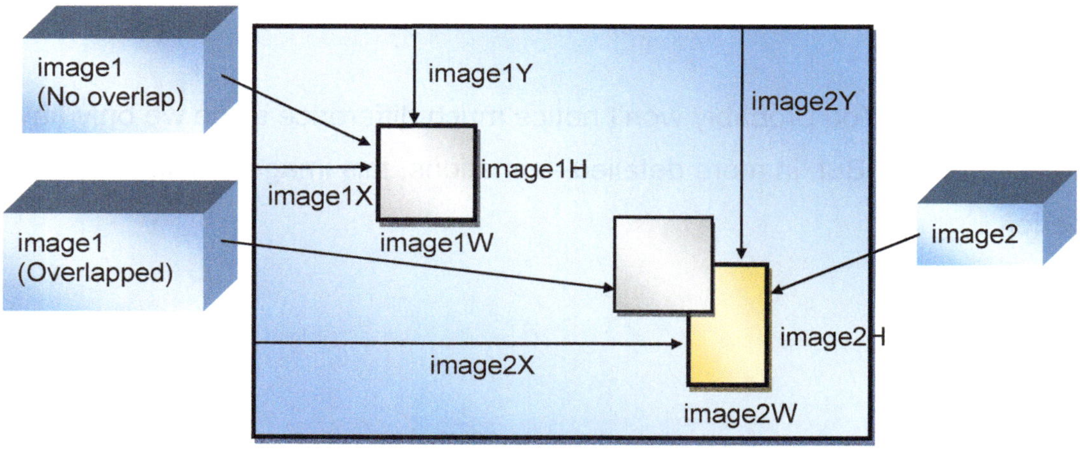

image1 is positioned at (**image1X**, **image1Y**), is **image1W** wide and **image1H** high. Similarly, **image2** is positioned at (**image2X**, **image2Y**), is **image2W** wide and **image2H** high.

Looking at this diagram, you should see there are four requirements for the two rectangles to overlap:

1. The right side of image1 (**image1X + image1H**) must be "farther right" than the left side of image2 (**image2X**)
2. The left side of image1 (**image1X**) must be "farther left" than the right side of image2 (**image2X + image2W**)
3. The bottom of image1 (**image1Y + image1H**) must be "farther down" than the top of image2 (**image2Y**)
4. The top of image1 (**image1Y**) must be "farther up" than the bottom of image2 (**image2Y + image2H**)

All four of these requirements must be met for a collision.

The C# code to check if these rectangles overlap is:

```
if ((image1X + image1W) > image2X)
{
     if (image1X < (image2X + image2W))
     {
          if ((image1Y + image1H) > image2Y)
          {
               if (image1Y < (image2Y + image2H))
               {
                    [C# code for overlap, or collision]
               }
          }
     }
}
```

This code checks the four conditions for overlap using four "nested" if structures. The C# code for a collision is executed only if all four conditions are found to be true.

Let's try some collision detection with the bouncing soccer ball example. Add a button (default name **button2**) control near the bottom of the panel – narrow the width a bit. Blank out the Text property of the button so no text is on it. Make sure the button is "attached" to the panel. Yes, we know a button is not an image, but it is a rectangle and the same overlap rules apply. We want to see if the image will collide with the button control and bounce up. Your form should look something like this:

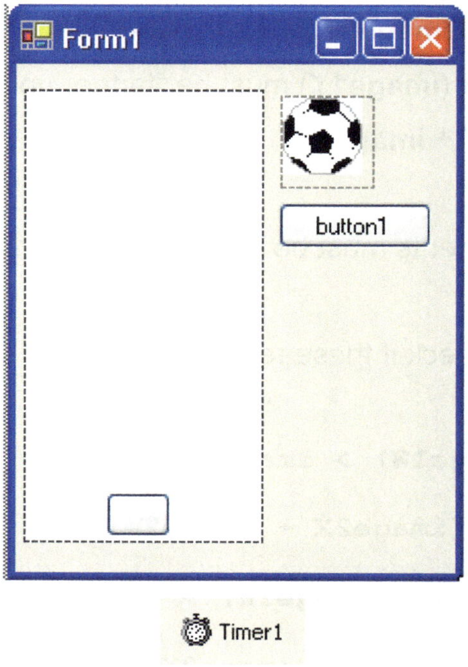

Change the **timer1_Tick** event code to (added code is shaded):

```
private void timer1_Tick(object sender, EventArgs e)
{
    int imageX = 10;
    int imageW = 30;
    int imageH = 25;
    bool collision;
    myGraphics.FillRectangle(blankBrush, imageX, imageY,
imageW, imageH);
    imageY = imageY + imageDir * panel1.Height / 40;
    myGraphics.DrawImage(pictureBox1.Image, imageX, imageY,
imageW, imageH);
```

```
    collision = false;
    if ((imageX + imageW) > button2.Left)
    {
        if (imageX < (button2.Left + button2.Width))
        {
            if ((imageY + imageH) > button2.Top)
            {
                if (imageY < (button2.Top + button2.Height))
                {
                    collision = true;
                }
            }
        }
    }
    if (collision)
    {
        imageY = button2.Top - imageH;
        imageDir = -1;
        System.Media.SystemSounds.Beep.Play();
    }
    else if (imageY < 0)
    {
        imageY = 0;
        imageDir = 1;
        Console.Beep();
    }
}
```

We declare a method level bool variable **collision** to indicate an overlap (true for overlap, false for no overlap). The overlap code [using the button control properties for location (Left, Top) and size (Width, Height)] follows the DrawImage method. If a collision is detected, the image is repositioned so it just touches the top of button2, its direction is reversed and a beep is played. The code for bouncing off the top of the panel is unchanged. Run the project. Notice the image now bounces off the button. Stop the project. Move button2 out of the panel control so the image won't collide with it. The image should just drop off the screen. See how close the image can pass by button2 without colliding to make sure the overlap routine works properly. Stop and save the project.

Now that you know how to detect collisions, you're well on your way to knowing how to build a simple video game. Next, we'll learn how to detect keyboard events from the user. One possible use for these events, among many, is to allow a user to move a little paddle to "hit" a dropping ball. The collision technique we just learned will come in handy for such a task.

Keyboard Events

In Class 8, we looked at ways for a user to interact with a Visual C# Express project using the mouse for input. We studied three mouse events: MouseDown, MouseMove, and MouseUp. Another input device available for use is the computer keyboard. Here we look at **keyboard events** which give our projects the ability to detect user input from the keyboard. Two keyboard events are studied: the **KeyDown** event and the **KeyPress** event.

Several Visual C# Express controls can recognize keyboard events, notably the form and the text box. Yet, only the control that has **focus** can receive a keyboard event. (Recall the control with focus is the active control.) When trying to detect a keyboard event for a certain control, we need to make sure that control has focus. We can give a control focus by clicking on it with the mouse. But, another way to assign focus to a control is with the **Focus** method. The format for such a statement is:

```
controlName.Focus();
```

This command in C# will give **controlName** focus and make it the active control. It has the same effect as clicking on the control. The control can then recognize any associated keyboard events. We use the Focus method with keyboard events to insure proper execution of each event.

To detect keyboard events on the form, you need to set the form **KeyPreview** property to **True**. This bypasses any keystrokes used by the controls to generate events.

KeyDown Event

The **KeyDown** event has the ability to detect the pressing of any key on the computer keyboard. It can detect:

- Special combinations of the Shift, Ctrl, and Alt keys
- Insert, Del, Home, End, PgUp, PgDn keys
- Cursor control keys
- Numeric keypad keys (it can distinguish these numbers from those on the top row of the keyboard)
- Function keys
- Letter, number and character keys

The KeyDown event for a control **controlName** is executed whenever that control has focus and a key is pressed. The form of this event method is:

```
private void controlName_KeyDown(object sender, KeyEventArgs
e)
{

    [C# code for KeyDown Event]

}
```

The KeyDown event has two arguments: **sender** and **e**. We won't be concerned with the sender argument in this class. And, we won't be concerned with the status of any of the control keys (such as Shift, Ctrl, Alt). We only want to know what key was pressed down to invoke this method.

The property **e.KeyCode** can be used to determine which key was pressed down. There is a **KeyCode** value for each key on the keyboard. By evaluating the **e.KeyCode** argument, we can determine which key was pressed. There are nearly 100 KeyCode values, some of which are:

e.KeyCode	**Description**
Keys.Back	The BACKSPACE key.
Keys.Cancel	The CANCEL key.
Keys.Delete	The DEL key.
Keys.Down	The DOWN ARROW key.
Keys.Enter	The ENTER key.
Keys.Escape	The ESC key.
Keys.F1	The F1 key.
Keys.Home	The HOME key.
Keys.Left	The LEFT ARROW key.
Keys.NumPad0	The 0 key on the numeric keypad.
Keys.PageDown	The PAGE DOWN key.
Keys.PageUp	The PAGE UP key.
Keys.Right	The RIGHT ARROW key.
Keys.Space	The SPACEBAR key.
Keys.Tab	The TAB key.
Keys.Up	The UP ARROW key.

Using the KeyDown event is not easy. There is a lot of work involved in interpreting the information provided in the KeyDown event. For example, the KeyDown event cannot distinguish between an upper and lower case letter. You need to make that distinction in your C# code. You usually use a switch or if structure (based on e.KeyCode) to determine which key was pressed. Let's see how to use KeyDown to recognize some keys.

Start Visual C# Express and start a new project. Put a text box control (**textBox1**) on the form. Use this **textBox1_KeyDown** event (make sure you pick the correct event):

```
private void textBox1_KeyDown(object sender, KeyEventArgs e)
{
    textBox1.Text =
Convert.ToString(Convert.ToInt32(e.KeyCode));
}
```

Run the project. Type a letter. The letter and its corresponding e.KeyCode (a numeric value) are shown (there is no space between the two values). Press the same letter while holding down the <Shift> key. The same code will appear – there is no distinction between upper and lower case. Press each of the four arrow keys to see their different values. Notice for such 'non-printable' keys, only a number displays in the text box. Type numbers using the top row of the keyboard and the numeric keypad (make sure your **NumLock** key is selected). Notice the keypad numbers don't display and have different KeyCode values than the "keyboard numbers." This lets us distinguish the keypad from the keyboard. Try various keys on the keyboard to see which keys have a KeyCode (all of them). Notice it works with function keys, cursor control keys, letters, number, everything! Stop the project.

Add a second text box (**textBox2**) to the form. Run the project. Click on this new text box and type some text. Notice the **textBox1_KeyDown** event does not detect any key press. Why not? textBox2 has focus - textBox1 does not. The **textBox2_KeyDown** event is being executed instead (but, there's no code there). Click on textBox1 with the mouse - this gives it focus. Now, press a key. The key detection works again. Remember, for a keyboard event to be detected, the corresponding control must have focus.

KeyPress Event

The **KeyPress** event is similar to the KeyDown event, with one distinction. Many characters in the world of computers have what are called Unicode values. Unicode values are simply numbers (ranging from 0 to 255) that represent all letters (upper and lower case), all numbers, all punctuation, and many special keys like Esc, Space, and Enter. The KeyPress event can detect the pressing of any key that has a corresponding Unicode code. A nice thing about the KeyPress event is that you immediately know what the user input is - no interpretation of any other key(s) is required (like with the KeyDown event). For example, there are different Unicode values for upper and lower case letters. Unicode values are related to ASCII (pronounced "askey") codes you may have seen in other languages.

The KeyPress event method for a control named **controlName** has the form:

```
private void controlName_KeyPress(object sender, KeyEventArgs
e)
{

        [C# code for KeyPress Event]

}
```

Again, there are two arguments, **sender** and **e**. We are interested in what key was pressed. That information is in the value of **e.KeyChar**. e.KeyChar is a **char** type variable (a type we haven't seen before), returning a single character, corresponding to the pressed key. The pressed key can be a readable character (letter, number, punctuation) or a non-readable character (Esc, Enter). It's easy to look at a readable character and know what it is. How can we distinguish one non-readable character from another?

Recall each possible key recognized by the KeyPress event has a Unicode value. If you want to know a Unicode value of a particular character, you simply cast the character to an int type. So, to determine the Unicode (**myCode**) value for a **char** type variable (named **myChar**), use:

```
myCode = (int) myChar;
```

For example:

```
myCode = (int) 'A';
```

returns the Unicode value (myCode) for the upper case A (65, by the way). Notice a character (**char**) type variable is enclosed in a pair of single quotes. To convert a Unicode value (myValue) to the corresponding character, cast the value to a **char** type::

```
myChar = (char) myCode;
```

For example:

```
myChar = (char) 49;
```

returns the character (myChar) represented by a Unicode value of 49 (a "1").

So, to recognize key presses of non-readable characters, known as control keys, we can examine the corresponding Unicode values. Two values we will use are:

Definition	**Unicode Value**
Backspace	8
<Enter>	13

Let's try an example with the KeyPress event. Start a new project. Add a label control (**label1**) and a text box (**textBox1**) control. Add this code to the **textBox1_KeyPress** event method:

```
private void textBox1_KeyPress(object sender,
KeyPressEventArgs e)
{
    label1.Text = Convert.ToString(e.KeyChar) + " " +
Convert.ToString((int) e.KeyChar);
}
```

Run the project. Press a key. The character typed (if it's printable) and its corresponding Unicode value (a space separates the two values) will appear in the label control. Press as many keys as you like. Notice different values are displayed for upper and lower case letters. Notice not every key has a Unicode value. In particular, press a function key or one of the arrow keys. What happens? Nothing. You can't detect function key or arrow key presses with a KeyPress event. That's why we needed to talk about the KeyDown event. Stop and save the project.

Let's look at a very powerful use of the KeyPress event. Say we have an application where we only want the user to be able to type numbers in a text box. In that text box's KeyPress event, we would like to examine e.KeyChar and determine if it's a number. If it is a number, great! If not, we want to ignore that key! This process of detecting and ignoring unwanted key strokes is called **key trapping**. By comparing the input e.KeyChar with acceptable values, we can decide (in C# code) if we want to accept that value as input. Key trapping is a part of every sophisticated Visual C# Express application.

The only question remaining is: if we decide a pressed key is <u>not</u> acceptable, how do we ignore it? We do that using the **e.Handled** property. If an unacceptable key is detected, we set **e.Handled** to **true**. This 'tricks' Visual C# Express into thinking the KeyPress event has already been handled and the pressed key is ignored. If a pressed key is acceptable, we set the **e.Handled** property to **false**. This tells Visual C# Express that this method has not been handled and the KeyPress should be allowed (by default, e.Handled is false, allowing all keystrokes).

Go back to the Visual C# Express example we've been using. Change the code in the example **textBox1_KeyPress** event to this:

```
private void textBox1_KeyPress(object sender,
KeyPressEventArgs e)
{
    if (e.KeyChar < '0' || e.KeyChar > '9')
    {
        e.Handled = true;
        label1.Text = "Not a number";
    }
    else
    {
        e.Handled = false;
        label1.Text = Convert.ToString(e.KeyChar) + " " +
Convert.ToString((int)e.KeyChar);
    }
}
```

Look at what's happening here. If e.KeyChar is outside the range of values from '0' to '9' (again, note **char** types are enclosed in single quotes), **e.Handled** is set to **true**, ignoring this key press. This method will only accept a typed value from 0 to 9. We are restricting our user to just those keys. This comes in handy in applications where only numerical input is allowed. Run the project. Try typing numbers. Try typing non-numerical values - nothing will appear in the text control, indicating the key press was ignored.

Project – Beach Balls

In our final class project, we will build a little video game. Colorful beach balls are dropping from the sky. You maneuver your popping device under them to make them pop and get a point. You try to pop as many balls as you can in one minute. This project is saved as **BeachBalls** in the projects folder (**\VCSEKids\VCSEK Projects**).

Project Design

All of the game action will go on in a panel control. There will be five possible balls, the image used is contained in a picture box. An picture box control will also hold the “popping arrow” image. This image will be moved using keys on the keyboard. A button will control starting and stopping the game. Another button will stop the program. The current score (number of balls popped) will be displayed in a titled text box.

Place Controls on Form

Start a new project in Visual C# Express. Place a panel control on the form - make it fairly wide and tall. This is where the game will be played. Place two picture box controls on the form. Add a label control. Add a text box under the label for keeping score. Add larger text box to tell us when the game is over. Add two buttons. And, add two timer controls to use for animation and for timing the overall game.

Try to make your form look something like this when done:

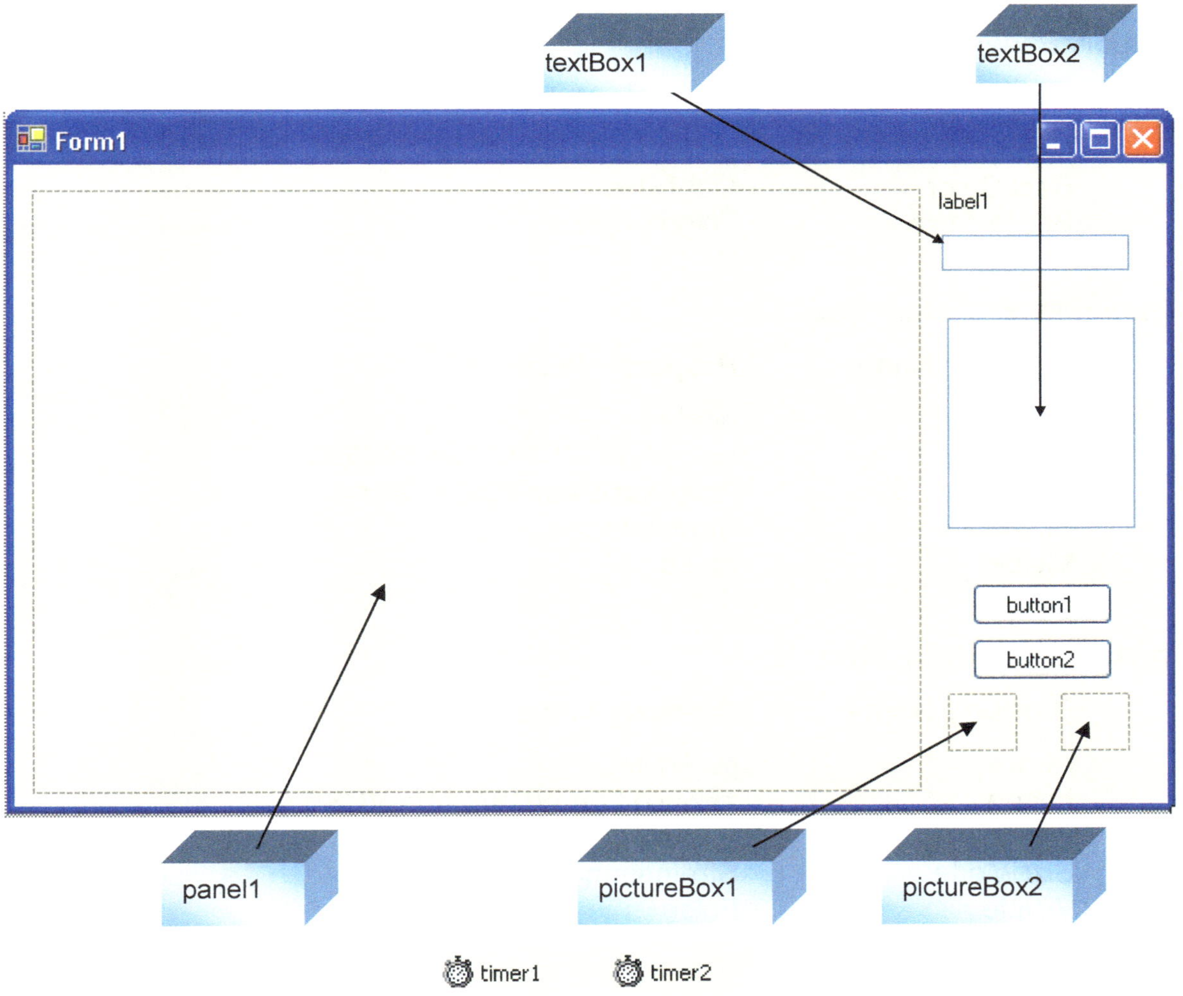

Set Control Properties

Set the control properties using the properties window:

Form1 Form:

Property Name	**Property Value**
BackColor	Light Red
Text	Beach Balls
FormBorderStyle	FixedSingle
StartPosition	CenterForm
KeyPreview	True (this allows us to detect key presses)

panel1 Panel:

Property Name	**Property Value**
Name	pnlBeachBalls
BackColor	Light Blue
BorderStyle	FixedSingle

pictureBox1 Picture Box:

Property Name	**Property Value**
Name	picBall
Image	ball.gif (in **\VCSEKids\VCSEK Projects\BeachBalls** folder)
SizeMode	StretchImage
Visible	False

pictureBox2 Picture Box:

Property Name	**Property Value**
Name	picArrow
Image	arrow.gif (in **\VCSEKids\VCSEK Projects\BeachBalls** folder)
SizeMode	StretchImage
Visible	False

label1 Label:

Property Name	Property Value
Name	lblHead
Text	Balls Popped
Font Size	10
Font Style	Bold

textBox1 Text Box:

Property Name	Property Value
Name	txtScore
Text	0
Font Size	18
ReadOnly	True
TabStop	False
TextAlign	Center
BackColor	White
ForeColor	Blue

textBox2 Text Box:

Property Name	Property Value
Name	txtOver
Text	Game Over
Font Size	18
ReadOnly	True
TabStop	False
TextAlign	Center
BackColor	White
ForeColor	Red

button1 Button:

Property Name	Property Value
Name	btnStart
BackColor	Light Yellow
Text	Start

button2 Button:

Property Name	**Property Value**
Name	btnExit
BackColor	Light Yellow
Text	Exit

timer1 Timer:

Property Name	**Property Value**
Name	timBalls
Interval	100

timer2 Timer:

Property Name	**Property Value**
Name	timGame
Interval	60000

When done setting properties, my form looks like this:

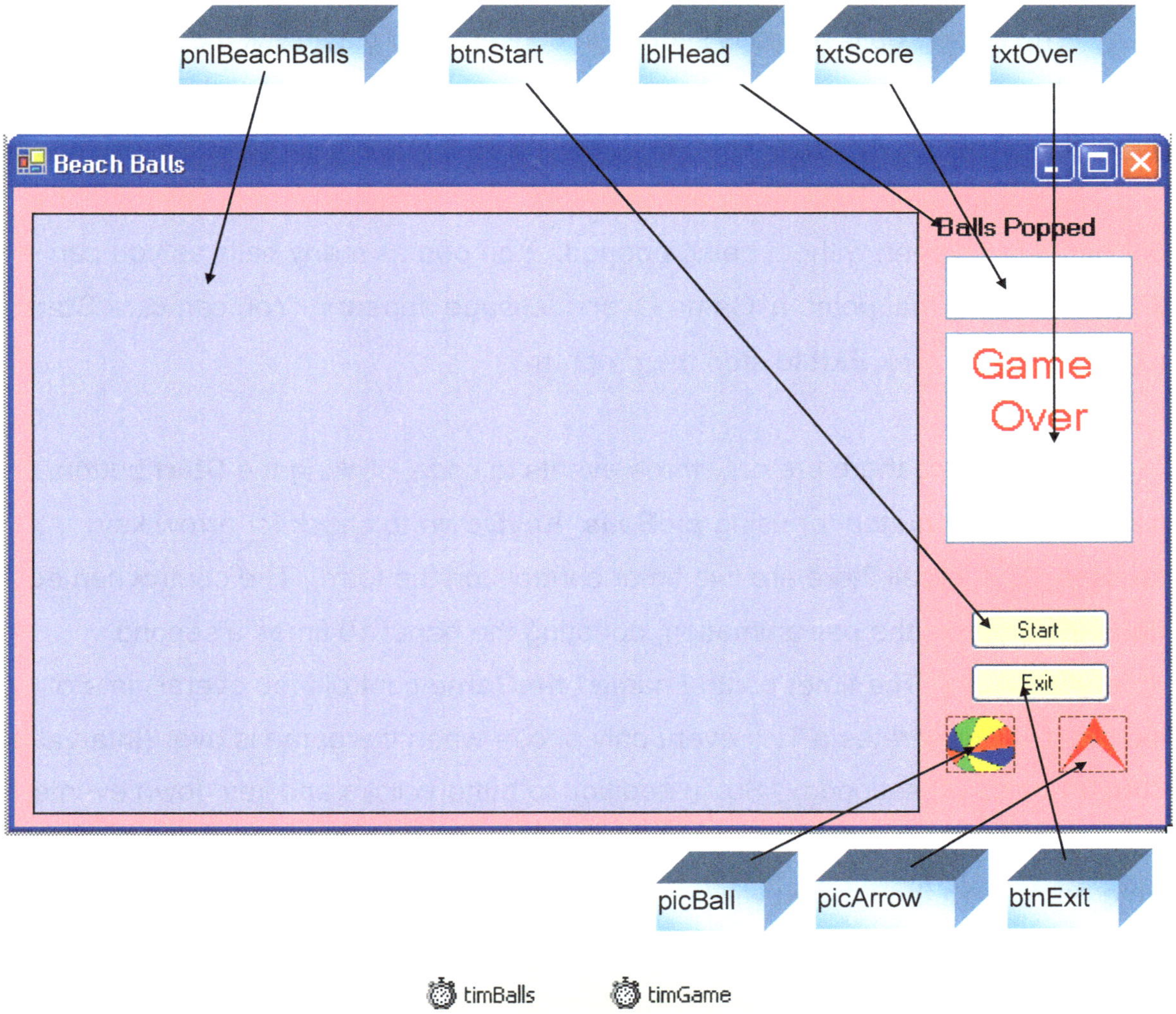

We have used **gif** files for our graphics (the ball and the arrow). With such graphics types, you can select one color to be transparent, allowing the background color to come through. How this is done is beyond the scope of this course. Do a little study on your own using paintbrush programs – PaintShop Pro by JASC (look on the Internet) is a great program for graphics.

Write Event methods

The Beach Balls game is simple, in concept. To play, click the **Start** button. Five balls will drop down the panel, each at a different speed. Use the keyboard to move the arrow. If the arrow is under a ball when a collision occurs, the ball pops and you get a point. Balls reappear at the top after popping or after reaching the bottom of the screen without being popped. You pop as many balls as you can in 60 seconds. At that point, a 'Game Over' message appears. You can click **Start** to play again or click **Exit** to stop the program.

It looks like there are only three events to code, clicking the **Start** button, clicking the **Exit** button, or using **picBalls_KeyDown** to check for arrow key presses. But, recall there are two timer controls on the form. The control named **timBalls** controls the ball animation, updating the panel 10 times a second (Interval is 100). The timer control named **timGame** controls the overall time of the game. It generates a Tick event only once - when the game is over (Interval is 60000 - that's 60 seconds). So, in addition to button clicks and key down events, we need code for two Timer events. There is a substantial amount of C# code to write here, even though you will see there is a lot of repetition. We suggest writing the event methods in stages. Write one method or a part of a method. Run the project. Make sure the code you wrote works. Add more code. Run the project again. Make sure the added code works. Continue adding code until complete. Building a project this way minimizes the potential for error and makes the debugging process much easier. Let's go.

Each ball will occupy a square region. We will compute the size (ballSize) of the ball to fit nicely on the panel. We need array variables to keep track of each ball's location (ballX, ballY) and dropping speed (ballSpeed). We need to know the arrow's size (arrowSize) and position (arrowX). We also need a graphics object to draw the balls (myGraphics) and a blank brush object (blankBrush, for erasing balls). Lastly, we need a random number object (myRandom). Add this code to the **general declarations** area:

```
int ballSize;
int[] ballX = new int[5];
int[] ballY = new int[5];
int[] ballSpeed = new int[5];
int arrowSize;
int arrowX;
Graphics myGraphics;
Brush blankBrush;
Random myRandom = new Random();
```

The array **ballSpeed** holds the five speeds, representing the number of pixels a ball will drop with each update of the viewing panel. We want each ball to drop at a different rate. In code, each speed will be computed using:

```
myRandom.Next(4) + 3
```

Or, it will be a random value between 3 and 6. A new speed will be computed each time a ball starts its trip down the panel. How do we know this will be a good speed, providing reasonable dropping rates? We didn't before the project began. This expression was arrived at by 'trial and error.' We built the game and tried different speeds until we found values that worked. You do this a lot in developing games. You may not know values for some numbers before you start. So, you go ahead and build the game and try all kinds of values until you find ones that work. Then, you build these numbers into your code.

Use this **Form1_Load** method:

```
private void Form1_Load(object sender, EventArgs e)
{
    int x;
    // Have the balls spread across the panel with 20 pixels
borders
    ballSize = (int) ((pnlBeachBalls.Width - 6 * 20) / 5);
    x = 10;
    for (int i = 0; i < 5; i++)
    {
        ballX[i] = x;
        x = x + ballSize + 20;
    }
    // Make arrow one-half the ball size
    arrowSize = (int) (ballSize / 2);
    myGraphics = pnlBeachBalls.CreateGraphics();
    blankBrush = new SolidBrush(pnlBeachBalls.BackColor);
    // Give form focus
    this.Focus();
}
```

In this code, initial horizontal positions for each of the balls are computed (ballX array). The balls are spread evenly across the panel (see if you can understand the code). The arrow is made to be one-half the ball size (arrowSize). Lastly, the graphics object and brush object are created and the form is given focus so KeyDown events can occur.

Add this code to the **Form1_FormClosing** event to dispose of our objects:

```
private void Form1_FormClosing(object sender,
FormClosingEventArgs e)
{
    myGraphics.Dispose();
    blankBrush.Dispose();
}
```

To move the arrow (using DrawImage), we need a **Form1_KeyDown** event method (the panel control does not have a KeyDown event). Make sure you have set the form's **KeyPreview** property to **True**, so the KeyDown event will be "seen." Pick a key that will move the arrow to the left and a key that will move it to the right. I chose **F** for **left** movement and **J** for **right** movement. Why? The keys are in the middle of the keyboard, with F to the left of J, and are easy to reach with a natural typing position. You could pick others. The arrow keys are one possibility. I hardly ever use these because they are always at some odd location on a keyboard and just not "naturally" reached. Also, the arrow keys are often used to move among controls on the form and this can get confusing. The code I use is (change the key code values if you pick different keys for arrow motion):

```
private void Form1_KeyDown(object sender, KeyEventArgs e)
{
    // Erase arrow at old location
    myGraphics.FillRectangle(blankBrush, arrowX,
pnlBeachBalls.Height - arrowSize, arrowSize, arrowSize);
    // Check for F key (left) and J key (right) and compute
arrow position
    if (e.KeyCode == Keys.F)
    {
        arrowX = arrowX - 5;
    }
    else if (e.KeyCode == Keys.J)
    {
        arrowX = arrowX + 5;
    }
    // Position arrow
    myGraphics.DrawImage(picArrow.Image, arrowX,
pnlBeachBalls.Height - arrowSize, arrowSize, arrowSize);
}
```

Notice if the F key is pressed, the arrow (**imgArrow**) is moved to the left by 5 pixels. The arrow is moved right by 5 pixels if the J key is pressed. Again, the 5 pixels value was found by 'trial and error' - it seems to provide smooth motion. After typing in this method, save the project, then run it. Make sure the arrow moves as expected. Press the J key to see it. It should start at the left side of the form (arrowX = 0) since we have not given it an initial position. This is what we meant when we suggested building the project in stages. Notice there is no code that keeps the arrow from moving out of the panel - you could add it if you like. You would need to detect a left or right border crossing. Stop the project. Now, let's do the button events.

The **btnExit_Click** method is simple, so let's get it out of the way first. It's the usual one line (well, two with the comment) that stops the project:

```
private void btnExit_Click(object sender, EventArgs e)
{
    this.Close();
}
```

Let's outline the steps involved in the **btnStart_Click** event. We use this button for two purposes. It either starts the game (**Text** is **Start**) or stops the game (but, not the program - **Text** is **Stop**). So, the Click event has two segments. If Text is Start, the steps are:

- Hide 'Game Over' message
- Set btnStart Text to "Stop"
- Disable btnExit button
- Clear balls off screen
- Set score to 0
- Initialize each ball's position and speed
- Initialize arrow position
- Give form focus (so KeyDown can be recognized)
- Start the timers

If the Text is Stop when the button is clicked, the program steps are:

- Display 'Game Over' message
- Set btnStart Text to "Start"
- Enable btnExit button
- Stop the timers

Look at the **btnStart_Click** event method and see if you can identify all of the outlined steps. Notice the balls are positioned just above the panel and the speeds are set using the formula given earlier:

```
private void btnStart_Click(object sender, EventArgs e)
{
    if (btnStart.Text == "Start")
    {
        // New Game
        myGraphics.Clear(pnlBeachBalls.BackColor);
        txtOver.Visible = false;
        btnStart.Text = "Stop";
        btnExit.Enabled = false;
        txtScore.Text = "0";
        // set each ball off top of panel and give new speed
        for (int i = 0; i < 5; i++)
        {
            ballY[i] = -ballSize;
            ballSpeed[i] = myRandom.Next(4) + 3;
        }
        // Set arrow near center
        arrowX = (int)(pnlBeachBalls.Width / 2);
        myGraphics.DrawImage(picArrow.Image, arrowX,
pnlBeachBalls.Height - arrowSize, arrowSize, arrowSize);
        // Give form focus so it can accept KeyDown events
        this.Focus();
    }
    else
    {
        // Game stopped
        txtOver.Visible = true;
        btnStart.Text = "Start";
        btnExit.Enabled = true;
```

```
    }
    // Toggle timers
    timBalls.Enabled = !(timBalls.Enabled);
    timGame.Enabled = !(timGame.Enabled);
}
```

Save and run the project. There should be no balls displayed. Make sure you get no run-time errors. The arrow should be centered on the panel. Make sure the arrow motion keys (F and J) still work OK. Stop the project.

The **btnStart_Click** event method toggles the two timer controls. What goes on in the two Tick events? We'll do the easy one first. Each game lasts 60 seconds. This timing is handled by the timGame timer. It has an Interval of 60000, which means it's Tick event is executed every 60 seconds. We'll only execute that event once - when it is executed, we stop the game. The code to do this is identical to the code executed if the btnStart button is clicked when its Text is **Stop**. The **timGame_Tick** event method should be:

```
private void timGame_Tick(object sender, EventArgs e)
{
    // 60 seconds have elapsed - stop game
    timBalls.Enabled = false;
    timGame.Enabled = false;
    txtOver.Visible = true;
    btnStart.Text = "Start";
    btnExit.Enabled = true;
}
```

Save the project. Run it. Click **Start**. Play with the arrow motion keys or just sit there. After 60 seconds, you should see the 'Game Over' notice pop up and see the buttons change appearance. If this happens, the timGame timer control is working properly. If it doesn't happen, you need to fix something. Stop the project.

Now, to the heart of the Beach Balls game - the **timBalls_Tick** event. We haven't seen any dropping balls yet. Here's where we do that, and more. The timBalls timer control handles the animation sequence. It drops the balls down the screen, checks for popping, and checks for balls reaching the bottom of the panel. It gets new balls started. There's a lot going on. The method steps are identical for each ball. They are:

- Move the ball.
- Check to see if ball has popped. If so, sound a beep, make the ball disappear, increment score and make ball reappear at the top with a new speed.
- Check to see if ball has reached the bottom without being popped. If so, start a new ball with a new speed.

The steps are easy to write, just a little harder to code. Moving a ball simply involves erasing it at its old location and redrawing it at its new location (determined by the ballY value). To check if the ball has reached the bottom, we use the border crossing logic discussed earlier. The trickiest step is checking if a ball has popped. One way to check for a ball pop is to check to see if the ball image rectangle overlaps the arrow rectangle using the collision detection logic developed earlier. This would work, but a ball would pop if the arrow barely touched the ball. In our code, we modify the collision logic such that we will not consider a ball to be popped unless the <u>entire</u> width of the arrow is within the width of the ball.

Here's the complete **timBall_Tick** event implementing these steps. The balls are handled individually within the structure of a for loop:

```
private void timBalls_Tick(object sender, EventArgs e)
{
    for (int i = 0; i < 5; i++)
    {
        // erase ball
        myGraphics.FillRectangle(blankBrush, ballX[i],
ballY[i], ballSize, ballSize);
        // move ball
        ballY[i] = ballY[i] + ballSpeed[i];
        // check if ball has popped
        if ((ballY[i] + ballSize) > (pnlBeachBalls.Height -
arrowSize))
        {
            if (ballX[i] < arrowX)
            {
                if ((ballX[i] + ballSize) > (arrowX +
arrowSize))
                {
                    // Ball has popped
                    // Increase score - move back to top
                    System.Media.SystemSounds.Beep.Play();
                    txtScore.Text =
Convert.ToString(Convert.ToInt32(txtScore.Text) + 1);
                    ballY[i] = -ballSize;
                    ballSpeed[i] = myRandom.Next(4) + 3;
                }
            }
        }
        // check for moving off bottom
        if ((ballY[i] + ballSize) > pnlBeachBalls.Height)
        {
            // Ball reaches bottom without popping
            // Move back to top with new speed
            ballY[i] = -ballSize;
            ballSpeed[i] = myRandom.Next(4) + 3;
        }
        // redraw ball at new location
        myGraphics.DrawImage(picBall.Image, ballX[i],
ballY[i], ballSize, ballSize);
    }
}
```

Do you see how all the steps are implemented? We added a Beep statement for some audio feedback when a ball pops.

Run the Project

Run the project. Make sure it works. Make sure each ball falls. Make sure when a ball reaches the bottom, a new one is initialized. Make sure you can pop each ball. And, following a pop, make sure a new ball appears. Make sure the score changes by one with each pop. Here's what my screen looks like in the middle of a game:

By building and testing the program in stages, you should now have a thoroughly tested, running version of Beach Balls. So relax and have fun playing it. Show your friends and family your great creation. If you do find any bugs and need to make any changes, make sure you resave your project.

Other Things to Try

I'm sure as you played the Beach Balls game, you thought of some changes you could make. Go ahead - give it a try! Here are some ideas we have.

When a ball pops, it just disappears from the screen. Can you think of a more dramatic way to show popping? Maybe change the Image property of the picture box control. Or flash the panel background color.

Add selectable difficulty levels to the game. This could be used to make the game easy for little kids and very hard for experts. What can you do to adjust the game difficulty? One thing you could do is adjust the size of the popping arrow. To pop a ball, the entire arrow width must fit within the width of a ball. Hence, a smaller (narrower) arrow would make it easier to pop balls before they reach the bottom of the picture box. A larger (wider) arrow makes popping harder. The ball dropping speed also affects game difficulty. Slowly dropping balls are easy to pop - fast ones are not. Play with the game to see what speeds would work for different difficulty levels.

Make it possible to play longer games and, as the game goes on, make the game more difficult using some of the ideas above (smaller arrow, faster balls). You've seen this in other games you may have played - games usually get harder as time goes on.

Players like to know how much time they have left in a game. Add this capability to your game. Use a text box control to display the number of seconds remaining. You'll need another timer control with an Interval of 1000 (one second). Whenever this timer's Tick event is executed, another second has gone by. In this event, subtract 1 from the value displayed in the label. You should be comfortable making such a change to your project.

Another thing players like to know is the highest score on a game. Add this capability. Declare a new variable to keep track of the highest score. After each game is played, compare the current score with the highest score to see if a new high has been reached. Add a text box control to display the highest score. One problem, though. When you stop the program, the highest score value will be lost. A new high needs to be established each time you run the project. As you become a more advanced Visual C# Express programmer, you'll learn ways to save the highest score.

In this final class, we found that the timer control is a key element in computer animation. By periodically changing the display in a panel control, the sensation of motion was obtained. We studied "animation math" - how to detect if an image disappeared from a panel, how to detect if an image crosses the border of a panel, and how to detect if two images (rectangles) collide. We learned how to detect keyboard events. And, you built your first video game.

The **Visual C# Express for Kids** class is over. You've come a long way. Remember back in the first class when you first learned about events? You're an event expert by now. But, that doesn't mean you know everything there is to know about programming. Computer programming is a never-ending educational process. There are always new things to learn - ways to improve your skills. Believe it or not, you've just begun learning about Visual C# Express.

Our company, Kidware Software, offers several intermediate and advanced Visual C# Express courses that cover more advanced topics and lets you build more projects- **Programming Games With Visual C# Express, Programming Home Projects With Visual C# Express, Learn Visual C# and Visual C# and Databases**. These courses are all self-paced study guides that provide an overview of Visual C# and more detailed programming instructions. Fun projects are built with step-by-step details. What would you gain from these courses? Here are a few new things you would learn:

- More C# and more controls
- How to do many programming tasks using Visual C# Express
- Object-oriented programming concepts
- How to distribute your projects (develop SETUP programs)
- How to use the Visual C# Express debugger
- How to read files from disk and write files to disk (this could be used to save high scores in games)
- How to do more detailed animations
- How to play elaborate sounds (the Beep is pretty boring)
- How to add menus and toolbars to your projects
- How to use your printer
- Lastly, you will have many practical projects you can use (or modify).

Contact us if you want more information about these self-study courses. Or, visit our website at the address that is shown on the title page for this course. Before you leave, try the bonus projects. They give you some idea of what you can learn in the next Visual C# Express class.

Bonus Projects

Preview

By now, you should feel pretty comfortable with the steps involved in building a Visual C# Express project. In this bonus chapter, we give you more projects you can build and try. We'll present the steps involved in building each project - **Project Design**, **Place Controls on Form**, **Set Control Properties**, **Write Event methods**, **Run the Project**, and **Other Things to Try**. But, we won't give you detailed discussion of what's going on in the code (we will point out new ideas). You should be able to figure that out by now (with the help of the code comments). Actually, a very valuable programming skill to have is the ability to read and understand someone else's code.

The five new projects included are: Computer Stopwatch, Tic-Tac-Toe, Dice Rolling, State Capitals, and Memory Game. And, as another bonus, we'll throw in a Visual C# Express version of the first video game ever – Pong!

Project 1 - Computer Stopwatch

Project Design

In this project, we will build a computer stopwatch that measures elapsed time in seconds. One button will start and stop the timing and one will reset the display (a label). Elapsed time is measured using the C# **Now** function that provides the current time and date in a **Date** type function. The project you are about to build is saved as **Stopwatch** in the project folder (**\VCSEKids\VCSEK Projects**).

Place Controls on Form

Start a new project in Visual C# Express. Place a text box control on the form. Then place two buttons on the form. Add a timer control. When done, your form should look something like this:

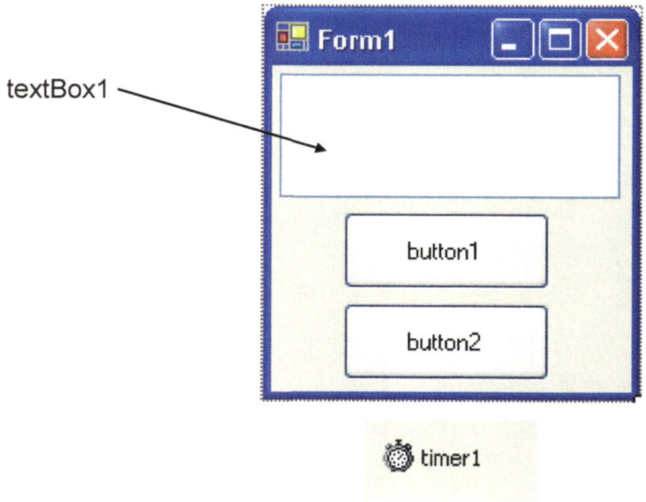

Set Control Properties

Set the control properties using the properties window:

Form1 Form:

Property Name	Property Value
Text	Stopwatch
FormBorderStyle	Fixed Single
StartPosition	CenterScreen

textBox1 Text Box:

Property Name	Property Value
Name	txtTime
Text	00:00:00
BackColor	White
Font	Arial
Font Size	24
Font Style	Bold
ReadOnly	True
TextAlign	Center
TabStop	False

button1 Button:

Property Name	Property Value
Name	btnStartStop
Text	Start
Font	Arial
Font Size	12

button2 Command Button:

Property Name	Property Value
Name	btnReset
Text	Reset
Enabled	False
Font	Arial
Font Size	12

timer1 Timer:

Property Name	**Property Value**
Name	timDisplay
Interval	1000

When done setting properties, my form looks like this (I resized the text box a bit):

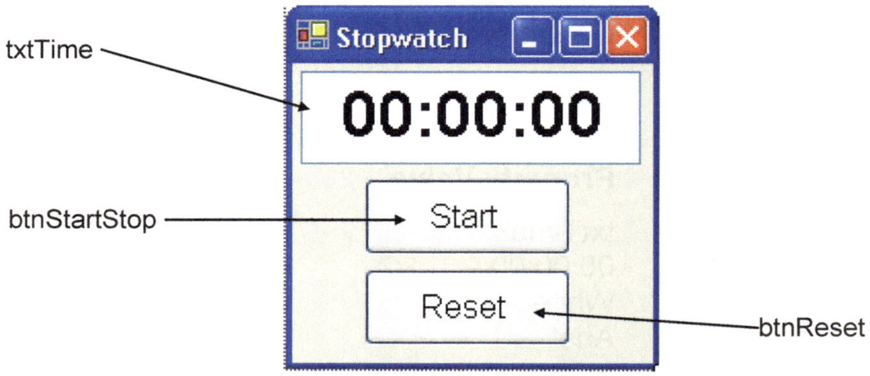

Write Event methods

To start the stopwatch, click **Start**. To stop, click **Stop**. Click **Reset** to reset the display to zero. Each of these buttons has a **Click** event. The timer control **Tick** event controls the display of the time.

Add this code to the **general declarations** area:

```
DateTime startTime;  // time when stopwatch started
```

The **btnStartStop_Click** event method:

```
private void btnStartStop_Click(object sender, EventArgs e)
{
    // Starting timer?
    if (btnStartStop.Text == "Start")
    {
        // Reset Text on Start/Stop button
        btnStartStop.Text = "Stop";
        // Start timer and get starting time
        timDisplay.Enabled = true;
        startTime = DateTime.Now;
    }
    else
    {
        // Stop timer
        timDisplay.Enabled = false;
        // Disable Start/Stop button, enable Reset button
        btnStartStop.Enabled = false;
        btnReset.Enabled = true;
    }
}
```

The **btnReset_Click** event method:

```
private void btnReset_Click(object sender, EventArgs e)
{
    // Reset display to zero
    txtTime.Text = "00:00:00";
    // Reset button Text and enable Start, disable Reset
    btnStartStop.Text = "Start";
    btnStartStop.Enabled = true;
    btnReset.Enabled = false;
}
```

The **timDisplay_Tick** event method:

```
private void timDisplay_Tick(object sender, EventArgs e)
{
    TimeSpan elapsedTime;
    // Determine elapsed time since Start was clicked
    elapsedTime = DateTime.Now - startTime;
    // Display time in label box
    txtTime.Text = Convert.ToString(elapsedTime);
}
```

Run the Project

Save your work. Run the project. Click **Start** to start the timer. Make sure the display updates every second. Here's a run I made:

Study the Tick event if you're unsure of how this is done – especially look at how to subtract two date (**DateTime**) types (using the C# **TimeSpan** type) to get the elapsed time. Click **Stop** to stop the timer. Make sure the **Reset** button works properly.

Other Things to Try

Many stopwatches allow you to continue timing after you've stopped one or more times. That is, you can measure total elapsed time in different segments. Modify this project to allow such measurement. You'll need a separate Stop button and a variable to keep track of total elapsed time. You'll also need to determine which buttons you want to have enabled at different times in the project. Add a "lap timing" feature by displaying the time measured in each segment (a segment being defined as the time between each Start and Stop click).

Project 2 - Tic-Tac-Toe

Project Design

In this project, you build a form where you and someone else can play the classic Tic-Tac-Toe game against each other. You take turns marking a 3 x 3 grid with X's and O's. The computer will monitor play. The project you are about to build is saved as **TicTacToe** in the project folder (**\VCSEKids\VCSEK Projects**).

Place Controls on Form

Start a new project in Visual C# Express. Place one larger text box (textBox1), four very skinny text box controls (textBox2 - textBox5) to be used for the game grid), nine square text box controls (textBox6 – textBox14), and two buttons on the form. When done, your form should look something like this:

Set Control Properties

Set the control properties using the properties window:

Form1 Form:

Property Name	Property Value
Text	Tic-Tac-Toe
FormBorderStyle	FixedSingle
StartPosition	CenterScreen

textBox1 TextBox:

Property Name	Property Value
Name	txtMessage
Text	X's Turn
BackColor	White
Font	Arial
Font Size	24
TextAlign	Center
ReadOnly	True
TabStop	False

textBox2 Text Box:

Property Name	Property Value
BackColor	Black
ReadOnly	True
TabStop	False

textBox3 Text Box:

Property Name	Property Value
BackColor	Black
ReadOnly	True
TabStop	False

textBox4 Text Box:

Property Name	Property Value
BackColor	Black
ReadOnly	True
TabStop	False

textBox5 Text Box:

Property Name	Property Value
BackColor	Black
ReadOnly	True
TabStop	False

textBox6 Text Box:

Property Name	Property Value
Name	txtTopLeft
ForeColor	Blue
Font	Comic Sans MS
Font Style	Bold
Font Size	28
TextAlign	Center
ReadOnly	True
TabStop	False

textBox7 Text Box:

Property Name	Property Value
Name	txtTopMiddle
ForeColor	Blue
Font	Comic Sans MS
Font Style	Bold
Font Size	28
TextAlign	Center
ReadOnly	True
TabStop	False

textBox8 Text Box:

Property Name	**Property Value**
Name	txtTopRight
ForeColor	Blue
Font	Comic Sans MS
Font Style	Bold
Font Size	28
TextAlign	Center
ReadOnly	True
TabStop	False

textBox9 Text Box:

Property Name	**Property Value**
Name	txtMiddleLeft
ForeColor	Blue
Font	Comic Sans MS
Font Style	Bold
Font Size	28
TextAlign	Center
ReadOnly	True
TabStop	False

textBox10 Text Box:

Property Name	**Property Value**
Name	txtMiddleMiddle
ForeColor	Blue
Font	Comic Sans MS
Font Style	Bold
Font Size	28
TextAlign	Center
ReadOnly	True
TabStop	False

textBox11 Text Box:

Property Name	**Property Value**
Name	txtMiddleRight
ForeColor	Blue
Font	Comic Sans MS
Font Style	Bold
Font Size	28
TextAlign	Center
ReadOnly	True
TabStop	False

textBox12 Text Box:

Property Name	**Property Value**
Name	txtBottomLeft
ForeColor	Blue
Font	Comic Sans MS
Font Style	Bold
Font Size	28
TextAlign	Center
ReadOnly	True
TabStop	False

textBox13 Text Box:

Property Name	**Property Value**
Name	txtBottomMiddle
ForeColor	Blue
Font	Comic Sans MS
Font Style	Bold
Font Size	28
TextAlign	Center
ReadOnly	True
TabStop	False

textBox14 Text Box:

Property Name	Property Value
Name	txtBottomRight
ForeColor	Blue
Font	Comic Sans MS
Font Style	Bold
Font Size	28
TextAlign	Center
ReadOnly	True
TabStop	False

button1 Button:

Property Name	Property Value
Name	btnReset
Text	Reset Game

button2 Button:

Property Name	Property Value
Name	btnMark

Now, resize the form so the second button (**btnMark**) does not appear on the form – you'll see why when we discuss coding. When done setting properties, my form looks like this:

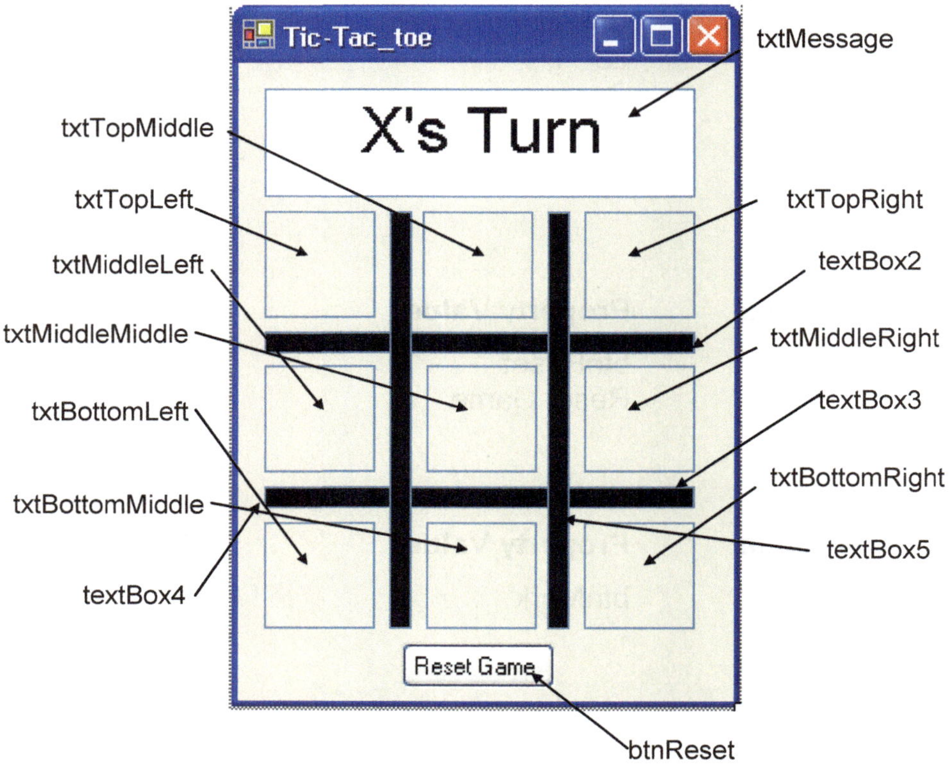

Notice how the "skinny text boxes" form the playing grid.

Write Event methods

We need **Click** event methods for each of the text boxes where the X's and O's will be drawn. And, we need a **Click** event for the **Reset** button.

Add this code to the **general declarations** area:

```
bool xTurn; // if true, it's X's turn
TextBox squareClicked;  // tells which text box is clicked
```

Use this in the **Form1_Load** event to initialize the XTurn variable:

```
private void Form1_Load(object sender, EventArgs e)
{
    // make it X's turn
    xTurn = true;
}
```

The **btnReset_Click** event method clears the grid and starts another game:

```
private void btnReset_Click(object sender, EventArgs e)
{
    // Clear board
    txtTopLeft.Text = "";
    txtTopMiddle.Text = "";
    txtTopRight.Text = "";
    txtMiddleLeft.Text = "";
    txtMiddleMiddle.Text = "";
    txtMiddleRight.Text = "";
    txtBottomLeft.Text = "";
    txtBottomMiddle.Text = "";
    txtBottomRight.Text = "";
    // Make it X's turn
    xTurn = true;
    txtMessage.Text = "X's Turn";
}
```

Whenever one of the nine text box controls is clicked, we need to first make sure there is no mark there yet. If there is no mark, we decide whether to place an X or an O in the space. Then, we make it the other player's turn. Notice you would need essentially the same code in nine different text box **Click** events. I don't think you want to write lots of duplicate code. We'll create what is known as a **general method** (one not directly accessible to the user through some event) to do this check. We'll do this with the "hidden" button we placed on the form named **btnMark**. In this button's **Click** event, we write the code to go through the marking method. Then, each time a text box is clicked, we will go to this general method to do the marking. The form level variable (a **TextBox** type) **squareClicked** tells us which particular text box control has been clicked and should be marked.

For our problem, the **btnMark_Click** event method is:

```
private void btnMark_Click(object sender, EventArgs e)
{
    // Place mark in SquareClicked (if none there already)
    if (squareClicked.Text == "")
    {
        if (xTurn)
        {
            squareClicked.Text = "X";
            xTurn = false;
            txtMessage.Text = "O's Turn";
        }
        else
        {
            squareClicked.Text = "O";
            xTurn = true;
            txtMessage.Text = "X's Turn";
        }
    }
}
```

Now that we have the **btnMark_Click** method, how and when do we access it? It's simple. In each text box **Click** event, we will identify which text box has been clicked (using SquareClicked) and then add this single line of code:

```
btnMark.PerformClick();
```

This code simulates clicking our hidden button and the general method code is executed. Pretty neat, huh?

The code for each text box control's **Click** event is straightforward:

```
private void txtTopLeft_Click(object sender, EventArgs e)
{
    squareClicked = txtTopLeft;
    btnMark.PerformClick();
}

private void txtTopMiddle_Click(object sender, EventArgs e)
{
    squareClicked = txtTopMiddle;
    btnMark.PerformClick();
}

private void txtTopRight_Click(object sender, EventArgs e)
{
    squareClicked = txtTopRight;
    btnMark.PerformClick();
}

private void txtMiddleLeft_Click(object sender, EventArgs e)
{
    squareClicked = txtMiddleLeft;
    btnMark.PerformClick();
}

private void txtMiddleMiddle_Click(object sender, EventArgs
e)
{
    squareClicked = txtMiddleMiddle;
    btnMark.PerformClick();
}

private void txtMiddleRight_Click(object sender, EventArgs e)
{
    squareClicked = txtMiddleRight;
    btnMark.PerformClick();
}
```

```
private void txtBottomLeft_Click(object sender, EventArgs e)
{
    squareClicked = txtBottomLeft;
    btnMark.PerformClick();
}

private void txtBottomMiddle_Click(object sender, EventArgs
e)
{
    squareClicked = txtBottomMiddle;
    btnMark.PerformClick();
}

private void txtBottomRight_Click(object sender, EventArgs e)
{
    squareClicked = txtBottomRight;
    btnMark.PerformClick();
}
```

Run the Project

Save your work. Run the project. Playing the game is obvious. X goes first and clicks the desired square. Then, it's O's turn. Alternate turns until there is a winner or the grid is full without a winner (a tie). Click **Reset** at any time to start a new game. Here's the middle of a game I tried:

Other Things to Try

Two adaptations to this project jump out. First, there is no logic to detect a win. The players must look at the grid and decide if someone has won. See if you can add logic to check if there is a winner after each move. The code would be added at the end of the existing **btnMark_Click** general method. This code would see if the symbols in the three horizontal directions, three vertical directions or two diagonal directions are the same. If so, a win is declared and the game is stopped.

The second modification (a much tougher one) would be to program the computer to play the game against a human player. You could let the computer have either X's or O's and use some kind of logic (maybe even just random moves for a simple minded computer) for the computer to use in generating moves. You would probably want another **general method** to compute the computer moves. This is one of the first games ever programmed by little Billy Gates!

Project 3 – Dice Rolling

Project Design

It happens all the time. You get your favorite game out and the dice are missing! This program comes to the rescue – it uses the C# random number generator to roll two dice for you. Simply click a button to see the two dice displayed. A group of picture box controls will hold the six possible die values. This project is saved as **DiceRoll** in the project folder (**\VCSEKids\VCSEK Projects**).

Place Controls on Form

Start a new project in Visual C# Express. Place two large picture box controls (to display the dice) and six small picture box controls (to hold the six possible die pictures) on the form. Place one button on the form. When done, you form should resemble this:

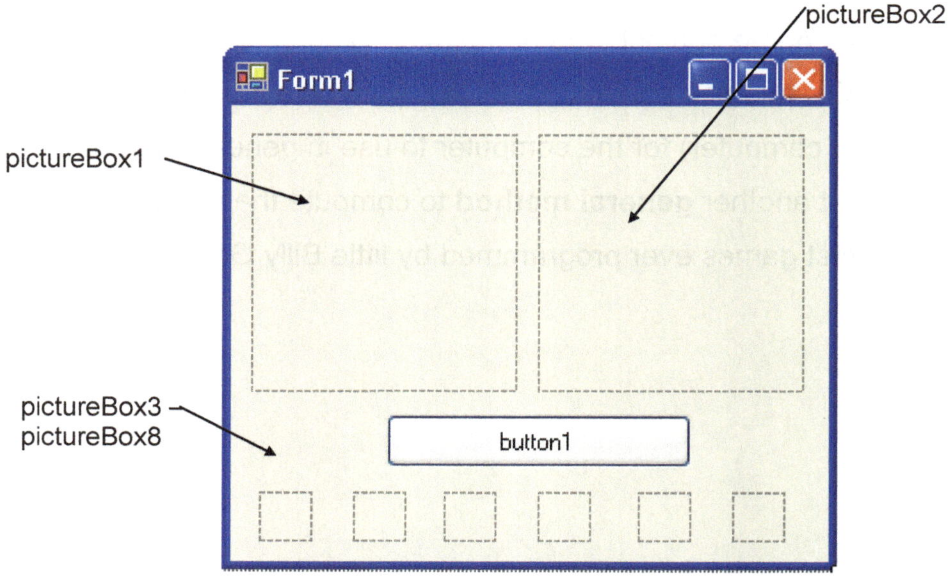

Set Control Properties

Set the control properties using the properties window:

Form1 Form:

Property Name	**Property Value**
Text	Dice Rolling
BackColor	Red
FormBorderStyle	FixedSingle
StartPosition	CenterScreen

pictureBox1 Picture Box:

Property Name	**Property Value**
Name	picDice1
SizeMode	StretchImage

pictureBox2 Picture Box:

Property Name	**Property Value**
Name	picDice2
SizeMode	StretchImage

pictureBox3 Picture Box:

Property Name	**Property Value**
Name	picDots1
Image	Dice1.gif (in **\VCSEKids\VCSEK Projects\DiceRoll** folder)
SizeMode	StretchImage
Visible	False

pictureBox4 Picture Box:

Property Name	Property Value
Name	picDots2
Image	Dice2.gif (in **\VCSEKids\VCSEK Projects\DiceRoll** folder)
SizeMode	StretchImage
Visible	False

pictureBox5 Picture Box:

Property Name	Property Value
Name	picDots3
Image	Dice3.gif (in **\VCSEKids\VCSEK Projects\DiceRoll** folder)
SizeMode	StretchImage
Visible	False

pictureBox6 Picture Box:

Property Name	Property Value
Name	picDots4
Image	Dice4.gif (in **\VCSEKids\VCSEK Projects\DiceRoll** folder)
SizeMode	StretchImage
Visible	False

pictureBox7 Picture Box:

Property Name	Property Value
Name	picDots5
Image	Dice5.gif (in **\VCSEKids\VCSEK Projects\DiceRoll** folder)
SizeMode	StretchImage
Visible	False

pictureBox8 Picture Box:

Property Name	Property Value
Name	picDots6
Image	Dice6.gif (in **\VCSEKids\VCSEK Projects\DiceRoll** folder)
SizeMode	StretchImage
Visible	False

button1 Button:

Property Name	Property Value
Name	btnRoll
Text	Roll Dice

When, done my form looks like this:

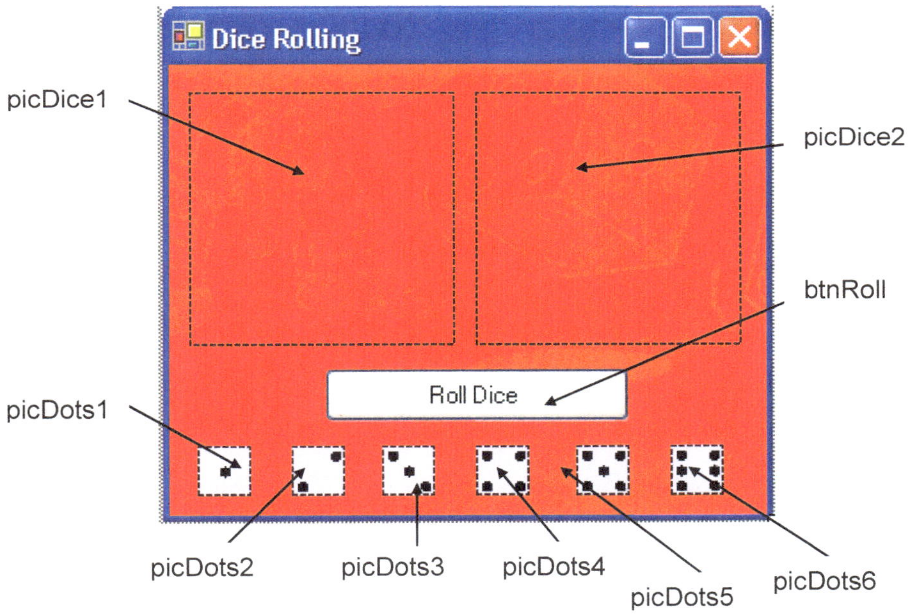

Notice we use two sets of picture boxes. The first, picDice1 and picDice2, is used to display the two dice. The second, picDots1 – picDots6, is used to store the six possible die pictures. This second group has a Visible property of False. Hence, you only see them displayed at design time.

Write Event methods

To roll the dice, simply click **Roll Dice**.

Declare an array of images (named **dots**) in the **general declarations** area. This array will be used to choose which of the six possible images to display. You also need a random number object:

```
Image[] dots = new Image[6];
Random myRandom = new Random();
```

Add this code to the **Form1_Load** event. Here, we establish the image array and 'click' the **btnRoll** button to 'roll' the dice before the display is activated:

```
private void Form1_Load(object sender, EventArgs e)
{
    // initialize display
    dots[0] = picDots1.Image;
    dots[1] = picDots2.Image;
    dots[2] = picDots3.Image;
    dots[3] = picDots4.Image;
    dots[4] = picDots5.Image;
    dots[5] = picDots6.Image;
    btnRoll.PerformClick();
}
```

The **btnRoll_Click** event method:

```
private void btnRoll_Click(object sender, EventArgs e)
{
    // Roll Dice 1 and set display
    picDice1.Image = dots[myRandom.Next(6)];
    // Roll Dice 2 and set display
    picDice2.Image = dots[myRandom.Next(6)];
}
```

Run the Project

Save your work. Run the project. Click **Roll Dice** to see the dice change with each click. Look at the code to see how the random number (1 through 6) is generated and how the image array (**Dots**) sets the display. Here's one of my rolls:

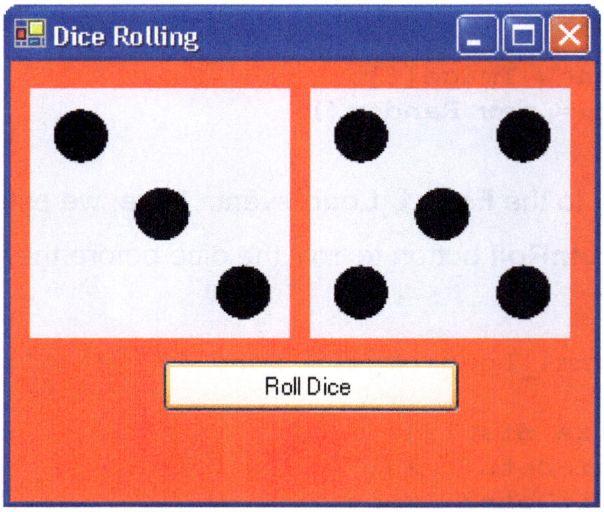

Other Things to Try

The game of Yahtzee requires 5 dice. Modify the project to roll and display five dice. Or, let the user decide how many dice to display (you could more 'display' picture boxes and use the **Visible** property to specify whether a particular die is displayed). Add a label control that displays the sum of the displayed dice.

A fun change would be to have the die displays updated by a **Timer** control to give the appearance of rolling dice. You would need a Timer control for each die (every 100 milliseconds or so, randomly display from 1 to 6 dots). And, then you would need a Timer control to stop the 'rolling' (use an **Interval** of about 2000 milliseconds). The **btnRoll** button would control enabling on the Timer controls. All Timer controls are turned off (Enabled is set to false) by the Timer event that stops the rolling.

Project 4 – State Capitals

Project Design

In this project, we build a fun game for home and school. You will be given the name of a state in the United States and four possible choices for its capital city. You click on the guess of your choice to see if you are right. (We apologize to our foreign readers – perhaps you can modify this project to build a similar multiple choice type game). Click on **Next State** for another question. This project is saved as **StateCapitals** in the project folder (**\VCSEKids\VCSEK Projects**).

Place Controls on Form

Start a new project in Visual C# Express. Place two label controls, five text boxes and two buttons on the form. When done, you form should resemble this:

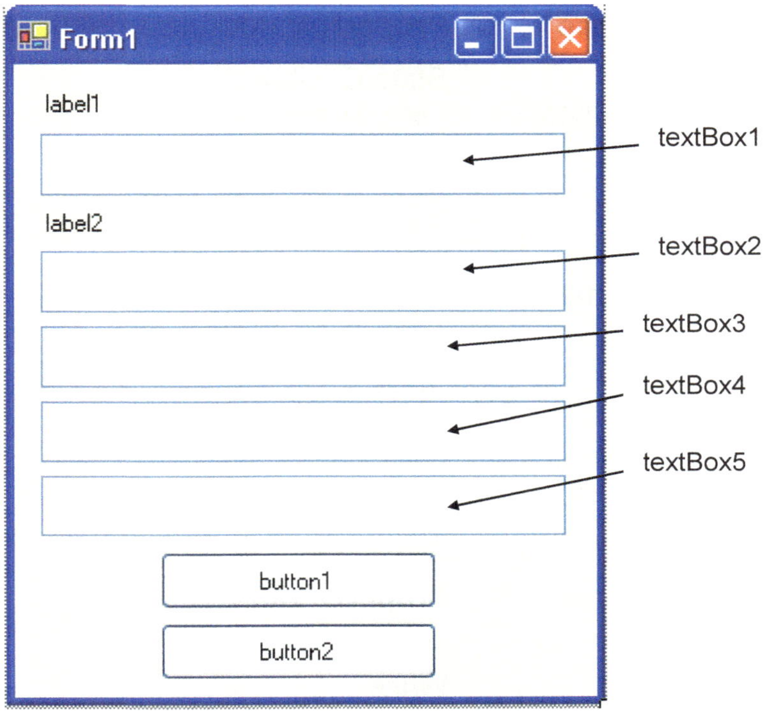

Set Control Properties

Set the control properties using the properties window:

Form1 Form:

Property Name	**Property Value**
Text	State Capitals
FormBorderStyle	FixedSingle
StartPosition	CenterScreen

label1 Label:

Property Name	**Property Value**
Name	lblHeadState
Text	State:
Font Size	14
Font Style	Italic

textBox1 Text Box:

Property Name	**Property Value**
Name	txtState
BackColor	White
Font Size	14
ReadOnly	True
TextAlign	Center
TabStop	False

label2 Label:

Property Name	**Property Value**
Name	lblHeadCapital
Text	Capital:
Font Size	14
Font Style	Italic

textBox2 Text Box:

Property Name	**Property Value**
Name	txtCapital0
BackColor	White
Font Size	14
ReadOnly	True
TextAlign	Center
TabStop	False

textBox3 Text Box:

Property Name	**Property Value**
Name	txtCapital1
BackColor	White
Font Size	14
ReadOnly	True
TextAlign	Center
TabStop	False

textBox4 Text Box:

Property Name	**Property Value**
Name	txtCapital2
BackColor	White
Font Size	14
ReadOnly	True
TextAlign	Center
TabStop	False

textBox5 Text Box:

Property Name	**Property Value**
Name	txtCapita3
BackColor	White
Font Size	14
ReadOnly	True
TextAlign	Center
TabStop	False

button1 Button:

Property Name	**Property Value**
Name	btnNext
Text	Next State

button2 Button:

Property Name	**Property Value**
Name	btnCheck

Resize the form so **btnCheck** does not appear (we'll use this as a general method button). When done, the form looks like this :

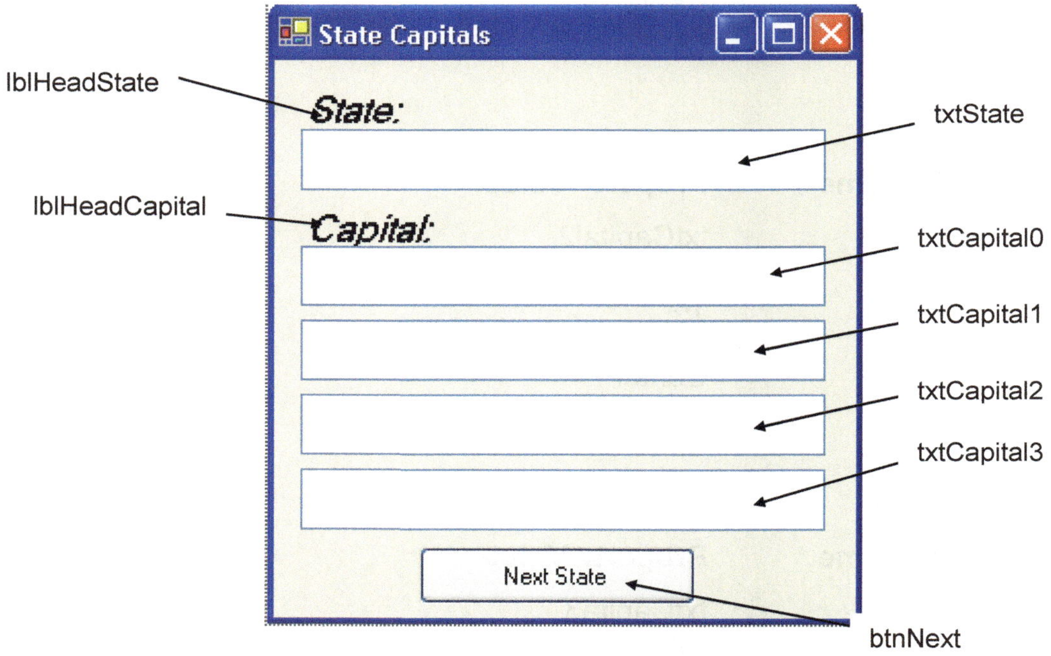

Write Event methods

To display a state and possible capitals, click **Next State**. Click on your choice for answer.

Put this code in the general declarations area:

```
int answer;
string[] state = new string[50];
string[] capital = new string[50];
TextBox[] listedCapital = new TextBox[4];
int capitalClicked;
Random myRandom = new Random();
```

Add this code to the **Form1_Load** event (yes, it's a lot of typing or just copy and paste from these notes):

```
private void Form1_Load(object sender, EventArgs e)
{
    // load state and capital arrays
    state[0] = "Alabama"; capital[0] = "Montgomery";
    state[1] = "Alaska"; capital[1] = "Juneau";
    state[2] = "Arizona"; capital[2] = "Phoenix";
    state[3] = "Arkansas"; capital[3] = "Little Rock";
    state[4] = "California"; capital[4] = "Sacramento";
    state[5] = "Colorado"; capital[5] = "Denver";
    state[6] = "Connecticut"; capital[6] = "Hartford";
    state[7] = "Delaware"; capital[7] = "Dover";
    state[8] = "Florida"; capital[8] = "Tallahassee";
    state[9] = "Georgia"; capital[9] = "Atlanta";
    state[10] = "Hawaii"; capital[10] = "Honolulu";
    state[11] = "Idaho"; capital[11] = "Boise";
    state[12] = "Illinois"; capital[12] = "Springfield";
    state[13] = "Indiana"; capital[13] = "Indianapolis";
    state[14] = "Iowa"; capital[14] = "Des Moines";
    state[15] = "Kansas"; capital[15] = "Topeka";
    state[16] = "Kentucky"; capital[16] = "Frankfort";
    state[17] = "Louisiana"; capital[17] = "Baton Rouge";
    state[18] = "Maine"; capital[18] = "Augusta";
    state[19] = "Maryland"; capital[19] = "Annapolis";
```

```
    state[20] = "Massachusetts"; capital[20] = "Boston";
    state[21] = "Michigan"; capital[21] = "Lansing";
    state[22] = "Minnesota"; capital[22] = "Saint Paul";
    state[23] = "Mississippi"; capital[23] = "Jackson";
    state[24] = "Missouri"; capital[24] = "Jefferson City";
    state[25] = "Montana"; capital[25] = "Helena";
    state[26] = "Nebraska"; capital[26] = "Lincoln";
    state[27] = "Nevada"; capital[27] = "Carson City";
    state[28] = "New Hampshire"; capital[28] = "Concord";
    state[29] = "New Jersey"; capital[29] = "Trenton";
    state[30] = "New Mexico"; capital[30] = "Santa Fe";
    state[31] = "New York"; capital[31] = "Albany";
    state[32] = "North Carolina"; capital[32] = "Raleigh";
    state[33] = "North Dakota"; capital[33] = "Bismarck";
    state[34] = "Ohio"; capital[34] = "Columbus";
    state[35] = "Oklahoma"; capital[35] = "Oklahoma City";
    state[36] = "Oregon"; capital[36] = "Salem";
    state[37] = "Pennsylvania"; capital[37] = "Harrisburg";
    state[38] = "Rhode Island"; capital[38] = "Providence";
    state[39] = "South Carolina"; capital[39] = "Columbia";
    state[40] = "South Dakota"; capital[40] = "Pierre";
    state[41] = "Tennessee"; capital[41] = "Nashville";
    state[42] = "Texas"; capital[42] = "Austin";
    state[43] = "Utah"; capital[43] = "Salt Lake City";
    state[44] = "Vermont"; capital[44] = "Montpelier";
    state[45] = "Virginia"; capital[45] = "Richmond";
    state[46] = "Washington"; capital[46] = "Olympia";
    state[47] = "West Virginia"; capital[47] = "Charleston";
    state[48] = "Wisconsin"; capital[48] = "Madison";
    state[49] = "Wyoming"; capital[49] = "Cheyenne";
    // Set listed capital labels
    listedCapital[0] = txtCapital0;
    listedCapital[1] = txtCapital1;
    listedCapital[2] = txtCapital2;
    listedCapital[3] = txtCapital3;
    // set first question
    btnNext.PerformClick();
}
```

The **btnNext_Click** event method generates the next multiple choice question:

```
private void btnNext_Click(object sender, EventArgs e)
{
    int[] vUsed = new int[50];
    int[] index = new int[4];
    int j;
    // Generate the next question at random
    btnNext.Enabled = false;
    answer = myRandom.Next(50);
    // Display selected state
    txtState.Text = state[answer];
    // Vused array is used to see which state capitals have
    // been selected as possible answers
    for (int i = 0; i < 50; i++)
    {
        vUsed[i] = 0;
    }
    // Pick four different state indices (J) at random
    // These are used to set up multiple choice answers
    // Stored in the Index array
    for (int i = 0; i < 4; i++)
    {
        // Find index not used yet and not the answer
        //Find value not used yet and not the answer
        do
        {
            j = myRandom.Next(50);
        }
        while (vUsed[j] != 0 || j == answer);
        vUsed[j] = 1;
        index[i] = j;
    }
    // Now replace one index (at random) with correct answer
    index[myRandom.Next(4)] = answer;
    // Display multiple choice answers in text boxes
    for (int i = 0; i < 4; i++)
    {
        listedCapital[i].Text = capital[index[i]];
    }
}
```

A new concept in this routine is the **do** loop (shaded line) to pick the different possible answers. Let's explain how this particular loop works.

The form used in this code is:

```
do
{
        [C# code]
}
while condition;
```

In this "loop," the C# code between the **do** line and the **while** line is repeated as long as the specified **condition** is true. See if you can see how this loop allows us to pick four distinct capital cities for the multiple choice answers (no repeated values).

The event methods for clicking the capital city text box controls simply identify which text box was clicked and "clicks" the hidden **btnCheck** button:

```
private void txtCapital0_Click(object sender, EventArgs e)
{
    capitalClicked = 0;
    btnCheck.PerformClick();
}

private void txtCapital1_Click(object sender, EventArgs e)
{
    capitalClicked = 1;
    btnCheck.PerformClick();
}

private void txtCapital2_Click(object sender, EventArgs e)
{
    capitalClicked = 2;
    btnCheck.PerformClick();
}

private void txtCapital3_Click(object sender, EventArgs e)
{
    capitalClicked = 3;
    btnCheck.PerformClick();
}
```

We write a **btnCheck_Click** “hidden” general method to check the answer (when it is selected by clicking a text box control):

```
private void btnCheck_Click(object sender, EventArgs e)
{
    // If already answered, ignore click
    if (listedCapital[capitalClicked].Text != "" &&
btnNext.Enabled == false)
    {
        // Check clicked answer
        if (listedCapital[capitalClicked].Text ==
capital[answer])
        {
            // Correct answer - clear out other answers and
enable Next button
            for (int i = 0; i < 4; i++)
            {
                if (i != capitalClicked)
                {
                    listedCapital[i].Text = "";
                }
            }
            btnNext.Enabled = true;
            btnNext.Focus();
        }
        else
        {
            // Incorrect answer - clear out selected answer
            listedCapital[capitalClicked].Text = "";
        }
    }
}
```

Run the Project

Save your work. Run the project. A state name and four possible capital cities will be displayed. (Study the code used to choose and sort the possible answers – this kind of code is very useful.) Choose an answer. If correct, the other answers will be cleared. Click **Next State** to continue. If incorrect, your choice will be cleared. Keeping answering until correct. Here's a run I made where I missed on my first guess:

Other Things to Try

This would be a fun project to modify. How about changing it to display a capital city with four states as the multiple choices? Allow the user to type in the answer (use a text box) instead of picking from a list. Add some kind of scoring system.

This program could also be used to build general multiple choice tests from any two lists. You could do language translations (given a word in English, choose the corresponding word in Spanish), given a book, choose the author, or given an invention, name the inventor. Use your imagination.

Project 5 – Memory Game

Project Design

In this game for little kids, sixteen squares are used to hide eight different pairs of pictures. The player chooses two squares on the board and the pictures behind them are revealed. If the pictures match, those squares are removed from the board. If there is no match, the pictures are recovered and the player tries again. The play continues until all eight pairs are matched up. The game is saved as **MemoryGame** in the project folder (**\VCSEKids\VCSEK Projects**).

Place Controls on Form

Start a new project in Visual C# Express. Place sixteen large picture box controls and nine smaller picture box controls on the form. Place two buttons and a timer on the form. When done, you form should resemble this:

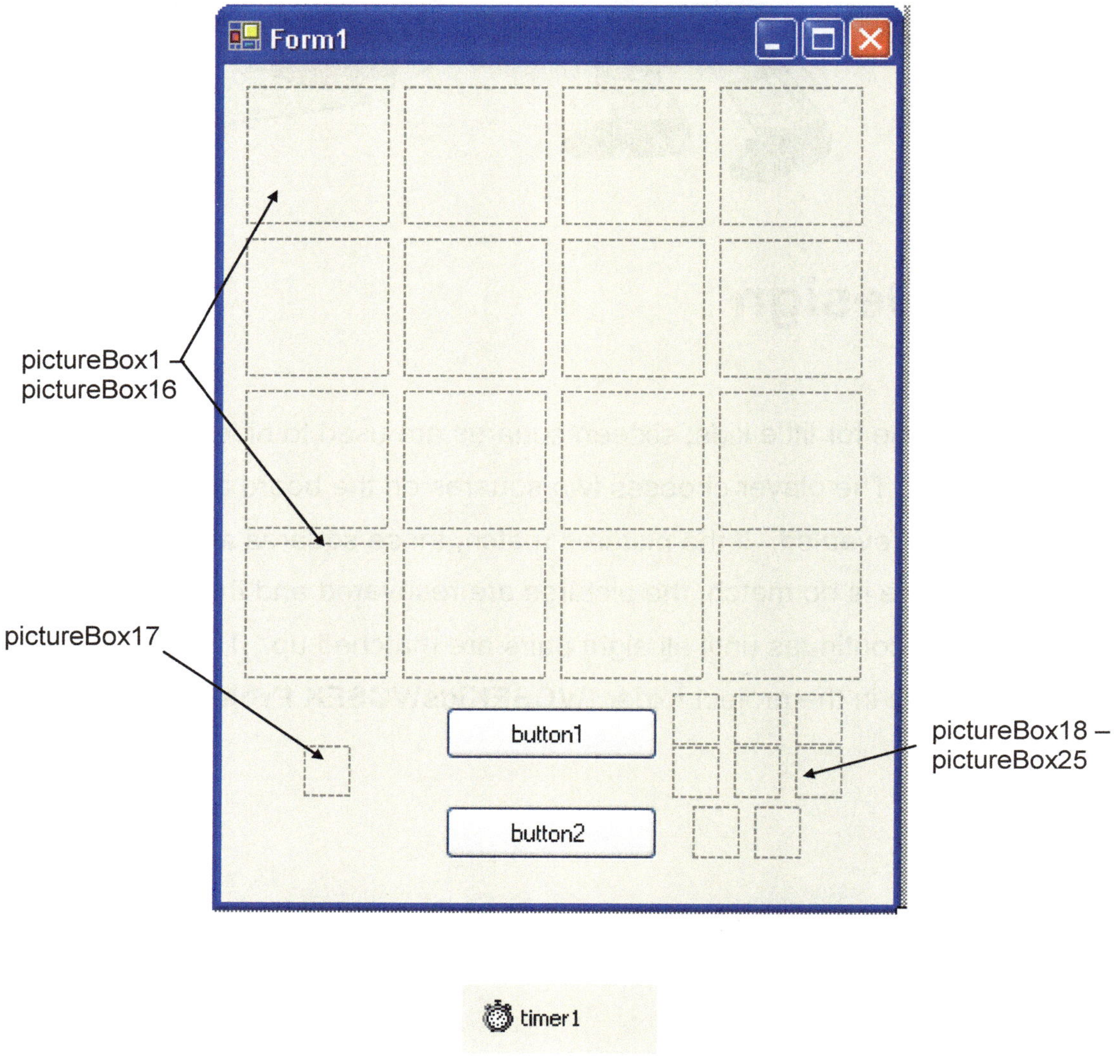

Set Control Properties

Set the control properties using the properties window:

Form1 Form:

Property Name	Property Value
Text	Memory Game
FormBorderStyle	FixedSingle
StartPosition	CenterScreen
BackColor	Light Blue

pictureBox1 Picture Box:

Property Name	Property Value
Name	picHidden0
SizeMode	StretchImage

pictureBox2 Picture Box:

Property Name	Property Value
Name	picHidden1
SizeMode	StretchImage

pictureBox3 Picture Box:

Property Name	Property Value
Name	picHidden2
SizeMode	StretchImage

pictureBox4 Picture Box:

Property Name	Property Value
Name	picHidden3
SizeMode	StretchImage

pictureBox5 Picture Box:

Property Name	Property Value
Name	picHidden4
SizeMode	StretchImage

pictureBox6 Picture Box:

Property Name	Property Value
Name	picHidden5
SizeMode	StretchImage

pictureBox7 Picture Box:

Property Name	Property Value
Name	picHidden6
SizeMode	StretchImage

pictureBox8 Picture Box:

Property Name	Property Value
Name	picHidden7
SizeMode	StretchImage

pictureBox9 Picture Box:

Property Name	Property Value
Name	picHidden8
SizeMode	StretchImage

pictureBox10 Picture Box:

Property Name	Property Value
Name	picHidden9
SizeMode	StretchImage

pictureBox11 Picture Box:

Property Name	**Property Value**
Name	picHidden10
SizeMode	StretchImage

pictureBox12 Picture Box:

Property Name	**Property Value**
Name	picHidden11
SizeMode	StretchImage

pictureBox13 Picture Box:

Property Name	**Property Value**
Name	picHidden12
SizeMode	StretchImage

pictureBox14 Picture Box:

Property Name	**Property Value**
Name	picHidden13
SizeMode	StretchImage

pictureBox15 Picture Box:

Property Name	**Property Value**
Name	picHidden14
SizeMode	StretchImage

pictureBox16 Picture Box:

Property Name	**Property Value**
Name	picHidden15
SizeMode	StretchImage

pictureBox17 Picture Box:

Property Name	Property Value
Name	picBack
SizeMode	StretchImage
Image	Back.gif (in **\VCSEKids\VCSEK Projects\MemoryGame**folder)
Visible	False

pictureBox18 Picture Box:

Property Name	Property Value
Name	picChoice0
SizeMode	StretchImage
Image	Ball.gif (in **\VCSEKids\VCSEK Projects\MemoryGame**folder)
Visible	False

pictureBox19 Picture Box:

Property Name	Property Value
Name	picChoice1
SizeMode	StretchImage
Image	Gift.gif (in **\VCSEKids\VCSEK Projects\MemoryGame**folder)
Visible	False

pictureBox20 Picture Box:

Property Name	Property Value
Name	picChoice2
SizeMode	StretchImage
Image	Bear.gif (in **\VCSEKids\VCSEK Projects\MemoryGame**folder)
Visible	False

pictureBox21 Picture Box:

Property Name	Property Value
Name	picChoice3
SizeMode	StretchImage
Image	Block.gif (in **\VCSEKids\VCSEK Projects\MemoryGame**folder)
Visible	False

pictureBox22 Picture Box:

Property Name	Property Value
Name	picChoice4
SizeMode	StretchImage
Image	Ducky.gif (in **\VCSEKids\VCSEK Projects\MemoryGame**folder)
Visible	False

pictureBox23 Picture Box:

Property Name	Property Value
Name	picChoice5
SizeMode	StretchImage
Image	Burger.gif (in **\VCSEKids\VCSEK Projects\MemoryGame**folder)
Visible	False

pictureBox24 Picture Box:

Property Name	Property Value
Name	picChoice6
SizeMode	StretchImage
Image	Hotdog.gif (in **\VCSEKids\VCSEK Projects\MemoryGame**folder)
Visible	False

pictureBox25 Picture Box:

Property Name	Property Value
Name	picChoice7
SizeMode	StretchImage
Image	Cake.gif (in **\VCSEKids\VCSEK Projects\MemoryGame**folder)
Visible	False

button1 Button:

Property Name	Property Value
Name	btnNew
Text	New Game

button2 Button:

Property Name	Property Value
Name	btnCheck

timer1 Timer:

Property Name	Property Value
Name	timDelay
Interval	1000

The completed form appears like this:

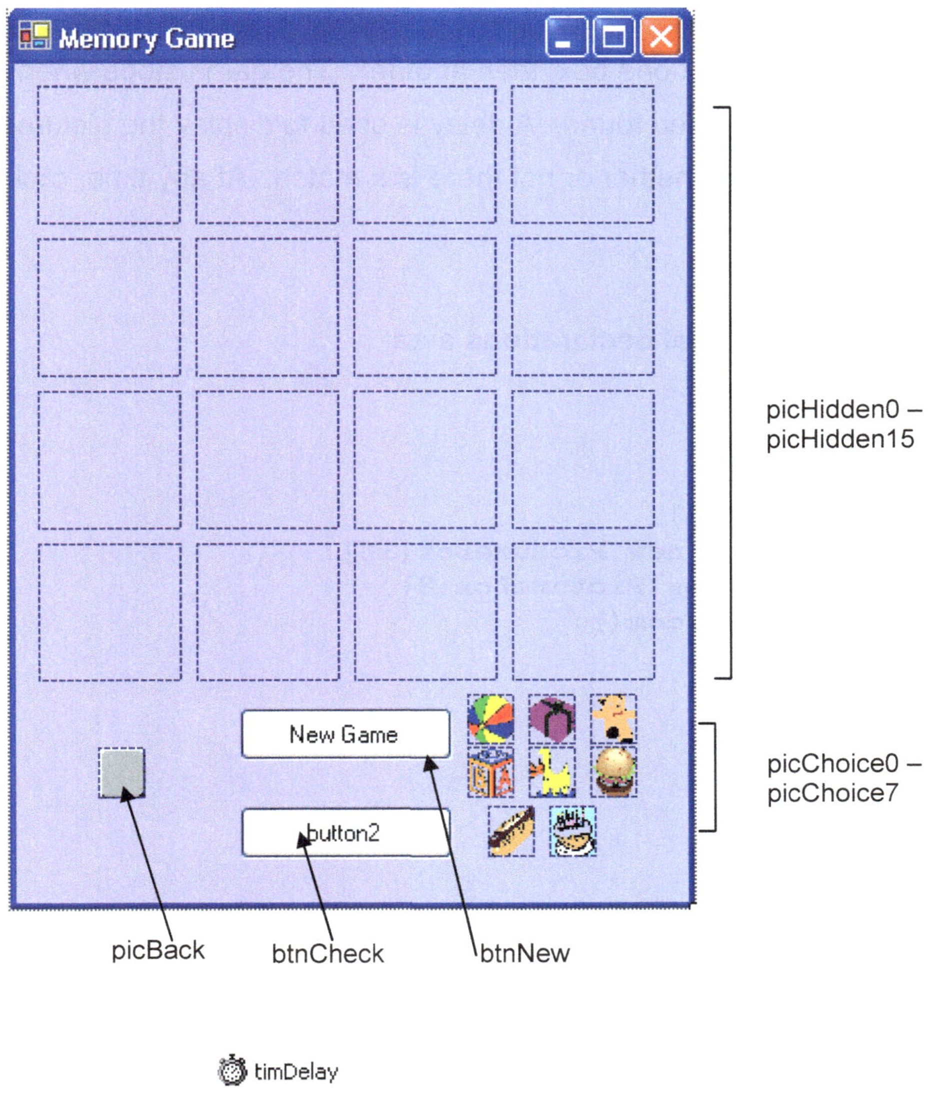

Before continuing, resize the form to hide **btnCheck**, a button we use for a general method. A few of the graphics will disappear, but that's okay since their Visible property is False anyway.

Write Event methods

When the game starts, pick one box, then another. The game stops when all matching picture pairs have been found. A delay is used to display the pictures for one second before deciding whether or not there is a match. At any time, click **New Game** to start again.

Add this code to the **general declarations** area:

```
int choice;
int[] picked = new int[2];
int[] behind = new int[16];
PictureBox[] displayed = new PictureBox[16];
PictureBox[] choices = new PictureBox[8];
Random myRandom = new Random();
```

The **Form1_Load** event establishes images to pick from

```
private void Form1_Load(object sender, EventArgs e)
{
    //establish display and choices picture boxes
    displayed[0] = picHidden0;
    displayed[1] = picHidden1;
    displayed[2] = picHidden2;
    displayed[3] = picHidden3;
    displayed[4] = picHidden4;
    displayed[5] = picHidden5;
    displayed[6] = picHidden6;
    displayed[7] = picHidden7;
    displayed[8] = picHidden8;
    displayed[9] = picHidden9;
    displayed[10] = picHidden10;
    displayed[11] = picHidden11;
    displayed[12] = picHidden12;
    displayed[13] = picHidden13;
    displayed[14] = picHidden14;
    displayed[15] = picHidden15;
    choices[0] = picChoice0;
    choices[1] = picChoice1;
    choices[2] = picChoice2;
    choices[3] = picChoice3;
    choices[4] = picChoice4;
    choices[5] = picChoice5;
    choices[6] = picChoice6;
    choices[7] = picChoice7;
    // start new game
    btnNew.PerformClick();
}
```

The **btnNew_Click** event method sets up the hidden pictures:

```
private void btnNew_Click(object sender, EventArgs e)
{
    for (int i = 0; i < 16; i++)
    {
        // replace with card back
        displayed[i].Image = picBack.Image;
        displayed[i].Visible = true;
        behind[i] = i;
    }
    // Randomly sort 16 integers (0 to 15) using Shuffle
routine from Class 9
    // behind array contains indexes (0-7) for hidden
pictures
    // Work through remaining values
    // Start at 16 and swap one value
    // at each for loop step
    // After each step, remaining is decreased by 1
    for (int remaining = 16; remaining >= 1; remaining--)
    {
        // Pick item at random
        int itemPicked = myRandom.Next(remaining);
        // Swap picked item with bottom item
        int tempValue = behind[itemPicked];
        behind[itemPicked] = behind[remaining - 1];
        behind[remaining - 1] = tempValue;
    }
    for (int i = 0; i < 16; i++)
    {
        if (behind[i] > 7)
        {
            behind[i] = behind[i] - 8;
        }
    }
    choice = 0;
}
```

The **Click** event methods for the 16 picture boxes:

```
private void picHidden0_Click(object sender, EventArgs e)
{
    picked[choice] = 0;
    btnCheck.PerformClick();
}

private void picHidden1_Click(object sender, EventArgs e)
{
    picked[choice] = 1;
    btnCheck.PerformClick();
}

private void picHidden2_Click(object sender, EventArgs e)
{
    picked[choice] = 2;
    btnCheck.PerformClick();
}

private void picHidden3_Click(object sender, EventArgs e)
{
    picked[choice] = 3;
    btnCheck.PerformClick();
}

private void picHidden4_Click(object sender, EventArgs e)
{
    picked[choice] = 4;
    btnCheck.PerformClick();
}

private void picHidden5_Click(object sender, EventArgs e)
{
    picked[choice] = 5;
    btnCheck.PerformClick();
}

private void picHidden6_Click(object sender, EventArgs e)
{
    picked[choice] = 6;
    btnCheck.PerformClick();
}
```

```
private void picHidden7_Click(object sender, EventArgs e)
{
    picked[choice] = 7;
    btnCheck.PerformClick();
}

private void picHidden8_Click(object sender, EventArgs e)
{
    picked[choice] = 8;
    btnCheck.PerformClick();
}

private void picHidden9_Click(object sender, EventArgs e)
{
    picked[choice] = 9;
    btnCheck.PerformClick();
}

private void picHidden10_Click(object sender, EventArgs e)
{
    picked[choice] = 10;
    btnCheck.PerformClick();
}

private void picHidden11_Click(object sender, EventArgs e)
{
    picked[choice] = 11;
    btnCheck.PerformClick();
}

private void picHidden12_Click(object sender, EventArgs e)
{
    picked[choice] = 12;
    btnCheck.PerformClick();
}

private void picHidden13_Click(object sender, EventArgs e)
{
    picked[choice] = 13;
    btnCheck.PerformClick();
}
```

```
private void picHidden14_Click(object sender, EventArgs e)
{
    picked[choice] = 14;
    btnCheck.PerformClick();
}

private void picHidden15_Click(object sender, EventArgs e)
{
    picked[choice] = 15;
    btnCheck.PerformClick();
}
```

The **btnCheck_Click** “hidden” general method that displays the choices for a match:

```
private void btnCheck_Click(object sender, EventArgs e)
{
    // Only execute if not trying to pick same box
    if (choice == 0 || (choice == 1 && picked[0] !=
picked[1]))
    {
        // Display selected picture
        displayed[picked[choice]].Image =
choices[behind[picked[choice]]].Image;
        displayed[picked[choice]].Refresh();
        if (choice == 0)
        {
            // first choice - just display
            choice = 1;
        }
        else
        {
            // Delay for one second before checking
            timDelay.Enabled = true;
        }
    }
}
```

The **timDelay_Tick** method that checks for matches after a delay:

```
private void timDelay_Tick(object sender, EventArgs e)
{
    timDelay.Enabled = false;
    // After delay, check for match
    if (behind[picked[0]] == behind[picked[1]])
    {
        // If match, remove pictures
        displayed[picked[0]].Visible = false;
        displayed[picked[1]].Visible = false;
    }
    else
    {
        // If no match, blank picture, restore backs
        displayed[picked[0]].Image = picBack.Image;
        displayed[picked[1]].Image = picBack.Image;
    }
    choice = 0;
}
```

Run the Project

Save your work. Run the project. Sixteen boxes appear. Click on one and view the picture. Click on another. If there is a match, the two pictures are removed (after a delay). If there is no match, the boxes are restored (also after a delay). Once all matches are found, click **New Game** to play again. Here's the middle of a game I was playing (notice the form has been resized at design time to hide the lower of the two button controls:

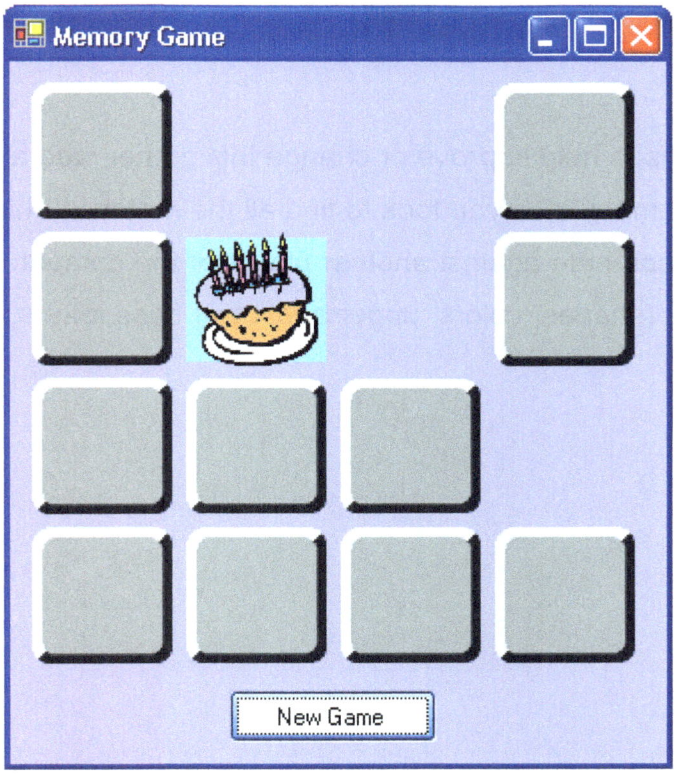

Other Things to Try

Some things to help improve or change this game: add a scoring system to keep track of how many tries you took to find all the matches, make it a two player game where you compete against another player or the computer, or set it up to match other items (shapes, colors, upper and lower case letters, numbers and objects, etc.).

Bonus Project - Pong!

In the early 1970's, while Bill Gates and Paul Allen were still in high school, a man named Nolan Bushnell began the video game revolution. He invented a very simple game - a computer version of Ping Pong. There were two paddles, one on each side of the screen. Players then bounced the ball back and forth. If you missed the ball, the other player got a point.

This first game was called Pong. And, Nolan Bushnell was the founder of Atari - the biggest video game maker for many years. (Nolan Bushnell also founded Chucky Cheese's Pizza Parlors, but that's another story!) In this bonus project, I give you my version of Pong written with Visual C# Express. I don't expect you to build this project, but you can if you want. Just load the project (named **Pong**) and run it. Skim through the C# code - you should be able to understand a lot of it. The idea of giving you this project is to let you see what can be done with Visual C# Express.

In this version of Pong, a ball moves from one end of a panel to the other, bouncing off side walls. Players try to deflect the ball at each end using a controllable paddle. In my simple game, the left paddle is controlled with the A and Z keys on the keyboard, while the right paddle is controlled with the K and M keys (detected using KeyPress events). My solution freely borrows code and techniques from several reference sources. The project relies heavily on lots of coding techniques you haven't seen. You will learn about these as you progress in your Visual C# Express studies.

Start Visual C# Express. Open the project named **Pong** in the project folder (**\VCSEKids\VCSEK Projects**). Look at the form. Here's what my finished form looks like (with control names identified):

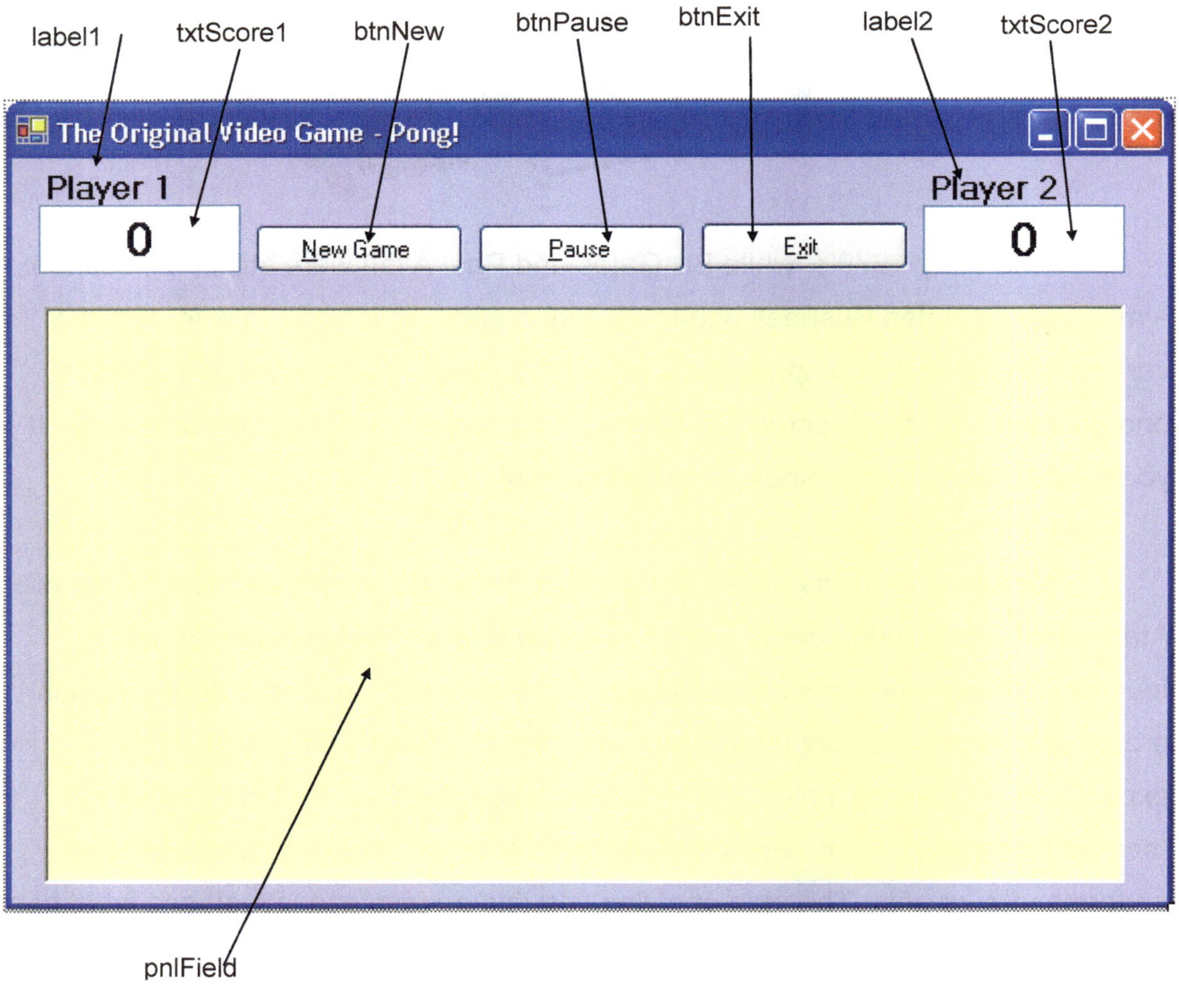

The graphics (paddles and ball) are loaded from files stored with the application. Try to identify controls you have seen before. Go to the properties window and look at the assigned properties. Run the project and play the game with someone. In particular, notice the cool sounds (if you have a sound card in your computer). This is something that should be a part of any Visual C# Express project – these sounds are also loaded from files. Have fun with Pong! Can you believe people used to spend hours mesmerized by this game? It seems very tame compared to today's video games, but it holds a warm spot in many people's gaming hearts.

We publish several Self-Study or Instructor-Led Computer Programming Tutorials for Microsoft® Small Basic:

Small Basic For Kids is an illustrated introduction to computer programming that provides an interactive, self-paced tutorial to the new Small Basic programming environment. The book consists of 30 short lessons that explain how to create and run a Small Basic program. Elementary students learn about program design and many elements of the Small Basic language. Numerous examples are used to demonstrate every step in the building process. The tutorial also includes two complete games (Hangman and Pizza Zapper) for students to build and try. Designed for kids ages 8 and up.

The Beginning Microsoft Small Basic Programming Tutorial is a self-study first semester "beginner" programming tutorial consisting of 11 chapters explaining (in simple, easy-to-follow terms) how to write Microsoft Small Basic programs. Numerous examples are used to demonstrate every step in the building process. The last chapter of this tutorial shows you how four different Small Basic games could port to Visual Basic, Visual C# and Java. This beginning level self-paced tutorial can be used at home or at school. The tutorial is simple enough for kids ages 10 and above yet engaging enough for beginning adults.

Programming Games with Microsoft Small Basic is a self-paced second semester "intermediate" level programming tutorial consisting of 10 chapters explaining (in simple, easy-to-follow terms) how to write video games in Microsoft Small Basic. The games built are non-violent, family-friendly, and teach logical thinking skills. Students will learn how to program the following Small Basic video games: Safecracker, Tic Tac Toe, Match Game, Pizza Delivery, Moon Landing, and Leap Frog. This intermediate level self-paced tutorial can be used at home or school. The tutorial is simple enough for kids yet engaging enough for beginning adults.

Programming Home Projects with Microsoft Small Basic is a self-paced programming tutorial explains (in simple, easy-to-follow terms) how to build Small Basic Windows applications. Students learn about program design, Small Basic objects, many elements of the Small Basic language, and how to debug and distribute finished programs. Sequential file input and output is also introduced.. The projects built include a Dual-Mode Stopwatch, Flash Card Math Quiz, Multiple Choice Exam, Blackjack Card Game, Weight Monitor, Home Inventory Manager and a Snowball Toss Game.

The Developer's Reference Guide to Microsoft Small Basic
While developing all the different Microsoft Small Basic tutorials we found it necessary to write The Developer's Reference Guide to Microsoft Small Basic. The Developer's Reference Guide to Microsoft Small Basic is over 500 pages long and includes over 100 Small Basic programming examples for you to learn from and include in your own Microsoft Small Basic programs. It is a detailed reference guide for new developers.

David Ahl's Small Basic Computer Adventures is a Microsoft Small Basic re-make of the classic *Basic Computer Games* programming *book* originally written by David H. Ahl. This new book includes the following classic adventure simulations; Marco Polo, Westward Ho!, The Longest Automobile Race, The Orient Express, Amelia Earhart: Around the World Flight, Tour de France, Subway Scavenger, Hong Kong Hustle, and Voyage to Neptune. Learn how to program these classic computer simulations in Microsoft Small Basic. This "intermediate" level self-paced tutorial can be used at home or school.

Basic Computer Games - Small Basic Edition is a re-make of the classic BASIC COMPUTER GAMES book originally edited by David H. Ahl. It contains 100 of the original text based BASIC games that inspired a whole generation of programmers. Now these classic BASIC games have been re-written in Microsoft Small Basic for a new generation to enjoy! The new Small Basic games look and act like the original text based games. The book includes all the original spaghetti code GOTO commands and it will make you appreciate the structured programming techniques found in our other tutorials.

We also publish several Self-Study or Instructor-Led Computer Programming Tutorials for Microsoft® Visual Basic® Express and Visual C#® Express:

Visual Basic® Express For Kids is a beginning programming tutorial consisting of 10 chapters explaining (in simple, easy-to-follow terms) how to build a Visual Basic Express Windows application. Students learn about project design, the Visual Basic Express toolbox, and many elements of the BASIC language. The tutorial also includes several detailed computer projects for students to build and try. These projects include a number guessing game, a card game, an allowance calculator, a drawing program, a state capitals game, Tic-Tac-Toe and even a simple video game. Designed for kids ages 12 and up.

Beginning Visual Basic® Express is a semester long self-paced "beginner" programming tutorial consisting of 10 chapters explaining (in simple, easy-to-follow terms) how to build a Visual Basic Express Windows application. The tutorial includes several detailed computer projects for students to build and try. These projects include a number guessing game, card game, allowance calculator, drawing program, state capitals game, and a couple of video games like Pong. We also include several college prep bonus projects including a loan calculator, portfolio manager, and checkbook balancer. Designed for students age 15 and up.

Programming Games with Visual Basic® Express is a semester long "intermediate" programming tutorial consisting of 10 chapters explaining (in simple, easy-to-follow terms) how to build Visual Basic Video Games. The games built are non-violent, family-friendly, and teach logical thinking skills. Students will learn how to program the following Visual Basic video games: Safecracker, Tic Tac Toe, Match Game, Pizza Delivery, Moon Landing, and Leap Frog. This intermediate level self-paced tutorial can be used at home or school. The tutorial is simple enough for kids yet engaging enough for beginning adults.

Programming Home Projects with Visual Basic® Express is a semester long self-paced programming tutorial explains (in simple, easy-to-follow terms) how to build a Visual Basic Express Windows project. Students learn about project design, the Visual Basic Express toolbox, many elements of the Visual Basic language, and how to debug and distribute finished projects. The projects built include a Dual-Mode Stopwatch, Flash Card Math Quiz, Multiple Choice Exam, Blackjack Card Game, Weight Monitor, Home Inventory Manager and a Snowball Toss Game.

Visual C#® Express For Kids is a beginning programming tutorial consisting of 10 chapters explaining (in simple, easy-to-follow terms) how to build a Visual C# Express Windows application. Students learn about project design, the Visual C# Express toolbox, and many elements of the C# language. Numerous examples are used to demonstrate every step in the building process. The projects include a number guessing game, a card game, an allowance calculator, a drawing program, a state capitals game, Tic-Tac-Toe and even a simple video game. Designed for kids ages 12 and up.

Beginning Visual C#® Express is a semester long "beginning" programming tutorial consisting of 10 chapters explaining (in simple, easy-to-follow terms) how to build a C# Express Windows application. The tutorial includes several detailed computer projects for students to build and try. These projects include a number guessing game, card game, allowance calculator, drawing program, state capitals game, and a couple of video games like Pong. We also include several college prep bonus projects including a loan calculator, portfolio manager, and checkbook balancer. Designed for students age 15 and up.

Programming Games with Visual C#® Express is a semester long "intermediate" programming tutorial consisting of 10 chapters explaining (in simple, easy-to-follow terms) how to build a Visual C# Video Games. The games built are non-violent, family-friendly and teach logical thinking skills. Students will learn how to program the following Visual C# video games: Safecracker, Tic Tac Toe, Match Game, Pizza Delivery, Moon Landing, and Leap Frog. This intermediate level self-paced tutorial can be used at home or school. The tutorial is simple enough for kids yet engaging enough for beginning adults.

Programming Home Projects with Visual C#® Express is a semester long self-paced programming tutorial explains (in simple, easy-to-follow terms) how to build a Visual C# Express Windows project. Students learn about project design, the Visual C# Express toolbox, many elements of the Visual C# language, and how to debug and distribute finished projects. The projects built include a Dual-Mode Stopwatch, Flash Card Math Quiz, Multiple Choice Exam, Blackjack Card Game, Weight Monitor, Home Inventory Manager and a Snowball Toss Game.

We also publish several Self-Study or Instructor-Led Computer Programming Tutorials for Oracle® Java®:

Java™ For Kids is a beginning programming tutorial consisting of 10 chapters explaining (in simple, easy-to-follow terms) how to build a Java application. Students learn about project design, object-oriented programming, console applications, graphics applications and many elements of the Java language. Numerous examples are used to demonstrate every step in the building process. The projects include a number guessing game, a card game, an allowance calculator, a state capitals game, Tic-Tac-Toe, a simple drawing program, and even a basic video game. Designed for kids ages 12 and up.

Beginning Java™ is a semester long "beginning" programming tutorial consisting of 10 chapters explaining (in simple, easy-to-follow terms) how to build a Java application. The tutorial includes several detailed computer projects for students to build and try. These projects include a number guessing game, card game, allowance calculator, drawing program, state capitals game, and a couple of video games like Pong. We also include several college prep bonus projects including a loan calculator, portfolio manager, and checkbook balancer. Designed for students age 15 and up.

Learn Java™ GUI Applications is a 9 lesson Tutorial covering object-oriented programming concepts, using a integrated development environment to create and test Java projects, building and distributing GUI applications, understanding and using the Swing control library, exception handling, sequential file access, graphics, multimedia, advanced topics such as printing, and help system authoring. Our **Beginning Java** tutorial is a pre-requisite for this tutorial.

Programming Games with Java™ is a semester long "intermediate" programming tutorial consisting of 10 chapters explaining (in simple, easy-to-follow terms) how to build a Visual C# Video Games. The games built are non-violent, family-friendly and teach logical thinking skills. Students will learn how to program the following Visual C# video games: Safecracker, Tic Tac Toe, Match Game, Pizza Delivery, Moon Landing, and Leap Frog. This intermediate level self-paced tutorial can be used at home or school. The tutorial is simple enough for kids yet engaging enough for beginning adults. Our **Beginning Java** and **Learn Java GUI Applications** tutorials are required pre-requisites for this tutorial.

Programming Home Projects with Java™ is a Java GUI Swing tutorial covering object-oriented programming concepts. It explains (in simple, easy-to-follow terms) how to build Java GUI project to use around the home. Students learn about project design, the Java Swing controls, many elements of the Java language, and how to distribute finished projects. The projects built include a Dual-Mode Stopwatch, Flash Card Math Quiz, Multiple Choice Exam, Blackjack Card Game, Weight Monitor, Home Inventory Manager and a Snowball Toss Game. Our **Beginning Java** and **Learn Java GUI Applications** tutorials are pre-requisites for this tutorial.

We also publish several advanced Honors Level Self-Study or Instructor-Led "College-Prep" and College Level Computer Programming Tutorials for Microsoft® Visual Basic® Professional Edition and Visual C#® Professional Edition:

LEARN VISUAL BASIC PROFESSIONAL EDITION is a comprehensive college prep programming tutorial covering object-oriented programming, the Visual Basic integrated development environment, building and distributing Windows applications using the Windows Installer, exception handling, sequential file access, graphics, multimedia, advanced topics such as web access, printing, and HTML help system authoring. The tutorial also introduces database applications (using ADO .NET) and web applications (using ASP.NET).

VISUAL BASIC AND DATABASES PROFESSIONAL EDITION is a tutorial that provides a detailed introduction to using Visual Basic for accessing and maintaining databases for desktop applications. Topics covered include: database structure, database design, Visual Basic project building, ADO .NET data objects (connection, data adapter, command, data table), data bound controls, proper interface design, structured query language (SQL), creating databases using Access, SQL Server and ADOX, and database reports. Actual projects developed include a book tracking system, a sales invoicing program, a home inventory system and a daily weather monitor.

LEARN VISUAL C# PROFESSIONAL EDITION is a comprehensive college prep computer programming tutorial covering object-oriented programming, the Visual C# integrated development environment and toolbox, building and distributing Windows applications (using the Windows Installer), exception handling, sequential file input and output, graphics, multimedia effects (animation and sounds), advanced topics such as web access, printing, and HTML help system authoring. The tutorial also introduces database applications (using ADO .NET) and web applications (using ASP.NET).

VISUAL C# AND DATABASES PROFESSIONAL EDITION is a tutorial that provides a detailed introduction to using Visual C# for accessing and maintaining databases for desktop applications. Topics covered include: database structure, database design, Visual C# project building, ADO .NET data objects (connection, data adapter, command, data table), data bound controls, proper interface design, structured query language (SQL), creating databases using Access, SQL Server and ADOX, and database reports. Actual projects developed include a books tracking system, a sales invoicing program, a home inventory system and a daily weather monitor.

CPSIA information can be obtained at www.ICGtesting.com
Printed in the USA
BVOW11s0138250315
393230BV00006B/11/P

9 781937 161590